DIRTY WINDSHIELDS

GRANT LAWRENCE

DIRTY
WINDSHIELDS

THE BEST AND THE WORST OF
THE SMUGGLERS TOUR DIARIES

Douglas & McIntyre

Douglas and McIntyre (2013) Ltd.
P.O. Box 219, Madeira Park, BC, VON 2H0
www.douglas-mcintyre.com

Edited by Barbara Pulling and Silas White
Cover and text design by Naomi MacDougall
Printed and bound in Canada
Printed on paper made from 100% post-consumer fibre

Douglas and McIntyre (2013) Ltd. acknowledges the support of the Canada Council
for the Arts, which last year invested $153 million to bring the arts to Canadians
throughout the country. We also gratefully acknowledge financial support from
the Government of Canada through the Canada Book Fund and from the Province
of British Columbia through the BC Arts Council and the Book Publishing Tax Credit.

Library and Archives Canada Cataloguing in Publication
Lawrence, Grant, 1971–, author
Dirty windshields : the best and worst of the Smugglers tour diaries / Grant Lawrence.

Issued in print and electronic formats.
ISBN 978-1-77162-148-9 (softcover)
ISBN 978-1-77162-149-6 (HTML)

1. Smugglers (Musical group). 2. Lawrence, Grant, 1971–.
3. Rock musicians--Canada—Biography.
4. Radio broadcasters—Canada—Biography I. Title.

ML421.S666L42 2017   782.42166092′2   C2017-901010-7   C2017-901011-5

CONTACT THE AUTHOR OR THE BAND:
www.grantlawrence.ca
www.thesmugglers.com
gtwelve@aol.com

Contents

PART 3: SUSHI AND SQUATS

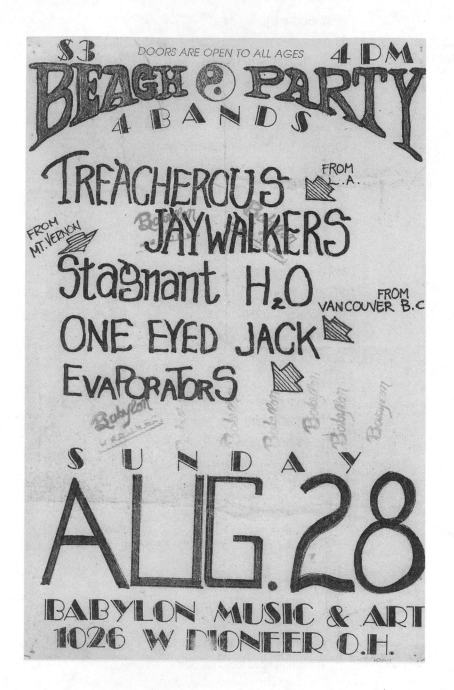

Prologue

"**D**OES ANYONE HAVE a G-string I can borrow?"

That's the question Nick begged of the audience, panic in his voice, as the last out-of-tune chord of the Sonics' "Have Love, Will Travel" painfully rang in the air to a smattering of applause.

The broken string hung off Nick's guitar like the bouncing whisker of a tiger. We were only halfway through our ramshackle set of songs, played at full volume to the mostly empty Babylon Music and Art, a theatre in Oak Harbor, Whidbey Island, Washington. It was Sunday, August 28, 1988, the One-Eyed Jacks' first-ever show in the United States of America.

Thanks to our friend and mentor Nardwuar the Human Serviette, we had landed a cross-border opening slot on a Sunday matinee show for two American bands: Stagnant Water, a pop-punk group from Mount Vernon, and a jazz-punk trio from Los Angeles called the Treacherous Jaywalkers. It was a searingly hot afternoon. For our band, average age sixteen, a broken string on an electric guitar was enough to bring our show to an unprofessional, crashing halt. Nick broke strings all the time in practice, but we had never thought to prepare for such a quandary during a live concert.

Nick's request was answered by silence. I assumed the minuscule audience was amused at his wholly unconfident, wavering voice, which hadn't quite broken yet but still boomed throughout the cavernous theatre as if he suddenly possessed the pipes of a demonic Peter Brady. Scrambling, he pulled off his heavy black 1979 Gibson Les Paul Standard guitar, which he'd recently purchased for $425, his entire savings from a summer of dishwashing side by side with me at the Big Scoop, and pushed open the back doors of the theatre.

The gayest of sunbeams poured in, illuminating row upon row of empty seats. The unfortunate few in attendance shielded their eyes, no doubt reminded of the many better things they could have been doing on Whidbey Island at that moment. Nick dashed like a frightened rabbit through the doors. They slammed shut behind him, echoing through the room and blocking out the sun again. The rest of the One-Eyed Jacks stood onstage like teenage statues, staring into an entertainment abyss.

NICK THOMAS AND I had formed the One-Eyed Jacks in grade nine, musical ability nil. We desperately wanted to look and sound as cool as the bands plastered on the record covers we adored: the Rolling Stones on *England's Newest Hit Makers*, the Sonics on *Boom*, the Gruesomes on *Tyrants of Teen Trash*. The members of those bands all *matched*. They looked like a collective unit, a team, a gang. But this was high school in West Vancouver, BC, in the 1980s, and hardly any other kids in our grade were into British Invasion beat, weird 1950s rock 'n' roll or 1960s garage rock. Hard rock and hair metal bands ruled the planet like braggart dinosaurs, packing stadiums from Calgary to Calcutta and dominating the musical taste of most of the kids we knew.

To fill out a five-person band in the classic Rolling Stones formation of lead singer, rhythm guitarist, lead guitarist, bassist and drummer, Nick and I were forced to be flexible. I took on the role of lead singer, Nick played rhythm and our drummer was a band class dropout named Craig Frew. Craig wasn't really into the music, but he could play the drums. What we *really* needed was a lead guitarist. Nick had only picked up the guitar a few months earlier, and while he was making strumming strides and could play the chords of just about any rocker we chose, we needed somebody, *anybody*, who could play those awesome Chuck Berry leads.

Enter guitarist Sean Harper Powers. Sean hated his middle name long before a Canadian prime minister would forever tarnish it for artists and art lovers. Sean's gloves were studded and fingerless, *Warriors*-style. A loud, proud, stocky little headbanger, he rocked incredibly tight, faded and torn-up jeans, and massive white sneakers. He rarely wore a shirt, no matter what the season. His banger pride and joy was his cut-off denim vest festooned with a huge Def Leppard patch sewn expertly on the back (by his mom) and smaller patches sewn pell-mell on the front: AC/DC, Mötley Crüe, Skid Row and our one glimmer of hope—the Who. Sean's blond Nigel Tufnel haystack mullet looked constantly electrified, standing up in all directions as if he had stuck his penis into a light socket. He had a glazed-over, distant look, hung out primarily in the smoke hole at school and communicated in high-pitched half-sentences that were almost unintelligible.

And he repeatedly flunked his classes. That's because Sean Harper Powers cared about only one thing: playing the electric guitar. He was known as the best guitar shredder in our suburb. On weekends, it was rumoured he would practise his scales and metal licks for fourteen hours straight. His mom was concerned, wondering why all the metal band posters that adorned his walls featured "people in pain." Sean loved the mockumentary *This Is Spinal Tap* far beyond the humour, rigging his amp and guitar to go to 11 with the deepest respect.

The bassist we lined up for the band happened to be Sean Powers's best friend. Jason Carthy was a rare crossover-banger. Jason loved the party lifestyle, rocked a mullet and a Mack jacket, but was also a history buff, did well in school and, most importantly, liked all sorts of music, including the seemingly wacko, dated sixties shit Nick and I worshipped. Best of all, Jason was an excellent bassist. He could also screech out Creedence Clearwater Revival songs into our RadioShack practice mics in my parents' basement as well as John Fogerty himself. It was Jason who had convinced Nick and me, against our better judgment, to give Sean Powers a shot.

WHEN NICK DISAPPEARED through those theatre doors, it was Sean Powers who stepped up to the lip of the stage, carnally sensing that this was his long-awaited moment of metal glory. As long as Nick was madly searching the trunk of his mom's Honda Civic for a G-string, Sean Powers was freed from the shackles of our Eddie Cochran and Animals covers.

Sean Harper Powers, metal maniac. It was rumoured that Sean could practise his metallic hammer-on solos for fourteen hours straight. Our first band needed a lead guitarist, and Sean was our bassist's best friend, so he was in. A mistake, but it proved to be the match strike that ignited the Smugglers, in a painful way.

NICK THOMAS PHOTO

With a single practised flick of the wrist, he turned all three knobs on his guitar to 11. He shook out his mane and licked his lips like a lion ready to kill. Craning his head back, he let out a devil yell at the bewildered audience and launched into a note-for-note-for-note rendition of Eddie Van Halen's "Eruption" solo. Thirty seconds into his outrageous, string-bending riffage, Sean's hairless banger chest glistened with beads of sweat. He gritted his teeth, shut his eyes tight, spread the legs of his white leopard-print spandex show pants and leaned back like he was withstanding a bomb blast.

The full-volume, mathematical solo went on and on and on, each hammer-on note bleeding from his leased-to-own Roland cube amp like a screeching weasel. His blinding finger-tapping increased in ferocity and scale as the solo continued. Sean Harper Powers completely lost himself, spiralling deep within the deafening, symphonic metal, the soundtrack of his wildest wet dreams. It was as if he'd melded with his candy-apple red Kramer guitar: the exact same body, year and model as Eddie Van Halen's.

Nick had slipped back into the theatre by now, tightly gripping a pack of strings, but it was too late. To add insult to injury, the tiny crowd had actually started to get into it. As Sean Powers's solo climbed to dizzying, seizure-inducing, dog-whistle frequencies, the scant audience came alive, and were soon out of their seats and down on the theatre floor, fists and lighters in the air, screaming their appreciation for the birth of the metal monster. No. NO!

Sean Powers had no idea at the time, but his performance was fateful, a kind of Custer's Last Stand. The alternative era was right around the corner, a meteoric extinction for metal dinosaurs like Sean and the licks he roared. The Treacherous Jaywalkers, the band we were opening for on Whidbey Island, would perform in Seattle the very next night with an unknown opening group called Nirvana.

As Nick and I watched our rock 'n' roll dreams go up in a plume of headbanger mania, we knew that our first band, the One-Eyed Jacks, was over. We would do what all bands did when they didn't have the guts to fire a particular member. We would break up and start over from scratch on Monday, nobody's feelings hurt. This was not the American musical debut we had imagined, and we wondered if we would ever have another chance at crossing the forty-ninth parallel in the name of rock 'n' roll.

The new band Nick and I formed was called the Smugglers. Our original intention was an homage to darker garage rock, a musical cross between the Sonics, the Velvet Underground and the Cramps, built on the blueprint of the Rolling Stones with a decidedly Northwest twist. Our sound and look would evolve over time, but our music stayed rooted in rock 'n' roll. The One-Eyed Jacks had lasted barely eighteen months and collapsed in a metal meltdown. The Smugglers would straddle three different decades over sixteen years.

PART

1

CLAM CHOWDER AND ICE

I Drove the Coquihalla

THE VOLKSWAGEN VAN rumbled out of my parents' driveway, up the hill and onto the Trans-Canada Highway East. Behind the wheel, David Carswell, our hulking, ex-pat English-born guitarist, picked up some speed and shifted the rust bucket into fourth gear, leaving a loud blast of black exhaust in our wake. The five of us let out whoops and cheers, the freedom of the open road literally under our feet. The floor of the VW van was so corroded that depending on where you sat, you could actually look down and see the asphalt. Didn't matter. We were on tour! Dave slammed a dubbed cassette tape of the Rolling Stones' *Exile on Main St.* into the deck and cranked it. To the soundtrack of "Rocks Off," cans of lukewarm Black Label beer were passed around and cracked, bags of chips were ripped open, cigarettes and joints were lit.

Our babbling conversation mixed with blue smoke and laughter. Only our new bassist, Beez, sat in apprehension, perched on top of his bass amp in his black leather trench coat and jackboots. His long black hair hung over his thick, black-framed Buddy Holly glasses. What the hell he

9

was doing in a van full of totally unprepared teenagers, he worried, climbing into the rugged mountain terrain of British Columbia?

Showing the complete opposite body language was our harmonica player, Adam "Doobie" Woodall, the youngest member of the band.

It was Nick who had suggested we throw a wild-card musician into the Smugglers. I wasn't so sure. Adam was way too much of a hippie for my taste. I had a narrow vision of how I wanted our band to appear and an ingrained unease about the hippie lifestyle from childhood summers spent in the draft-dodger bottleneck of Desolation Sound, BC. Adam's favourite band was the Grateful Dead. He and his older sister were Deadheads, travelling far and wide to as many of the band's concerts as they possibly could every summer.

Like any Deadhead worth his patchouli oil, Adam eventually procured himself a Volkswagen van, complete with pop-up camper that could sleep several. We needed a van. And as Nick pointed out, Adam was an outstanding harmonica player. No other band we knew of had its own harmonica player. Maybe he would be our secret weapon. Adam, his harmonicas and his VW bus were in.

So began the first tour the Smugglers ever embarked on, just over a year after our formation. We were booked for a weekend of shows in

Our harmonica player, Adam Woodall, was a hippie, right down to his Volkswagen bus. I wasn't into the hippie scene, but Adam was an excellent harmonica player, a very funny guy, and we needed a touring van, so he was in.
NICK THOMAS PHOTO

Left to right: Adam Woodall (harmonica), Nick Thomas (guitar) and Paul Preminger (drums) trying desperately to look like a cool 1960s garage band in one of our first promo photo shoots.
SARAH EDMONDS PHOTO

Regina, a mere eighteen hundred kilometres away from our parental suburban nests. It would also be our first attempt at crossing the Rocky Mountains. We had no idea what we were getting into, nor did we really have any business attempting it. The Smugglers didn't have an album out, or even a cassette, but there we were, on the highway rolling east. Regina was in the faraway land of Saskatchewan. There was no time or money to stop at a motel; we had to keep moving.

Beez was already a seasoned touring veteran from his years in his established band, Sarcastic Mannequins. He was ten years older than the rest of us. Our hippie harmonica player, Adam, was still in high school; the rest of us had freshly escaped. Beez had tried desperately to warn us about what possible weather might lie east of Vancouver in March, but we willfully ignored him. It was spring break. Daffodils and cherry blossoms were in full bloom on the West Coast. That meant spring had sprung across the rest of Canada, too, right? What could possibly go wrong driving from Vancouver to Regina? *Ambition, good times, denial.*

Two hours east of Vancouver, near Hope, the steep, dark walls of the Coast Mountains surrounded us. To everyone but Beez's surprise, we

Adam Woodall (left) and Paul Preminger minutes after leaving on our first tour, from Vancouver to Regina for spring break. The party was on as soon as we hit the highway. The party was over as soon as we hit the mountains. NICK THOMAS PHOTO

stared out the windows as snow began to fall. As we ascended, the temperature slid in the opposite direction, plummeting to below zero. When I reached over to switch on the dashboard heat (something we never had to use when driving the van to our crappy gigs around temperate Vancouver), it was as if I had opened a refrigerator door. I swivelled to face Adam. "How does the heat work?" I asked urgently.

"I . . . don't . . . know . . . man," Adam answered, between long drags on a juicy, fat joint he and our drummer, Paul Preminger, were passing back and forth. They were already as baked as a pair of PEI potatoes.

"Does this thing have snow tires?" Dave asked just as urgently, glancing at Adam in the rear-view mirror.

Choking on a mouthful of smoke, Adam repeated himself. "I . . . don't . . . know . . . man."

We never considered for a second that we should actually stop and try to get the heat fixed or check if we did or did not have snow tires. Instead, we simply unfurled our sleeping bags, spread them over top of us and kept going. We were wearing our Vancouver-in-March street clothes: Value

Village jean jackets, tattered three-button blazers, T-shirts, corduroy pants, suede desert boots and Chuck Taylor sneakers. Paul lit up another joint.

Way past Hope, the highway became so steep and the VW van so slow, weighed down with the five of us and our equipment, that Dave had to constantly gear down to keep us chugging in an upwardly direction. Even the slowest eighteen-wheeler rigs roared past us like freighters passing a rowboat. With flakes as big as loonies dusting the windshield, it was difficult to tell if we were moving at all. On one extremely steep grade, Dave turned down the NoMeansNo cassette just long enough to announce that he would have to punch the clutch and shift down to second gear. But the incline didn't relent. The gear change was punctuated by a loud backfire of black smoke and a forward lurch. We glanced at each other nervously as the van continued to lose momentum, even with Dave's Converse sneaker pinned flat to the floor on the accelerator. "Shit! I might have to go down to first gear!" shouted Dave over the music.

"What happens after first gear?" I yelled back, reaching out to further turn down the tunes.

"After first gear we roll back down the mountain," Dave grunted, once again hammering his sneaker to the gas pedal. Finally, as it was getting dark, we crawled past a sign partially obscured by snow that read "Coquihalla Summit." A ten-dollar tollbooth was next. "You should be paying us, asshole!" our cantankerous drummer yelled at the attendant. The worst of the mountain terrain was behind us now, we figured. Beez rolled his eyes and hunkered down.

Hours later, our little Volkswagen van was hurtling down a mountainside in the inky blackness of night. The highway we so desperately tried to cling to was a ribbon of white. Snowflakes rushed towards us, caught in the van's one working headlight. Even though we faced plunging to a frozen death at any moment, all I could think of through clattering teeth was how the streaking snowflakes oddly created the same effect as the Millennium Falcon flipping to light speed.

Everyone but Dave, who was still at the wheel, was either drunk or stoned, and all of us were shivering violently. We climbed ever farther into the Rockies, slip-sliding down one pass only to ascend another. The snow fell fast and furious, the flakes swirling specks as the frigid temperature dictated. Luckily, old VW vans were built with their engines in the rear.

The heavy weight over our back axle allowed us just enough traction to keep rolling in the right direction.

On our right was a ninety-degree drop into a blackened abyss. To our left was a glimmering rock face. The van's headlight illuminated constant small avalanches of snow and ice that slid across the road in front of us like someone dumping a Slushie onto a tabletop. The van fishtailed on through or crunched over top, everyone gripping whatever we could hold on to. The downhill slides reminded me of the Matterhorn roller coaster at Disneyland. I was conflicted. On every plunge I longed for the rain-soaked pavement we had left behind on the West Coast. On every ascent I needed to see what would come next in the frozen wilderness. *Ambition, good times, denial.*

With the guys in the back all passed out, Dave and I were still up front, trying to keep our wits about us, as we listened to Shadowy Men on a Shadowy Planet on low volume. Just north of three-thirty A.M., we swerved into Golden, a glittering Rocky Mountain hamlet. Outside of town we were stopped at a roadblock. An RCMP officer dressed like Shackleton approached us, motioning for Dave to roll down his window. From the passenger seat, I glanced around for beer cans and drug paraphernalia, but it was a sea of sleeping bags and snoring bodies. The winter air and swirling snow blasting into the open driver's side window felt refreshing.

The cop informed us there had been a huge avalanche a few kilometres ahead. The Trans-Canada Highway was blocked in both directions, which meant we would be forced to detour several hours to the south and hundreds of kilometres in the wrong direction. I was sure the cop was going to nail us for the headlight, for something, but he just waved us in the direction of the detour. As we scaled yet another mountain pass, our headlight cast its beam on snow-covered trees guarding the highway like slumped sentries. I swore one of them stepped into the path of our van like an Ent from *The Lord of the Rings*. I was hallucinating, and despite my pledge to act as Dave's wingman to make sure he stayed awake through the night, I fell fast asleep in the passenger seat. I slipped into my recurring dream that I'd been asked to be the new lead singer of the Gruesomes.

two

Gruesomania!

T HE NIGHT THAT changed my life was a rainy Monday evening in June of 1987. My pal Nardwuar the Human Serviette and I snuck into Club Soda in downtown Vancouver to see the Gruesomes, a garage rock band from Montreal. I had attended concerts before—ZZ Top at the Coliseum and a bunch of first- and second-wave rock 'n' roll legends at Expo 86, artists like Jerry Lee Lewis, Fats Domino, Freddy Cannon, Jan and Dean, Ray Charles—but I had never experienced anything as exciting, as forbidden or as visceral as I did that Monday night.

Club Soda was "of age," meaning you had to be nineteen years or older to be allowed in. That could've been a problem, since I was fifteen. Nardwuar was eighteen, but he had already been to some shows downtown using an older friend's ID, so he was covered. I didn't have any friends over nineteen, and it was long before our skinhead friend Roger the Dodger would hook me up with a fake ID, so I was forced to put a plan of my own into action. Two months before the gig, in an attempt to rapidly age myself by at least three years, I began growing my first beard. By the night of the show, my lower face sported an embarrassing growth of patchy, near-pubic mange. But it was, by definition, a beard.

Together, Nardwuar and I heaved open the heavy wooden doors of

GRUESOMES pin-up
AN OFFICIAL
photo by J. WENK

Every musician has a band that changed their life, and for me it was Montreal garage rock band the Gruesomes. When Nardwuar and I snuck into their downtown Vancouver concert in the late 1980s, all I wanted to do was exactly what they did. Clockwise from top left: John "Jed" Knoll (drums), Gerry Alvarez (guitar and vocals), Bobby Beaton (guitar and lead vocals), John Davis (bass and vocals).

Club Soda and peered up the dark flight of stairs that led to the second storey. From the top, a gargantuan bouncer with a shaved head, a monobrow and arms hanging from his torso like sausage links glared down at us. We took a deep breath, but when we reached the top, the bouncer barely gave us a second glance, instead jabbing a muscular finger towards the box office where we nervously paid the six-dollar cover charge. Was . . . that it? Nardwuar and I stepped into the darkness of the room. We were in! Without getting ID'd! I'd keep that mangy facial hair for years because of it.

The Homer Street club was packed with people wearing the same colour as the paint on the windowless walls: black. Everyone had terrible posture. They slumped over like question marks in leather jackets with band logos hand-painted or sewn on the back: SNFU, the Blasters, D.O.A., the Cramps, Black Flag, Death Sentence, the Damned. Haircuts ranged from rockabilly pompadours to punk mohawks to angular gothic explosions of purple hair, a.k.a. "The Kennedy." The club reeked of cigarette smoke, stale beer and urinal pucks, a noxious smell that would eventually become my personal trigger of both nostalgia and post-traumatic stress disorder. Nardwuar and I sidestepped our way onto the dance floor until we were in a frothing swell of bodies, sweating and shoving, beer sloshing out of pint glasses. Looking up at the Gruesomes, we were in awe. They were a loud blur of cool; they were blowing our minds.

INDEPENDENT BANDS LIKE the Gruesomes were sketching out a new Canadian rock 'n' roll roadmap at the time. Thanks to huge support from campus radio and the fledgling MuchMusic TV station, by the late 1980s the Gruesomes were among the country's most popular touring club musicians. They were a sixties-purist garage-rock party band, and while they took their exacting impression of sixties punk seriously, their delivery and between-song banter was often hilarious. The four-piece group took their name from a band that appeared on an episode of *The Flintstones*. The image of the real-life Gruesomes was sharp, calculated and fun: a uniformed cross between the Music Machine and the Ramones. Their sound was a screamin' rave-up and mash-down of the Standells, the Syndicate of Sound and Les Lutins. They played a mix of originals and ultra-hip sixties covers and paid tribute to their native Quebec by singing a few songs in French.

Most of the Gruesomes had matching dark mushroom haircuts that hung perfect and straight over their eyes, a haircut I desperately wanted but could never pull off. The band wore a combination of black leather vests, mod suit jackets and turtlenecks, pointy black Beatle boots and tight black jeans. Their lead singer was the handsome, hugely charismatic, awkward and funny Bobby Beaton. Their live show was sensational. The Gruesomes packed every joint they played, from St. John's to Victoria. Nardwuar had stumbled upon them because they covered the Sonics' hit "The Witch" on their debut album *Tyrants of Teen Trash*. I became so obsessed with them that I dated a girl just to borrow her Gruesomes records.

Bobby Beaton was now on stage mere feet away from me, a god in his tight black suit jacket and skinny black tie, shaking his head back and forth like a dashboard Jesus on a logging road. He attacked the strings of his Rickenbacker guitar, supported by a black leather boot propped on

the edge of the stage monitor. His lips were pressed right up against the
wet metal microphone screen as he snarled the lyrics to "Get Outta My
Hair." Steam rose from his shoulders. Sweat dripped from his chin like a
leaking shower faucet.

My stunned adoration was violently interrupted when I was body-
checked from the side. I found myself face down on the sticky dance floor,
glasses bent. Colourful Doc Marten boots and Fluevog creepers with thick
rubber soles stomped all around me. As quickly as I got knocked down
I got up again, aided by several arms clad in black leather. The shove
wasn't an act of anger or bullying; we were dancing. Slam-dancing. Someone's spilt beer dripped from my patchy pubic beard. Nardwuar was a
few feet away, smacking shoulders with some skinny punk who looked
like a starving Christian Slater with a cigarette hanging out of his mouth.
Nardwuar leaned over with a smile and shouted, "Welcome to the pit!"

We slam-danced with reckless abandon, gleefully banging into each
other and into strangers on the packed dance floor. I found the camara-
derie that accompanied the violent action unifying. If I ever got smacked
over like that in my high school hallway, it was because a hockey jock had
meant to do it, and there was no way he was helping me to my feet. The
"pit" was enlightenment. I felt like I had found my people.

Eventually, Nardwuar and I tired out and took positions in the front row,
pressed right against the stage. We were shoved and pushed from behind
by the throbbing gristle on the dance floor, our torsos and ribs bruising as
we braced ourselves with wide smiles on our faces. After one final furious
song, "You Said Yeah," the Gruesomes dashed off the stage to a fantastic
roar. Nardwuar and I followed the lead of the sweaty punks around us
who banged their empty pint glasses on the stage in unison until the
dull thudding filled the club like jungle drums. A chant of "ONE MORE
SONG" fell in step with the thumping. To our delight, the Gruesomes
emerged once again: my first up-close exposure to an encore. The pounding ceased immediately, just like the jungle drums in the Tarzan movies,
then turned to wild cheers. The Gruesomes played two more wild songs
before the lights came on, cruel fluorescents that sent the patrons scur-
rying for the stairs like roaches, seeking the darkness of the rainy street.

At some point during that Gruesomes concert, I experienced the
Moment. It's the realization so many musicians have when we see a

certain band that we love: it's the *I can do that* moment. You have the sudden desire to try *that*, *up there*, for yourself, with your friends. The next day at school, I groggily raved about the Gruesomes concert to Nick. He had been desperate to go too, but he had such a baby face he wouldn't gain access into downtown clubs until many years later. I chattered excitedly about what I wanted to do for the rest of my life: play rock 'n' roll music and see the world. Nick wasn't completely convinced, but would be soon. We just needed some electric guitars, a drum set, a bass and a touring van, and we could be on our way.

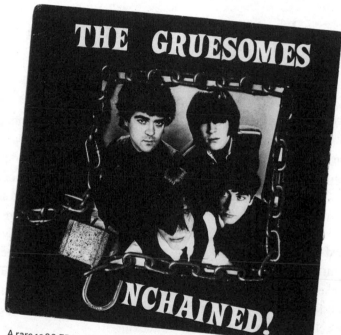

A rare 1988 EP by the Gruesomes, one of their records that I wore out by listening to it over and over again on my parents' record player. PHOTO COURTESY PRIMITIVE RECORDS

three

Roll On Saskatchewan

W HEN DAWN BROKE through our slush-splattered windshield, Dave was still at the wheel, deliriously singing along to Dolly Parton's *Greatest Hits*. Somehow, someway, our vw van had tobogganed down the eastern slope of the Rocky Mountains into the valleys and foothills of Alberta's wild rose country. The highway, while still covered in snow, had flattened out and become completely straight. To wake the rest of the band and celebrate hitting the prairies, Dave popped out Dolly and slammed in Stompin' Tom Connors's *My Stompin' Grounds*. The reflection of the sun on the snow was blinding, causing us to squint as we smacked our cracked lips together, still tasting the rolling party from the night before. Paul reached a gloved hand for a can of Black Label. It was frozen solid. He cracked it anyway and started sucking.

Just days after the One-Eyed Jacks' metal meltdown, Nick and I had been cruising down the main drag in my white 1962 Plymouth Valiant when we saw an older, tough-looking kid in a trench coat and desert boots hitchhiking outside West Vancouver's only Chinese restaurant. Who wears a trench coat in the summer? The dude looked like a cross between the Tasmanian Devil, the cast of *The Outsiders* and a beer fridge. We pulled over to pick him up, and he hopped in the back seat, lit up a cigarette

Paul Preminger, Smugglers drummer. Paul was a hard-hitting, hard-drinking, hard-eating kinda guy, and the best drummer we had played with to date. He had so many sordid stories, it was like having a merchant sailor join the band.

JULIET NICHOLL PHOTO

and started talking non-stop in a type of sly snarl, like he was constantly sharing malicious secrets. This was our introduction to Paul Preminger.

Paul had one artistic outlet: he was a drummer. When we picked him up hitchhiking that day, he had just been tossed from his last band, a surf combo called the Tidal Waves. When we asked why, he described in graphic detail being caught having sex with the lead guitarist's younger sister on a stepladder behind the garage they practised in, while on a ten-minute break from rehearsal. Paul was duly impressed when Nick reached into my Plymouth Valiant's dashboard and magically pulled out a lukewarm can of Black Label beer, tossing it back to him. (Nick and I had figured out that the space where an old radio speaker in the centre of the car's ultra-wide dashboard had once been could hide up to twenty-four cans of Black Label.) By the time we dropped off Paul Preminger at the Park Royal Mall in a cloud of cigarette smoke and burnt oil fumes, Nick and I knew he could be the perfect drummer for our new band. Paul did have one quirk, though. In spite of his bravado in everyday life, he had a surprisingly overpowering stage fright. He would vomit before every show, and eventually during them as well.

PAUL PREMINGER

Paul was a notorious local bad boy. He was one of those kids who was extremely smart but repeatedly got kicked out of high school, diverting his brain power instead into cons and manipulations aimed at getting as much sex, drugs, booze, money and free stuff as possible. He also had great taste in music. During our short introductory car ride, one of the first bands he mentioned he liked was the Pointed Sticks, one of the all-time great Canadian power-pop bands. Nick and I glanced at each other. Then Paul told us he was a drummer.

As we would soon learn, despite his overflowing vices, Paul was a voracious reader who devoured any book he could get his hands on, be it a textbook on geothermal energy or an anthology of *Penthouse Forum*. In the van, he would finish his book and then read our books over our shoulders, whispering every word to himself before urging us to turn the page. It became so annoying we'd usually surrender our books to him. He always had some pulp fiction paperback novel sticking out of his trench-coat pocket. On the day we met him, it was a well-worn copy of Henry Miller's *Tropic of Cancer*.

Paul hated authority of any kind. He was a Joe Pesci act-first-ask-questions-later kind of guy. His very short temper aside, Paul was a sweetheart under his tough exterior, and much more experienced than we were in every facet of life. It was like being on tour with a merchant mariner. He had hundreds of sordid stories. He also had the slightest hint of a lisp when he got excited, turning his Rs to Ws, which is why we called him "the Pwem."

Somehow, through all his misadventures and troubled family life, Paul kept up his drumming, and he could pound on those skins and cymbals as hard and fast as he could pound back his beers. He was by far the best drummer we had played with yet. Paul "The Pwem" Preminger also had an astounding appetite for just about any food or liquid you put in front of him. He could drink staggering amounts of alcohol, getting more and more quarrelsome with each gulp, and stopping only when the booze ran out or he passed out. Devilishly charming and sweet when he wanted to be, Paul would have sex with any girl, do any drug, knock back any drink and shove incredible amounts of food into his bulldog frame—he was able to devour a Quarter Pounder in one gargantuan bite and a six-inch Subway sandwich in just two.

To get physics on his side while chowing down, he would open his jaws as wide as possible and shove as much food into his mouth as he could, like a python trying to swallow a warthog. When he was near choking, he would stand up, holding on to any exposed food with both hands, then slam himself down in his seat as hard as he could, his jaws snapping together to cut through the food using the sheer force of gravity—a junk-food guillotine. Paul Preminger took his copious consumption very seriously. Whenever entrusting a 7-Eleven employee to heat an eighty-nine-cent burrito in the store's microwave, he insisted it be done just right. If it wasn't, he'd have a meltdown, screaming at the clerk as he tossed his hot, oozing burrito from hand to hand: "You ruined it, you idiot!" He'd still eat it, of course. We loved him.

```
Saturday, September 3, 1988
Great Canadian Scooter Portage
Chicago Pizza Works
Vancouver, BC

This was the Smugglers' premier gig. The
Smugglers are Nick and me, David Carswell
on bass, Adam Woodall on harmonica and Paul
Preminger on drums. We called Preminger
the day before the show and he is the best
drummer we ever had. I think this is also
the best gig we've ever done. The Smugglers
dress code is black navy pea jackets with
sunglasses and toques, playing songs like
"I'm Cramped," "Shot Down," "Parchman Farm,"
"What Goes On" and "Boss Hoss." Lots of
folks said "Ditch the One-Eyed Jacks. Go go
go Smugglers!" The Evaporators were very
good this time, and we also played with
The Saturday Boy from Seattle. They were
okay, all originals. Lots of mods showed up
on scooters. Hopefully the Smugglers will
continue. Paul Preminger said he'd like to
play with us again. Weird thing: Paul puked
right before the show!
```

Everyone but Beez had been certain that once we survived the Rocky Mountains, the snowy conditions would be but a bad memory. Out on the open prairie of southern Alberta, we came to the icy realization that the weather was actually getting worse. The winds howled without impediment and blew billowing white clouds across the road in front of us. Streaks of snow swivelled like snakes on what little we could see of the highway. The temperature plunged to staggering depths. The sunshine did nothing to warm us.

In the front seats, Dave and I were wrapped in our sleeping bags. Dave was still driving and had yet to be spelled off. His incredible endurance was possibly due to his British heritage—stiff upper lip and all that. Dave's arms stuck out of his sleeping bag to grip the steering wheel. He wore socks on his hands like puppets. His sneakers popped out of the bottom of the sleeping bag to work the pedals. Dave giddily complained that he was losing the feeling in his fingers and toes. In the back seat, the other guys huddled together for warmth. Beez had been stinking up the van for hours with outrageous farts that smelled oddly like chicken ("oddly" because Beez was a vegetarian). Dave admitted that he welcomed the farts as a source of heat. Paul complained that the smell was making him hungrier.

We spotted a Petro-Canada gas station on the horizon, a filthy oasis of brown snow on the otherwise porcelain-white prairie. Moments later, the van sloshed through a wall of muddy grey slush, skidding into the pit stop. I gingerly stepped outside, my joints rusty and stiff from sleeping in the passenger seat. The wind took my breath away, stabbing at me through the back of my corduroy Levi's jacket like a Roman senator. The van's side door was frozen shut, but after a few desert boot kicks from Paul on the inside, it reluctantly slid open. Empty beer cans clattered into the unnatural green puddles of salt around the pumps. The cans caught the wind and rattled across the parking lot, lodging themselves in the dirty snow banks.

The rest of the band emerged like miners who had been trapped for days, making a dash for the front door of the gas station. Dave and I stayed with the van, wrapping our sleeping bags around our shoulders like vagabonds as we pumped the gas, checked the oil and scraped off the windows. We agreed over the roar of the wind that neither of us had ever felt cold like this. Our Converse sneakers were like sponges, with the icy wetness seeping through to soak our cotton gym socks. Inside, the gas station attendant happily told us the temperature: minus twenty-eight degrees Celsius, minus forty with the wind chill.

"Bullshit!" Paul yelled at him. The attendant pointed to the large, round thermometer outside his frosted window to confirm it. "Oh fuck," Paul conceded.

Paul rushed from the gas station back to the van. In his haste to get warm, he mistakenly crawled into Adam's sleeping bag. When Adam arrived, he politely asked for his sleeping bag back. Paul waved him away, telling him to fuck off through a mouthful of shoplifted Doritos. It was too cold to worry about who was in which sleeping bag, he added with a snarl. Adam allowed Paul to get comfortably settled. A few moments later, Adam shared that the only way he'd been able to keep himself warm had been to quietly, repeatedly masturbate into that sleeping bag, never bothering to wipe up—and that the last time he'd done it was right before we pulled over into the gas station.

There was a mixed look of confusion and disbelief on Paul's face as Adam's revelation sunk in. "You disgusting little shit!" Paul freaked out further with a string of obscenities, spitting Doritos everywhere while squirming his stocky frame out of that sleeping bag. Dave immediately dubbed it "The Cheese Bag." Paul never lived it down.

Back on the road, it got so frigid in our van that the *inside* of the front windshield was soon covered in a sheet of smooth, translucent ice. We could no longer see the highway. We were in a rolling igloo. I spun around in the passenger seat and called for Adam's lighter to be thrown forward. I leaned over towards Dave and held Adam's BiC to the windshield for as long as my thumb could stand the heat. The flame melted an eyehole about the size of a hockey puck in the interior ice. Luckily, vw van windshields are in very close proximity to the driver's seat (the engine being in the rear of the vehicle), which allowed Dave to lean over the steering wheel and press his eye against the melted hole. We kept driving.

We slid into Moose Jaw, Saskatchewan, in time for a late lunch. The diner's linoleum floors were soaked with a mixture of melting Canada: snow, ice, salt and mud. The heat of the busy restaurant felt euphoric at first. The place smelled like cigarettes, bleach, cheap coffee and deep-fried comfort. But as soon as our extremities started to warm up, we were in writhing pain. We crowded into a single booth, our faces blue and expressionless. Beez quietly and dejectedly announced that it was his twenty-seventh birthday. A few of us managed "happy birthday" through chattering teeth. The booths at the diner were equipped with pay phones, so we all sat and listened as Beez called his parents back home in Ontario, explaining to them that he was in a diner in Moose Jaw, in a blizzard, while on tour with a teen band from Vancouver, in a van with no heat. The rest of us warmed up with steaming bowls of clam chowder, then pooled our money to pay for Beez's three-dollar plate of poutine, wondering if we'd ever get to Regina.

We spent many mornings after all-night drives in diners just like this one. A rare shot of Beez (right) without his trademark glasses. NICK THOMAS PHOTO

four

Regina, I Don't Want to Fight

A FEW HOURS AFTER Beez's birthday poutine in Moose Jaw, we rejoiced upon seeing the glowing lights of the prairie metropolis of Regina on the horizon. Paul, ever the reader, had never been to Regina but knew its history, eagerly explaining it to us between slurps of another beer Slushie. "The name of this place used to be Pile o' Bones, because of the massive mounds of buffalo bones explorers and fur traders found here, left over from buffalo hunts. The founding fathers were concerned people would make fun of that name, so they came up with REGINA." Everyone burst into shivering laughter as we ploughed into the place country singer Carolyn Mark would one day christen "The City That Rhymes with Fun."

Regina had two places for bands to play in the late 1980s. One was called the Venue and the other was called the Club. We were scheduled to play both places, the Venue on Friday night and the Club on Saturday night, both evenings opening for a like-minded, sixties-style garage band from Calgary called the Vindicators. Our enthusiasm about finally making it to Regina was extinguished when we realized there was no fanfare awaiting us, not a single poster or advertisement for the show, NOTHING to indicate that the Vindicators and the Smugglers were performing that night at the Venue. Consequently we played to an empty bar. Somehow the Vindicators still felt the need to do an encore.

We had driven eighteen hundred kilometres over twenty-four hours through winter conditions that would have made a wampa shudder, and yet the bartender didn't have a cent to pay either band. Instead he compensated us with whatever he could find around the club, which turned out to be a twelve-pack of stale cranberry muffins in a clear plastic container, left over from the hospitality rider of a popular ska band from Montreal called Me, Mom and Morgentaler, who had packed the place the night before. Disgusted, the Vindicators refused the muffins, so we kept the full pack. The Venue had a deal with a local hotel, so thankfully we at least had free rooms for the weekend.

On our way to the hotel, a salt-stained, dirt-encrusted Chevy Nova rumbled up alongside our VW van. Steam rose from the Nova's headlights like the nostrils of a bull as its engine revved and roared. The muscle car was crammed with a teenage scourge: headbangers, metalheads, heshers. We dealt with and avoided many West Coast headbangers on a daily basis back in Vancouver, so we weren't surprised when these prairie bangers gave us a distinctly drunken stink eye. The mulleted girl riding shotgun rolled down her window and leaned out. "GET THE FUCK OUT OF MY REGINA, YOU DIRTY FUCKIN' HIPPIES!"

The light turned green. The tires of the Nova screeched, burning ice from the frozen pavement. The car fishtailed through the intersection and down Broad Street. We looked at each other in dumbfounded silence, then sprang into action. Always up for a scrap, Paul shouted, "CATCH UP TO THEM, DAVE!" Dave slammed it into first, and our van jolted forward. We sidled up to the Nova at the next intersection, thanks to a red light, the great equalizer of street races.

Paul leaned out the van's side window into the frosty Regina night. "WAIT," urged Beez, glancing around at us with panic flashing behind his glasses. "What the hell are you guys doing?"

Ignoring him, Paul yelled, "Who the fuck you calling hippies? Here's what we think of your frozen shithole town!" He hurled a cranberry muffin at the Nova. It sailed through the open passenger window, scoring a direct hit, the muffin exploding into the side of the driver's face. We burst

BEEZ

Beez was an adopted kid from the tiny town of Kleinburg, Ontario, a rural-suburban farming community forty minutes from downtown Toronto. Besides Beez, Kleinburg is the hometown of both famed Canadian author Pierre Berton and Stephen McBean, lead singer of Black Mountain. Everyone said Beez looked like Kurt Russell, the Hollywood movie star. Maybe it was the clunky Buddy Holly glasses, but I could never really see it.

As a teenager, one of Beez's first jobs was a security guard posting at the McMichael Canadian Art Collection, home to many works of the Group of Seven. He got into punk rock at an early age too, when he stumbled upon a photo shoot on a nearby country road for the offensively named Toronto band Battered Wives. Beez subsequently made pilgrimages to downtown Toronto clubs to see seminal, life-changing gigs by Teenage Head, the Viletones and the Diodes. He took up the bass guitar and formed a cool rockabilly band called Skinny Jim, named after an obscure song by the massively influential, dead-at-twenty-one, 1950s rock 'n' roller Eddie Cochran.

Beez's bass-playing style was a hybrid of high-energy rock 'n' roll, the slap-style of rockabilly, the driving melodies of the early Beatles and the pounding propulsion of punk. He also loved to sing and write songs, drawing on the spirit of everyone from Paul McCartney to Mel Tormé.

When Beez eventually landed a corporate day job in Vancouver, an Ontario pal moved with him, and they formed the avant-garde jazz-punk band Sarcastic Mannequins upon arrival. The colourful trio sounded like a cross between Devo, Wings, and the B-52s and quickly dominated the local scene with outrageous thematic gigs like "The Eye Swallow Ball" (every patron received a real cow's eyeball in a jar upon entry) and their "Surprise Party for Jesus" at the Penthouse Night Club, a notorious local strip joint. *X-Files* actor Dean Haglund, who played Richard "Ringo" Langly, one of the "Lone Gunmen" on the show, took to the stage dressed as Jesus, bottle of red wine and cigarette in hand, swearing profusely and "humbled" that a gig had been thrown in his honour.

Beez partied and be-bopped all over town, the coolest geeknik to hit the city in years. He knew everybody. His black horn-rimmed glasses made him instantly recognizable, and the geek-chic look worked. He dated a staggering succession of Vancouver's hottest punk rock babes (including one called—no joke—"Paula the Sex Goddess"). He also ran a series of highly successful, illegal, late-night "booze cans" out of the squalid Downtown Eastside rentals he happily called home, making a nightly splash of cash selling beer after the bars had closed. Having studied economics in university, Beez loved cash. He even started a tele-dating company in Vancouver with a couple of his university buddies that eventually became a massive success.

into laughter and high fives. Beez, generally a feel-good peacenik, was shocked at the rapidly unfolding events.

I first came into contact with Beez while I was still in high school. I was student council president at the time, following in the footsteps of my predecessor Nardwuar the Human Serviette. Like Nardwuar, I tried to import cool bands from downtown to play our high school dances. Occasionally, an enterprising band would realize that suburban high school student councils had considerable budgets for entertainment and would reach out to the schools.

One such strategizing band that contacted me was the Sarcastic Mannequins. I called the number on the back of the crude but funny photocopied brochure the band had mailed me and spoke to the bassist, a guy named Beez. He sounded energetic and friendly and eager for his band to play our high school. Thinking quickly, I turned the tables on Beez, informing him that I had a band called the Smugglers that was looking to branch out into playing shows in downtown Vancouver. Would it be possible for our bands to help each other out? Beez fell silent on the other end of the line, seemingly unprepared for a counter-offer.

Before he could answer, I suggested a deal: if Beez could get the Smugglers a show opening for the Sarcastic Mannequins, in return I would get them a sweet, high-paying gig at my West Vancouver high school. Beez hummed and hawed a little, but eventually agreed. It didn't take long before he made good on his end of the deal, landing the Smugglers our first-ever real club performance at the legendary Town Pump in downtown Vancouver. It was our first break. Even before the Smugglers started touring, I was writing recaps of every show in my diary.

```
January 9, 1989
The Town Pump
Vancouver, BC

Oh yeah guy, we made it! We played THE PUMP!
A stage that has played host to such legends
as Bo Diddley, J.J. Cale, the blind guy, Deja
Voodoo, the Raunch Hands, the Bluesbreakers
```

and the Gruesomes. We played with Shovlhed from Victoria and the Sarcastic Mannequins from Vancouver. We played first, but it didn't matter, the place was really full for us and folks danced for the last half of our set. I think we really rocked! Nick and Dave wore matching outfits and I wore a contrasting one. All the songs went well except for our Rolling Stones cover of "Citadel." We really screwed that one up. In our Elvis Presley cover of "Burning Love," our friend Glen Winter dressed up as Elvis, pretending to be mad, and tried to stop the show. On his way off stage, he knocked over the bass amp, and Nick and Dave both broke strings. It was really fun seeing the audience packed with all our friends, all minors who snuck in somehow. The Mannequins were good, but I didn't like Shovlhed, and everyone left by the time they played anyway. While loading our equipment through the back, Glen was really drunk at this point and pulled the main power switch for the entire Town Pump, and had the place in utter darkness. The furious manager and the bouncers came running back with flashlights, looking for a guy "who's really tall and dressed like Elvis." Great gig anyway. Beez from the Sarcastic Mannequins paid us $31.

Our first gig at the Town Pump, which was hallowed ground for both local and touring acts coming through Vancouver. When we weren't on tour, I'd spend up to three or four nights a week seeing bands at this venue, like John Mayall and the Young Fresh Fellows.

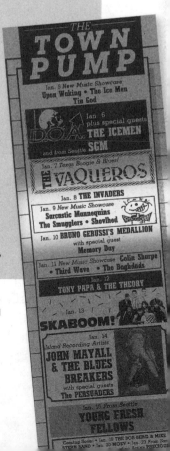

I wasn't as quick to fulfill my end of the bargain. Instead, I quizzed Beez during many subsequent phone calls. He was still trying to get that high-paying high school gig out of me, while I was trying to source as much music career advice as possible before he figured out that our school's entertainment budget for the year had already been spent. During those conversations, he offered a kernel of advice that has stuck with me ever since.

"Here's the deal," explained an exasperated Beez over the crackling phone line connecting my sheltered suburb to his downtown hipster abode. "Don't just put on *a gig*. Every band puts on a gig; the weeklies are full of bands playing regular gigs. *Put on an event*. Turn it into a *party*, every single time. Everybody wants to go to a party, right man? Everybody wants to be part of an event. Give people a *reason* that they *have* to be there, a part of the action, and if they're not, they're missing out. Hey, there's *always* a reason to celebrate, right?"

None of the Smugglers had ever met anyone quite like Beez. He was instantly likeable, and, when not facing an icy death, was mostly always smiling. Beez was a gifted musician, he *understood* rock 'n' roll and he could sing like a bird. He was ten years older than we were but certainly didn't seem it. We just had to convince him to play bass for us, even temporarily. That way, both Dave and Nick could be on guitars for a twin guitar, party-rock attack. A week before hitting the road to Regina, I called Beez and begged him to come with us. For reasons I am unclear about to this day, he agreed to come along.

I never did fulfill my end of the bargain to land the Sarcastic Mannequins that West Vancouver high school gig. Beez often summed up our initial interaction by telling people, "I contacted Grant to hustle him for a gig, and somehow I ended up working for him for the next sixteen years."

THE DRIVER OF the Nova had half-chewed cranberries from Paul's muffin streaked across his face, with chunks caught in his frizzy mullet. Crumbs littered the shoulder pads of the acid-washed jean jacket on the she-banger in the passenger seat. As the light turned green, she hung her torso out of the passenger window and shrieked like a banshee, "YOU'RE SO FUCKIN' DEAD!"

Both vehicles lurched forward. Dave kept one hand on the steering wheel, trying to control the van on the icy Saskatchewan streets, while he rolled down his window with the other. I leaned across his lap and hurled another muffin, again landing a baked bomb right into their banger mobile. The second muffin stayed relatively intact, and quickly became enemy fire. One of the bangers whipped it back, smacking Dave in the side of the face and causing the VW van to swerve. Paul fired a third muffin out of a side window. It skidded across the hood of the Nova, leaving a red streak of squished cranberries in the snow.

And so it went. The two vehicles raced down Broad Street in the early morning hours, a steady volley of cranberry muffins sailing back and forth. Finally, sensing a losing battle, Dave swerved down a side street to try and lose them, but he made a bad choice: cul-de-sac. He swung the van around and tried to U-turn back out, but the Nova cut us off. Our single headlight was no match for the Nova's blaring high beams in the deep freeze. A six-pack of bangers poured out of their muscle car as Paul kicked open the side door of our van.

"WHAT ARE YOU GUYS DOING?" yelled Beez from inside his zipped-up sleeping bag.

Paul stood in the snow with his arm cocked, another half-muffin ready to be launched. In his other hand he gripped our tire iron. I was right behind him, brandishing a cymbal stand. Dave revved the van's wimpy engine, ready to bolt. The bangers stood in their headlight beams, bow-legged silhouettes ready to scrap.

Seeing that we were outnumbered and in foreign territory, Beez scrambled out of his sleeping bag and jumped into the street, positioning himself between the two forces. "STOP!" he screamed, with enough nerdy responsibility and authority in his voice to remind us he was actually an adult. As both sides momentarily paused, an RCMP cruiser slid into the cul-de-sac, red and blue lights ablaze. The Mounties leapt out of their squad car.

"EVERYONE AGAINST THE VAN!" The police quickly surveyed the scene, assuming from the red streaks all over our faces, clothes and cars that they'd come across a bloody battle. It took Beez a while to convince them that none of us were wounded and no blood spatter expert was needed: it was all just squished cranberries. Once we were free to go our separate ways, Beez made us promise we'd never tangle with bangers again. It was a pledge we would not keep.

five

Oh My My

"THE ONLY TOURING bands people are interested in going out to see in Regina in this kind of weather are cool American groups," said Dave, the owner of X-Ray Records in Regina. "Canadian bands really don't do so well, unless you're like, say, Kick Axe, or Rush, or a ska band or something."

When I woke up earlier that afternoon at the hotel, it had struck me that we had some time to change our luck for our second show in Regina that night. I thought back to Beez's mantra: "Don't just put on a gig. Put on an event. Every time."

No advertising for the gig? No problem. We'd promote it ourselves. We approached the Vindicators with the idea, but they weren't inspired. They were content to hang out in their heated hotel room watching TV and plotting their next encore. The Smugglers braved the frostbitten elements, found a copy shop and made homemade posters. If the kids in Regina wanted touring bands from the USA, that's what we'd give them.

We spent the rest of the day battling the blizzard and plastering the city with our posters, handing them out to every teenager or remotely hip kid we saw. We hit the record store, the comic book shop, the pizza joint, liquor stores, the mall and the radio station. We did our very best

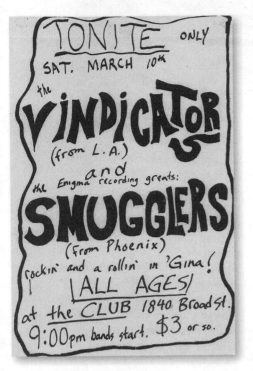

to turn on the teenage charm. (Oh, and the Enigma Records thing? We were big into the Cramps, and for a while in the late 1980s they were on Enigma).

Beez was right. It worked. An audience showed up! They lined up in the snow to pay the three-dollar cover charge! The show was packed, and Regina loved us! People danced! They cheered! It was one of the first-ever audiences who truly seemed to *enjoy* us. Immediately following the show, a very cute, very assertive girl walked up to Adam as he stepped off the stage covered in sweat. She grabbed him by his Guatemalan poncho, pulled him to her open lips and started making out with him right at the side of the stage. The rest of us tried not to stare, but our mouths were agape while watching their tongue tango. A moment later, the girl led Adam by the hand into the women's washroom, where she proceeded to give him a blow job with our last cymbal crash still ringing in the air. Even Beez was stunned. None of us had ever thought our event planning would go over *that* well.

A couple of days later, against all odds and elements, the Smugglers hissed and popped our way back to Vancouver for the rest of spring break. We had survived our first touring foray, braving some of the harshest winter conditions a group of Vancouverites could imagine. We had also experienced the alluring, escapist power of rock 'n' roll touring glory for the first time, prompting Dave to exclaim, "Can we do that again next weekend?"

THE LATE 1980S was a strange era for alternative music in Canada, an ebb between the creative punk rock riptide of the late 1970s and the alt-rock tidal wave that would occur in the early 1990s. Touring western Canada reflected that. Blues, bar rock and dance floor–oriented bands

BIO

ADAM WOODALL

Adam Woodall was a kind and absurdly funny fellow, always smiling, very charming and a big hit with the ladies. He had curly blond hair and a deep tan, and he loved the hippie lifestyle. Adam often dressed in colourful articles of clothing woven by Central American villagers, extra-large tie dye T-shirts, Rastafarian berets and beaded knee-high leather-fringed moccasins.

Adam was also a dedicated cyclist, so it wasn't surprising to see him sporting brightly coloured, skin-tight spandex short shorts that left nothing to the imagination. If he had just hopped off his bike for band practice, he looked like a sweaty cross between Bob Marley, Gallagher and Barbra Streisand. We did what we could to mold him into the Smugglers look, which worked to varying degrees of success.

Adam came by his hippie lifestyle honestly: both his parents were accomplished artists. His dad, a bear of a man, was Ron Woodall, the renowned painter, photographer, cartoonist and advertising genius who created the A&W Root Bear (some said in his own image). To his kids' great delight, Ron was also a dead ringer for Grateful Dead lead singer Jerry Garcia, so much so that he won a lookalike context, which sent the entire family to a Dead concert. The Woodalls also had a huge record collection, mostly original blues, jazz, folk and freedom rock LPs, and it was easy to conclude that Adam's parents were more understanding and supportive of their son's musical path than the rest of our parents combined.

Despite what I considered his fashion short-shortcomings, Adam was a savant-like harmonica player, honking out imaginative, rockin' solos in any key we threw at him. Plus, as Nick further pointed out when trying to secure Adam's place in the Smugglers, some of our all-time favourite songs had wicked harmonica solos: the Rolling Stones' "Midnight Rambler," the Doors' "Roadhouse Blues," the Gruesomes' "What's Your Problem?" Adam didn't love the music we played, but he really, really wanted to be in a band. He told us he could play the guitar if needed, and he practised his harp constantly. While delivering pizza on weekends in his parents' Volvo, he supposedly steered the car with his knees so he could blow along on his harmonica to the Grateful Dead's *American Beauty*.

ruled. Alternative punk and garage rock did not, with very rare exceptions like the Gruesomes.

By the time punk rock officially detonated in the mid-1970s, Vancouver was one of the epicentres of the riotous musical movement, arguably behind only New York, London and Los Angeles. Our Downtown Eastside core boasted bands like the Young Canadians, the Skulls, Death Sentence, Pointed Sticks, the Modernettes and, most famously, D.O.A., the band many punk rock historians credit with inventing the musical genre of hardcore and the do-it-yourself (DIY) punk rock work ethic of self-promotion, show booking, releasing records and van touring. The fertile Vancouver punk scene had a positive influence on nearby cities like Victoria, which spawned bands like NoMeansNo, the Dayglo Abortions and the Dishrags. Seattle, whose punk rock scene was but an emerald shadow to Vancouver's world-class acts, had a few good bands like the U-Men, the Pudz, the Fartz and the Fastbacks.

When the Smugglers came of age in the late 1980s, a full decade had passed since Vancouver's punk heyday, and besides D.O.A., many of the coolest and most infamous Vancouver punk and new wave bands were long gone; they had been replaced by art-rock and roots-oriented bands like Bob's Your Uncle (with enigmatic lead singer Sook-Yin Lee), the Hard Rock Miners (a high-energy Pogues-like acoustic folk-rock group), Roots Roundup (dance hall reggae, ska and hippie jams) and Beez's jazz-punk band, the Sarcastic Mannequins.

The Smugglers wanted an association with the original punks, but too much time had passed. We were kids, and they were grown-ups. We were a gap band between two major musical movements. When seeking out an original bassist for our band, Nick and I turned to David Carswell, who played guitar in Nardwuar's group, the Evaporators. They played a cool style of sixties garage surf punk. The Evaporators and the One-Eyed Jacks became friends, and when Dave suggested he was interested in playing bass for a band, Nick and I snapped him up. Dave would go on to do double duty in the Smugglers and the Evaporators for many years.

Dave was a fluid and funny bass player, pulling off hilariously twisted facial expressions while keeping his feet dancing and prancing. His prolific song writing often mined British influences like the Smiths and Depeche Mode. I preferred the Sonics and the Gruesomes, but Dave's songs had a more lasting melodic pop appeal than the three-chord garage rock songs Nick and I attempted to write. For a few months, Dave and Nick switched back and forth between bass and guitar while Adam honked on the harmonica, Paul pounded the drums and I squelched lyrics into the microphone. We tried a few short-term members but yearned for the fullness of Dave and Nick's twin-guitar attack. That's when we decided to target Beez.

The Smugglers began performing live immediately after forming, but the venues had shifted from the halls and church basements that dominated the late seventies all-ages punk scene to 19+ bars, pubs and clubs. A touring circuit had developed across the vast reaches of western Canada at places like the Town Pump in Vancouver, the Westward Hotel in Calgary, Amigos in Saskatoon, the Royal Albert Arms in Winnipeg and Crocks and Rolls in Thunder Bay. If you were willing to cross the epic geographic expanses between these rock 'n' roll outposts, the bars were not only open to booking live bands, but were also willing to supply the acts with free hot meals, free beer and free accommodation. This was the circuit the Smugglers desperately wanted to drill into. I started booking a western Canadian tour soon after our return from our blizzard blitz to Regina, hoping to add another five or six cities to a summer itinerary.

There was one significant catch: many of the western Canadian bars booked touring acts for multi-night stands and expected the bands to play, at minimum, three hour-long sets per night. Beez was aware of this, as he had done the expansive circuit with the Sarcastic Mannequins. They padded and stacked their sets into a living jukebox-like party-rock cover song party, he told us, and would occasionally slide in their jazz-punk originals and hope that people would keep on dancing. He advised the Smugglers to follow suit, but again we ignored the sage advice from our elderly bassist.

The covers we chose for our band to play were obscure/bad garage-rock songs by has-beens and never-weres, taken from weird vinyl compilation albums like *Back from the Grave* and *Pebbles*. The more esoteric the cover, the cooler it was to me. That made the good songs hard to find, though, so we only covered a handful, each about two minutes or less in length. "Louie Louie" and "Get Off My Cloud" were too mainstream for us. We completely missed Beez's universal point that live music audiences react positively to what they recognize: "Play the hits!" The Smugglers were used to being one of the many young and talentless bands on multi-act "new music" bills, where we were responsible for only thirty or forty-five minutes of music a night. Thus, we had barely forty minutes of material.

Undaunted, we continued our plans to get back out on the road. To book our first string of western Canadian tour dates, I cobbled together a list of clubs and phone numbers and started calling. Bands like the Hard Rock Miners and Bob's Your Uncle already had albums out, along with a booking agent who would do the work for a fee. The Smugglers didn't have an album or an agent, so I figured I could arrange the tour myself. I thought it would seem somewhat pathetic and unprofessional, however, if the lead singer of the band was the one calling up the clubs. It seemed un-Canadian to boast about how great we were, and I sure didn't have anyone else who would do it for us, so I came up with a persona: "Larry," a name I thought sounded like a booking agent's, and someone who could really sing the praises of the sheer musical genius of the Smugglers.

Unfortunately, I didn't consider that "Larry" was also short for "Lawrence." One of the first club bookers I got on the phone asked for my full name and contact information. I wasn't prepared for that, and I blurted out my actual last name. There was a pause. "Your name is Larry... Lawrence? As in, full name, Lawrence Lawrence?"

Caught off guard and wanting to keep up appearances, I maintained the charade. "Uh, yeah... my parents were very unimaginative. But hey, Jim, please call me Larry. Now, about this hot act outta Vancouver called the Smugglers. I think they'd be perfect for your Saskatoon New Music Monday series..." Somehow I managed to hustle several club owners for gigs, convincing many of them to book us because we were "the next Gruesomes."

Big mistake. The summer tour put us almost instantly into painful situations we were ill prepared for. Beez was right again. When we got fired after the first night of our first booking, a three-night stand in Calgary, we had to face the fact that we needed more songs, or at least a much longer set, immediately.

To achieve this, we added in horrible stretched-out "blues jams," often coming up with the riff and a lyric or two in the dressing room before the show or on-the-spot onstage. Beez sang one of them, a lament that repeated the chorus "It's a long, long, long, long, long, long, long, long way home" over and over. We added solo acoustic performances and attempts at stand-up comedy and audience trivia, as well as multiplying the length of ALL our guitar solos from the regular four bars into eight, twelve, sixteen or more. At times we simply played the same song twice in a row without stopping, hoping no one would notice.

People *did* notice, and the very few who had the misfortune to be in attendance at a Smugglers show on that tour expressed their discontent by booing, heckling, spitting, throwing things and eventually leaving—even our family members. Usually, by the middle of the second set, to our total denial, we had committed the cardinal sin of live rock 'n' roll: we'd cleared the room. By the third set we were often performing our blaring garage rock to the bartender and the manager, both of them glaring at us with arms crossed. Sometimes we wouldn't even get to the third set. "Your agent Larry Lawrence told me your act was the next Gruesomes!" the manager would shout at us between agitated drags on his cigarette as soon as we climbed off the stage. "What the hell was that shit?"

"We'll be more like the Gruesomes tomorrow night!" I promised in vain. There was rarely a "tomorrow night," since most of the second and third night bookings were cancelled. Forced out of the band accommodations and unable to afford a hotel, we'd often head back out to the Trans-Canada, puttering out of town for an hour or two, then turning off the highway down a country road under the infinite prairie night sky. There we'd shut down the van, pop up the built-in camper top, crack open a few lukewarm Black Labels and eventually pass out. When the chips were really down, I'd make a mental note to call Nardwuar the Human Serviette in the morning for some career advice.

six

Nardwuar the Human Serviette Presents...

EHIND THE MOST famous bands and musicians in rock 'n' roll, there is often a mentor or a visionary who, for better or worse, guides the young rockers through the early pitfalls and minefields of music. Elvis Presley had Colonel Tom Parker, a shady sideshow carny who applied everything he'd learned on the carnival circuit to music management. The Beatles had Brian Epstein, a Liverpudlian record store owner turned music mogul who was rumoured to have sexually propositioned at least two members of the band and who also convinced the lads to switch from jeans, pompadours and leather jackets to matching suits and mop-top haircuts. The Runaways had Kim Fowley, a deranged predator who stalked Sunset Strip in Los Angeles like a snarling wolf. The Velvet Underground had the gay pop-art luminary and scene-creator Andy Warhol. The Sex Pistols had Malcolm McLaren, the architect of punk. Green Day had greaser-turned-hippie-turned-punk prophet Larry Livermore.

Knowing that musical mentors helped add credibility and mystique, some bands created fictional backers who supposedly provided everything from songs to liner notes. The Hives had the elusive "Randy

Nardwuar the Human Serviette in all of his grade twelve glory. He was our newly elected student council president and brought all sorts of amazing bands like Grapes of Wrath and the Enigmas from downtown to play our high school dances. This is the only office Nardwuar has ever had. Note the Sonics and Subhumans posters on the wall. PHOTO COURTESY OF NARDWUAR PRODUCTIONS

Fitzsimmons." For the Gruesomes it was "Fuad Ramses." The Smugglers' mentor sounded made-up but was very real. We were far from famous, but we had the one-of-a-kind Nardwuar the Human Serviette looking out for us, and we were damn lucky for it.

Nardwuar was the most wonderfully peculiar character any of us had ever met. Highly intelligent and extremely positive, he had a manic energy that no one could ever hope to match. I had known the darkly hirsute Nardwuar since I was in grade two, but became close friends with him in high school when he reached out to me, a lonely loser barely surviving grade eight, to involve me in a hallway garbage can beautification project. We have been friends ever since. He adopted his bizarre pseudonym in his last year of high school, both as a tribute to the punk rockers he adored who used pseudonyms (Johnny Rotten, Lux Interior, Frankie Venom) and as a way to operate in the underground media and music scene. He and his friend Gary had coined "Nardwuar" as a nonsense word to yell at other people; "the Human Serviette" was tagged on as a tip of the toque to the Cramps song "Human Fly" and also as a Canadianism. Nardwuar was extremely funny, stubborn as a mule and deeply superstitious. He handed out lucky chestnuts, constantly touched wood and prayed to a "white light." Like me, he obsessed over 1960s rock 'n' roll culture. Nardwuar saw the world through an extremely curious, highly focused filter that would have exhausted Hunter S. Thompson.

Nardwuar not only booked many of the Smugglers' first gigs in Vancouver and released our first records on his label (aptly titled Nardwuar Records), but also suggested the name for our band. To this day, he insists I misheard him during the emergency phone call I made to him in the aftermath of the implosion of the One-Eyed Jacks. Nick and I were kind of on thin ice with Nardwuar that summer, since we had recently had his mom mistakenly arrested for allegedly pointing a firearm at a busload of school children (long story), but he agreed to help us nonetheless. Nardwuar says he suggested "the Snugglers" (after Snug Cove on Bowen Island, where his family had a cabin), but I heard "the Smugglers." I loved it, immediately picturing our new band's image: a West Coast dockworker look, with the band outfitted in dark wool, double-breasted navy pea jackets, black toques, rubber boots, dark turtlenecks and Velvet Underground-style wraparound shades. The look was meant to be a salute to our misty West Coast lifestyle and to the 1960s northwest garage bands in their matching outfits. Almost immediately, the choice of wearing heavy wool onstage would prove to be hazardous.

During Nardwuar's last few years at our high school, he got himself elected to student council, eventually becoming president. He used his power for the musical good, reinventing our school dances by firing the DJs with their canned music and instead booking live, original bands from downtown Vancouver: groups like the Grapes of Wrath (Canada's answer to R.E.M.), the Villains (a cool ska band that kept the mods skanking all night long), Poisoned (a post-punk/pre-grunge band featuring ex-Young Canadians front man Art Bergmann), and the Enigmas (a paisley-powered sixties garage rock explosion). Nardwuar tried to book iconic San Francisco punk band Dead Kennedys for our final dance of the year, but lead singer Jello Biafra replied with a personal letter saying they were unavailable. (Amazingly, twenty years later, Nardwuar's band, the

Evaporators, would end up signed to Alternative Tentacles, Jello Biafra's record label.) No matter who was playing, a healthy percentage of the student population would turn out for the dances, freaking out to whatever disaffected sounds were blasting from the PA.

After every dance, students came away inspired, many having experienced their very own I can do that moments. All sorts of bands began to emerge from various grades and cliques of our high school. While I thought Nardwuar and Dave's band, the Evaporators, was by far the coolest, the neo-hippies stopped playing hacky sack long enough to start a couple of bongo-beat bands called Sleepy Boy Floyd and the Hip Waiders. The mods formed two groups, a stripped-down, Who-inspired power trio entitled On the Go!, followed by a sax-driven, nattily attired combo called the Wee Beasties. Some hockey jocks and hosers merged talents to slap out a freedom rock combo called She Stole My Beer, while some of the truly weird, big-haired goths got together in a dark industrial unit called the Fourth Floor, who blew everyone away when they put out their own 12″ single while still in grade eleven. Not to be left out, the punks raged forward, creating TTSD, which stood for TURN THAT SHIT DOWN— exactly what the lead singer's dad screamed down the basement stairs during their rehearsals. Even the library geeks got involved, forming a shockingly pathetic, ego-driven Depeche-Mode-meets-Joy-Division synth-pop band called the Distress Signals. They probably had the best straight-up pop songs of any group in our school, and one of the best band names ever. Nick and I launched first the One-Eyed Jacks, and then the Smugglers.

Nardwuar took what he learned from booking bands at our high school dances and applied it to arranging and promoting all-ages shows under the brand "Nardwuar the Human Serviette Presents" around Vancouver, at any place he could find to rent. He started with local bands, branching out after a few years to cool touring groups like Deja Voodoo from Montreal, the Untamed Youth from Missouri and the Young Fresh Fellows from Seattle. Either the Evaporators or the Smugglers would always perform. The posters were hand-drawn, colourful, beautiful works of art by Evaporators drummer Scott Livingstone, recalling the psychedelic poster era of the late 1960s. Tickets to the shows were extremely cheap, usually just four dollars, and were sold in advance at record stores

Nardwuar swears this was the first circular gig poster in Vancouver music history. We cut every one out by hand. He also made clocks out of them. They advertised a two-night stand record release party for Nardwuar's first compilation album *Oh God My Mom's on Channel 10!*, which was the Smugglers' first appearance on vinyl. SCOTT LIVINGSTONE POSTER

and cafes. Nardwuar gave every gig a title, like "The Hip Flip," "Roger Ramjet's Rave Up," "That's Cool, That's Trash" and "Welcome to My Castle." True to his manic nature, every show started at an exact minute, such as 7:14 P.M., 7:27 P.M. or 7:29 P.M.

As Nardwuar's all-ages gigs grew in number and size, he realized he needed help. The kind of people who rented the spaces Nardwuar targeted for all-ages gigs (community centres, church basements and Masonic Halls) were often straitlaced older adults. The Masons were particularly strange. The last thing they wanted in their halls were punk rock bands and out-of-control teenagers.

Nardwuar came to me, and together we developed a game plan that would allow us to successfully provide independent, live rock 'n' roll music to underage kids in and around Vancouver. To convince The Man to rent us space, we needed a semantic spin, and thus I became the chief negotiator of Nardwuar the Human Serviette Presents. Nardwuar, who looked and acted like Prince Valiant with a squirrel in his pants, was too extreme, too excitable and too weird for most church ladies and all Masons. Through trial and error, we discovered that if Nardwuar waited outside in his mom's Volare station wagon, I could awkwardly proceed into the office wearing my nerdy glasses and collared shirts and explain the situation using reassuring terminology.

When anyone asked the name of our production company, I never dared utter the true gonzo moniker. Instead, Nardwuar and I came up with the vaguely Christian-sounding "Serve-Youth." I would describe a wholesome evening, a "teen talent show," during which "some of the kids will bring along a guitar or two for a group sing-along." We figured the venue managers didn't need to know that those guitars were Gibson SGs and Fender Mustangs, cranked to Biblical volumes. More often than not, after listening to my pitch, the managers would just hand over the keys and let us have the place for the night. Most of the time, everything went off with aplomb, like when my mom allowed us to hold a gig in her church's basement. The most important thing was that kids finally had access to great music usually reserved for the 19+ clubs. Our young audiences were usually fairly well behaved, and we'd fastidiously clean the place after an event so we could hopefully rent it again.

Unfortunately, everything went wrong at one notorious show Nardwuar held in another church basement, this one in the prestigious British Properties in West Vancouver. It was a weeknight event that turned into a congregation of chaos starring our all-time favourite band.

seven

Bama Lama Bama Loo!

NARDWUAR PACED THE floor in front of me as I waited for the motel operator to transfer my call. "It's ringing," I hissed. Nardwuar stopped in his tracks and gazed down at me as I cradled the receiver of his ancient rotary phone. Someone on the other end picked up. I heard a loud television laugh track in the background.

"Hello?"

"Uh . . . hi . . . is this . . . the Gruesomes?"

"Who wants to know?"

"Uh . . . this is Grant Lawrence from West Vancouver, BC, and we really want to book you for an all-ages gig on Wednesday, November 16, 1988, in Vancouver when you have a day off on your tour schedule and we can pay you three hundred dollars and you can stay at my parents' house and would you be able to do it?"

My question was followed by a long pause, but I knew he hadn't hung up, because I still heard *Gilligan's Island*.

"How the fuck did you get this number?"

"Uh . . ."

As with booking the venues, Nardwuar and I had to go to creative lengths to secure the headlining bands we loved. We had recently bought copies of the Gruesomes' astounding, life-changing third album, *Hey!* Inserted into the LP was a photocopied sheet of their cross-Canada tour dates. When we noticed the band was spending a whole week in the Vancouver area with a few days off, we immediately wanted one of those nights for our next "Nardwuar the Human Serviette Presents" all-ages concert.

The list of venues the Gruesomes were playing across Canada looked so exotic: Foufoune Electriques in Montreal. Lee's Palace in Toronto. The Flamingo in Halifax. On the very night Nardwuar and I were poring over the tour dates on the LP insert, we learned the Gruesomes were playing a club called Crocks and Rolls in Thunder Bay, Ontario, on the isolated northern shore of Lake Superior.

"Why don't we call the operator in Thunder Bay and ask for the number to this club?" I suggested to Nardwuar.

Nardwuar paused for a moment, staring at me. "Do it!" he shrieked.

Within a few minutes, we had the phone number for the club scrawled out. We nervously dialled it up, trying to keep our voices low so we wouldn't wake Nardwuar's dad. With the time change, unfortunately, the club was already closed for the night.

"They're probably staying in a hotel or motel right in Thunder Bay," I guessed. "Why don't we call a few?" On only our second call, we struck Gruesomes gold.

"Good evening, Sleeping Giant Travel Lodge, how may I help you?"

"I'm callin' from Crocks and Rolls," I lied, using a false deep voice and an inexplicable New York accent. "Can you put me through to the Gruesomes' room right away, doll? They forgot a few things down at da club."

"Sure, Frank, hang on."

What? Who was Frank? But the bluff worked. I was connected directly with the Gruesomes. After the first awkward moments, expecting at any second to hear a dial tone, I was shocked to be chatting clumsily with Gruesomes bassist John Davis as late-night reruns echoed loudly in the background. Within twenty minutes, the gig was booked and the Gruesomes had accepted the invitation to stay at my parents' house, eager to save money otherwise spent at a hotel. When I hung up the phone, Nardwuar and I collapsed on the floor, writhing in joy, screaming, "YES! THE GRUESOMES! YES!" Nardwuar's dad yelled at us down the stairs, "Stop

The Gruesomes performing at Nardwuar's all-ages concert Bama Lama Bama Loo in a church basement in West Vancouver. The gig turned out to be a complete melee. NICK THOMAS PHOTO

~~~~~~

acting crazy! Be quiet and go to bed." We celebrated in silence after that with high fives and fist pumps. The opening bands on the bill would, of course, be Nardwuar and his Evaporators and the Smugglers.

Even though the British Properties church was in a ridiculously hard-to-reach location, halfway up a mountainside with no access to public transit, we postered for Nardwuar the Human Serviette Presents Bama Lama Bama Loo (named after a Little Richard song) day and night for weeks leading up to the event, all over downtown and in every suburb within thirty kilometres. We specifically targeted all-girls schools, sneaking in to stick up posters in the hallways and the cafeteria, and were chased out of one by a ruler-swinging headmistress. By the week of the gig, there was a Gruesomes poster in every possible place we could think of.

When the night of Bama Lama Bama Loo arrived, Nardwuar and I reaped the results of our thorough promotional job. Hundreds of kids showed up to the church basement. Gig attendees came from kilometres around and from every sect imaginable: mods, punks, nerds, new wavers, goths, rockabilly teds, skinheads and more. The crowd encompassed all the underage kids who hadn't been able to see the Gruesomes at their downtown bar shows on previous tours.

In an echo of the Rolling Stones' ill-fated move of hiring Hells Angels to provide security for their disastrous 1969 Altamont concert, Nardwuar had drafted local skinheads to do our gig security in the last-minute planning stages of Bama Lama Bama Loo. A lanky, loud and often out-of-control skinhead named Roger the Dodger was their leader.

The first sign of trouble came when I spotted blood splattering across the linoleum floor of the church basement. Bodies slammed into each other in all directions as the Evaporators played. Communion this was not. I was shocked when my best friend and bandmate Nick emerged from the pit, doubled over in pain, his hands cupped under his blood-spurting nose. He had just been smacked in the face by one of the skinheads' high-flying elbows. The skinheads were supposed to be doing security, yet half of them were on the dance floor, elbows, knees and Doc Martens up.

While Nick mopped up his face in the bathroom, more and more kids poured in through the church basement doors. Roger the Dodger and his skinhead security team were supposed to be guarding the entrance, but instead they raged through the church and the adjacent parking lot like Satan's pilgrims, causing bloody mayhem everywhere. There were dozens of kids in the church parking lot, many of them drinking. Roger and his skinhead security force shoved their way through the crowd, starting fist fights with any kid—goth, rockabilly, mod or punk—who didn't hand over their booze to the skinheads (so they could drink it themselves).

With increasing urgency, Nardwuar demanded the skinheads guard the doors against the gatecrashers. When they finally got around to it, the skins made the most of that responsibility, too, letting fellow skinheads in for free and stealing most of the precious ticket money we'd collected. Naively, we'd left wads of cash sitting unattended on a table near the entrance, stuffed into a large glass container labelled in bright red letters, "Dad's Job Jar," which I had grabbed from our house on my way out in lieu of a cash register.

As the Smugglers performed, fights popped up across the dance floor like Whac-a-Moles, the skinheads always at the centre of the thuggery. By

NICK THOMAS

I'd known Nick Thomas since we were in grade one, and my first memory of him was of a tiny boy entertaining a group of us at recess with a party trick: he could wiggle his ears. Always a sporty kid, Nick got turned off athletics in high school when he was cut at team tryouts due to his diminutive size. He switched his attention to skateboarding and the music that provided the soundtrack: Suicidal Tendencies, Violent Femmes and Agent Orange. We became close friends when Nick's parents were in the midst of a separation and he was going through a tough time. Neither of us was comfortable in gym locker rooms, for various reasons, and music became not only our escape but also the source of a newfound confidence. We bonded over our love for rock 'n' roll music and our passion for digging deeper and deeper through generations of vinyl.

Nick was a kind-hearted, even-keeled guy, the perfect yin to my aggressively ambitious, at times dictatorial yang. His parents were wary of me, worried that I was coercing their son into a dead-end world of sex, booze and rock 'n' roll. Arguably, they were right, except the part about it being a dead end. Nick's mother eventually saw the proof of that first-hand: she was a travel agent who would prove invaluable to the Smugglers on tour. Nick's father was a doctor; once he got over his initial concerns, he quickly became the Smugglers' first superfan, and he never missed a local show. Nick blossomed from his physically awkward teen years into a golden boy of sorts, the Smugglers' de facto sex symbol. It was sometimes tough playing wingman to Nick's polite but potent charms.

He also evolved into a sturdy rock 'n' roll guitarist with such explosive physical energy it left him drenched in sweat. Onstage, he looked like he'd jumped into a lake fully clothed. After our shows, he could pour litres of perspiration out of his black rubber boots, to the amazement and disgust of anyone gathered backstage. Even though he had a very friendly disposition, Nick also had an odd knack for getting his handsome mug battered and bruised.

the time the Gruesomes finally took the stage, most of the skinheads had either passed out or were busy luring girls upstairs into the darkness of the main church to have sex in the pews, so the fun-time all-ages dance party was finally on.

The morning after Bama Lama Bama Loo, I awoke to the dream come true of having my rock 'n' roll heroes asleep throughout my family home. I desperately wanted to stay home from school and hang out with them, but Dad, who had been very reluctant to allow them to stay in the first place, forced me out the kitchen door. I ingloriously shuffled off to catch the school bus.

Although my mom had sung in her church choir for decades, neither of my parents came from a rich musical background. Neither played an instrument. When I was a kid, we had about three cassette tapes in the car: the greatest hits of ABBA and the Beach Boys, and Billy Joel's *Glass Houses*. I love all three artists to this day, probably due to Stockholm Syndrome-like repetition, but suffice to say the listening selection on family road trips was limiting. In the house, my parents had a couple of Rolling Stones LPs for parties, but that was about it. When I got turned on to music with an unbridled passion, it caught them both off guard.

My father was as straitlaced and conservative as they come. Elvis was about as wild as he got musically. My mother was a fashion-conscious preppie who loved Frankie Avalon and the colour pink. They were horrified when I grew my hair out, stopped shaving and started wearing fringed buckskin jackets and black Beatle boots. Mom did her best to hide her concern, but Dad challenged me on everything from my haircut to the economic black hole that is the music business. He had reason to: I used the family phone to book the Smugglers' tours. The bills were outrageous, and Dad was furious. In the face of it all, they allowed us to practise in the basement. We created a spine-altering racket, forcing them to listen to the same crappy songs over and over again.

Nardwuar had to hide his rock 'n' roll identity from his father, so with my parents' hesitant permission, our home phone number was printed on the Nardwuar concert posters as the "info" line. All four members of my family became adept at fielding inquiries at all hours, my mom with gusto and attention to detail, my dad and sister not so much.

When I nervously asked my folks if a touring band from Montreal could stay over for "a couple of nights," Mom was open to the idea. Predictably, Dad wasn't into it. Having already promised my family home as lodging to the Gruesomes, I begged until Mom convinced Dad behind closed doors and he relented. Little did they know the Hotel California-like rock 'n' roll cavalcade they had just agreed to. Years later Mom told me she thought allowing travelling bands to stay with us was "the right thing to do." She hoped another family would return the favour to the Smugglers someday.

Bama Lama Bama Loo was all any of my friends and bandmates could talk about at school, but I couldn't wait to get home again. The time ticked slowly by until the final bell mercifully rang. I was fearful the Gruesomes might already have left, like a circus in the night, but most of them were just getting up when I arrived home at three thirty P.M. They were all over the house, eating, doing their laundry, practising their instruments and watching TV. The Gruesomes LOVED TV, the cornier the show the better. I discovered the drummer John "Jed" Knoll, a big Fred Flintstone-type guy with a dry sense of humour, watching *The Brady Bunch* with my little sister, Heather, both of them laughing at the ironic moments. "Where do they keep their maid, Alice?" wondered John aloud. "Some windowless dungeon behind the kitchen in an otherwise gorgeous home? And why is she forced to wear the exact same uniform every day?"

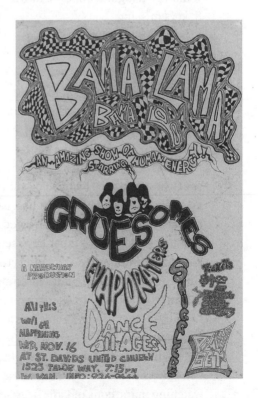

I joined the two of them on the couch just as the phone rang. My sister answered. After a moment, she cupped the phone receiver and whispered to me, "It's the lady from the church your band played at last night. She's really mad." I panicked, wondering what Nardwuar and I had forgotten or overlooked in our attempted cleanup during the disorganized aftermath of the show. I was too freaked out to take the call, so I passed the phone like a hot potato to John. "Hello there, John Knoll speaking. Grant can't come to the phone right now. May I address any concerns you may have regarding last evening's talent show?"

I could hear the church lady screaming at him over the phone. Not fazed in the least, John calmly scribbled down notes. I looked over his bulky shoulder as he numbered her complaints in point form:

1. broken altar
2. filthy conditions
3. cigarette butts inside
4. bathrooms: blood, vomit, diarrhea smeared on walls
5. missing pulpit mic
6. amplifier damaged
7. mother-daughter knocked down
8. keys missing
9. beer cans everywhere
10. never again

Our damage deposit paid for most of it. Money from our bank accounts paid for the rest. It was the last time Nardwuar and I would rent out a church basement. The potential Wrath of God and wrath of Mom (who was heavily involved in the church community) just wasn't worth it. On the positive side, the gig led to a long friendship and many more gigs with the Gruesomes. The band enjoyed the comfort of our family home for an entire week and made many subsequent visits. My parents worked during the day, and the Gruesomes gigged at night, so there wasn't too much crossover. Our house must have seemed like a luxurious pit stop compared to the ratty roadside motels the Gruesomes were used to, though they and many other bands who stayed over the years quickly found out that my dad kept our house at seventeen degrees, even in the winter. But free accommodation was still free accommodation.

Gruesomes lead singer Bobby Beaton became the object of one of my sister's first-ever crushes. She would stare longingly at his perfect brown bob haircut while the two of them sat bundled in blankets in our TV room watching marathons of Little House on the Prairie. Guitarist Gerry Alvarez thrilled the Smugglers when he sat in on guitar for a band practice in our basement. The Gruesomes did drive my dad crazy by arriving home at three A.M. after a downtown Vancouver show and putting their wet clothes in the dryer, including their Beatle boots, waking up my family with noise that sounded like someone repeatedly falling down the stairs. All was somewhat forgiven when bassist John Davis cooked up a burrito feast for my family and the band. Having everyone seated around our dinner table was surreal. So began a long tradition: from then on, my family home was the de facto accommodation for any band Nardwuar and I brought to town. In spite of my mom's fond hope, it was a courtesy that was rarely extended to the Smugglers during our first touring forays.

DEAR LAWRENCES,
THANK YOU VERY MUCH FOR MAKING US SO WELCOME IN YOUR HOME. OUR STAY IN VANCOUVER WAS GREAT ... WE HOPE WE WEREN'T TOO BOTHERSOME. THANK YOU AGAIN,

The GRUESOMES

The Gruesomes' lead singer, Bobby Beaton, unpacking his stuff to head into my parents' house, where the band would stay on tour stops in Vancouver for several years.
GRANT LAWRENCE PHOTO

eight

Big Black Bugs
Bleed Blue Blood

THE SMUGGLERS WERE in the middle of our first summer tour. We woke up slowly, one by one, groaning, squinting, soaked in sweat and spooning each other with unwelcome morning wood. The scorching July sunshine of the rolling Manitoba prairie had turned our little vw van into a noxious sauna. We were a couple of hours west of Winnipeg on a dirt road. In the distance, massive trucks shimmered by silently in the morning heat, looking destined for head-on collisions with the trucks coming the opposite direction but always sliding by.

We wrestled to open the van's tricky side door, gasping for air. The band staggered in all directions as we gagged and spat, coughed and puked, urinated and shat. I swayed and squinted while I peed over the vast crewcut of some freshly harvested green crop. The air smelled pleasantly of cow dung. We never knew what we'd wake up to when we parked in the darkness after a gig. We should have been playing our second show in Winnipeg that night, but we'd gotten fired again, this time from the Royal Albert Arms. You had to be really bad to get the boot from that notorious dump.

This would have been a typical morning on tour in the Canadian prairies. With nowhere to stay, we'd drive after the gig, get out of town, pull over on some random dirt road, pop the camper top and hunker down for the night. NICK THOMAS PHOTO

Our nerves were gradually adjusting to the disappointments that came with being in a band and to the stark realization that we were not the Gruesomes. Earlier that spring, we had entered a Vancouver indie rock talent contest, an infamous battle of the bands known as Shindig! held at a watering hole called the Railway Club. It was only our second time playing downtown, and it couldn't have gone any worse.

We had been knocked out in the first round in a chorus of boos. Harsh criticism from the judges was delivered after our performance in the form of anonymously written comment cards. "You are an absolutely, unforgivably, irrepressibly terrible band." "You are the worst group I've ever seen." "Please do everyone in Vancouver a favour and break up now." "What's with the drummer throwing up in the middle of the set?" "The lead singer is very ugly and should be fired immediately." Etc.

One particularly cruel judge had gone so far as to sketch out the band members on his comment card, putting little check marks beside those members he liked (Adam and Nick) and little X's beside those he didn't (the rest of us). He had reserved his most vicious doodling for me, repeatedly circling my little caricature, then scratching an X on top so furiously that his pen had broken right through the cardstock. While the nasty comments had stung like hornets, I was mostly insulted that the music-snob judges didn't have the balls to back up their brutal critiques by signing their names. Years later, we found out by chance that the caricature card was drawn by none other than Bill Baker, future owner of Mint Records, a label that would eventually sign the Smugglers and employ me.

It wasn't just on the road that we were getting fired. For example, the plug was pulled on a show we performed in the parking lot of a local mall for an event called Totally Cool, Back to School! Billed as "teen band," the Smugglers were expected to play a staggering three sets of an hour each to the supposed throngs of teenage shoppers 'n' boppers. In the middle of the second "set," we attempted to stretch out the proceedings with a particularly painful loop of Elvis Presley's "Burning Love," during which Paul once again vomited onstage from high anxiety but kept drumming. The parking lot was filled with cars but devoid of a human audience, our only "fan" a seemingly lost man-child who was rolling back and forth on the pavement in front of the stage, in a state of either bliss or seizure, we weren't sure which. Soon the mall manager emerged, waving his arms over his head like an air traffic controller. He fired us and threw us off mall property. He essentially paid us three hundred dollars to leave.

A Totally Cool, Back to School!

This Saturday

Rock to "The Smugglers" teen band

Pick up your teen COOL PACK

Catch the make-up and hair demos

Check out the mall wide back-to-school savings

AUGUST 24 - SEPTEMBER 9

Lynn Valley Centre

980-9354 1199 LYNN VALLEY RD. (at Mtn. Hwy.)

We were booked to play the Lynn Valley mall, and were expected to play three one-hour sets. The only problem was we barely had a forty-minute set, which we attempted to play over and over, until we were fired mid-song by the mall manager.

An even worse feeling than getting fired mid-gig was stepping up on stage with anticipation, then having a promoter attempt to yank us off-stage before a single note was performed. That's what almost happened at a short-lived all-ages venue in North Vancouver.

```
July 28, 1989
Youth Art Works
North Vancouver, BC


What a screwed-up gig. We were playing third
in a four-band lineup featuring Three Blind
Cats (hilarious), Glynda Fitzgerald and the
Desert Sons (frustrating and annoying), the
Smugglers and Velour Underwear, who never
even got to play. This gig was at the Youth
Art Works Warehouse in industrial North
Vancouver, right across the street from
the car insurance place. First of all, the
organizers let the all-ages kids drink
inside. So stupid! So the cops came down and
shut the gig down right after the Desert
Sons, seconds before we were to play. We were
onstage, and just about to hit the first beat
when this DORK "Marty" comes up and says,
"Sorry guys," which is so frustrating because
the crowd was just wild. He left and we stood
stunned. Then another guy comes up and says,
"Okay, you can play one song."
   So, we took our entire amount of energy
and played "She's So Satisfyin'." It was the
best ever. We jumped all over the place (I
landed on a monitor and caved it in) and the
crowd went crazy, it was great. Then at the
end of the song an organizer lady jumped
up on stage, pulled my mic cord out and
```

slapped Adam across the face! But it didn't
matter because the song was over. Dave was
absolutely overwhelmed with excitement, it
was pretty funny, but the gig wasn't. Turns
out the guy who told us "You can play one
song" was just some random dude, not an
organizer, so they were pretty mad at us.
Screw Youth Art Works!

The very worst scenario, however, was when we performed most of the set, got fired and weren't paid, like the time we were hired to play the bar at a North Vancouver curling rink but were canned after about five songs. The bar manager refused to pay us the agreed-upon fee of two hundred dollars. When the back door of the rink unceremoniously slammed shut behind us, Paul came up with the idea of simply seizing payment by helping ourselves to the massive stack of empty beer bottles piled up in the back alley. We loaded as many cases as possible into our van, Paul assuring us, based on plenty of experience, that the refund on the bottles would soar well over two hundred dollars. Working fast, we stuffed the van so full we could barely squeeze ourselves in.

Halfway home we heard the siren. There was nowhere to pull over safely, so Dave turned onto a side street but took the corner too hard. The momentum sent the stacked beer bottles, many of which had an inch or two of stale beer and floating cigarette butts in them, loudly crashing down. The reeking contents sloshed out all over us. When Dave rolled down the window to speak to the policeman, greeting him as politely as he could with stale beer dripping from the end of his nose, the cop recoiled at the stench.

We had been pulled over for faulty tail lights, but the cop quickly forgot about those and demanded we open the sliding side door of the van. When we complied, an avalanche of wet, sticky beer bottles cascaded out, many of them shattering when they hit the street. The cop lined us up against the van while Dave tried desperately to explain our way out of the situation. We got to keep most of the unbroken bottles, which in the end came to about twenty dollars.

DAVID CARSWELL

David Carswell, our genius guitarist, had moved to Canada with the rest of his family in the late 1970s. He was originally from Dover, England, home of the famed White Cliffs—the very cliffs seen in the climax of the Who's mod tribute movie *Quadrophenia*. Back at Dave's elementary school in England, his headmaster, Mr. Headon, had often talked about his musician son, Topper, who happened to be the drummer of a downtown London band called the Clash.

Dave was a handsome, whip-smart and solid lug with curly black hair, a rugby player's build and a lilting British accent that stuck with him well after his move to the New World. He behaved like a cross between Winston Churchill and Benny Hill, and looked like a cross between Elvis Presley and David Hasselhoff. Dave had been nicknamed "Carsy" by an overzealous gym teacher, and we loved him for his spot-on impressions and his nasty wit. But you had to watch yourself. Dave was admittedly a bit of a prude, and he could get ticked off if things went too far, particularly when it came to sex on the road.

Dave's friendly, working-class parents were patriotic music fans, particularly into the Rolling Stones and avant-garde British pop music like David Bowie, Roxy Music and ELO. We loved going over to Dave's house, the interior of which resembled a dark British pub, to listen to his parents' imported record collection. By the time Dave was in grade ten, he was already the guitarist in the Evaporators. It wasn't long before he joined the Smugglers full-time as well.

Dave had an exceptional natural ability on his Fender Mustang guitar, and a knack for matching chords and guitar melodies to just about any lyrics I sang to him. According to his mood, he had hilarious energy onstage and off. He possessed song-writing talent in abundance, often showing up at practice with four or five new songs at a time. On tour, he was most comfortable in the driver's seat, which was fine with the rest of us, because it meant we could party. "Carsy" was our rock, behind the guitar and the wheel.

If we were lucky when we got fired at an out-of-town gig, Dave would motor us into a nearby campground in places like Dinosaur Provincial Park or Riding Mountain National Park. When that happened, we could park our little van beside a picnic table or BBQ pit, bathe in a nearby lake and sit around a crackling fire under the shimmering northern lights while telling each other stories and jokes we already knew and confessing our deepest rock 'n' roll ambitions. Nick could always be counted upon for his party trick of lighting his farts. He'd lie down on his back, throw his legs over his head and hold Adam's lighter to his crotch. It never ceased to amaze us when a blue flame rippled over his denim in synchronicity with a loud raspberry. It was like a scene from *Backdraft* if it had starred Chris Farley. More often, though, we'd have to pull off the highway onto a side road in the middle of nowhere, which is where we found ourselves waking up on that sunny Manitoba morning.

Paul emerged last from the van, still wearing the trench coat he used as a blanket, a lit joint already in his mouth. Even though he partook in his usual wake 'n' bake ritual, Paul was cranky. While peeing, he yelled at Adam, "You still wanna earn that twenty bucks, harmonica bitch?"

"You know I do, you big fat pig!" Adam answered over his own steaming stream of urine.

After days of driving the sizzle-hot prairie highway, our van was splattered with dead bugs of all shapes and sizes. Dragonflies, bees, wasps, butterflies, grasshoppers, beetles, black flies, moths, mosquitoes and many other unidentifiable insects—some tiny, some Jurassic in scope—had violently squished to varying degrees of disfigurement and baked into layers of insect carnage on the front of the vehicle like a piecrust. The previous night, we'd stepped out to marvel at the fuzzy, green streaks overhead. The magnificent shafts of the aurora borealis framed Paul's hefty silhouette as he uttered a challenge: all Adam had to do to earn twenty dollars was to lick the front of the van, from bumper to windshield, without stopping.

Whether it was the unbelievable beauty of the prairie night sky or just the pot talking, Adam had agreed to attempt the challenge in the morning. He was broke as a joke, and twenty dollars was a lofty reward on such a cash-strapped tour, where the few dollars we made at shows went straight into the van for gas.

We gathered in a semi-circle in front of the van in the blazing sunshine. Adam dropped to his knees in the gravel. "Adam, please, you don't have to do this," offered Beez. Ignoring him, dollar signs in his eyes, Adam stuck out his tongue and craned his head back. The tip of his tongue made contact just above the bug-encrusted bumper.

With his eyes shut tight, Adam methodically licked the front of our van as if it were a giant ice cream cone. Two thousand kilometres' worth of exploded bugs piled up on his tongue. By the time he reached the windshield, his tongue was stacked and black, like fresh dirt on the blade of a bulldozer. Upon completion of the task, before even spitting out his roadkill tartare, Adam spun around towards Paul. "Gimmay muh twenney dollahs!" he yelled, hand and tongue outstretched.

Paul feigned a look of incredulousness we were getting used to. "What?! You think I have that kinda money on me? I'll pay you as soon as we get home, I promise, just don't bug me about it, eh?" He burst into maniacal laughter.

The ensuing fight was interrupted when Dave let out a shocked "HOLY SHIT!" Adam and Paul joined the rest of us as we gazed in wonderment at a dozen or so of North America's only grasslands antelope, the rare and elusive pronghorn. The stern little creatures bounded across the open prairie, their leaps so graceful and powerful it was as if they were flying.

After the pronghorns had disappeared over the horizon, Adam washed his mouth out with hot Bohemian beer and spat it at Paul, then climbed sullenly into the van. Dave got behind the wheel and slid the VW into second gear while the rest of us trudged to the back and started pushing. That was the only way we had been able to get the van to start for the past week. The battery was as dead as Louis Riel. Once we got it rolling, Dave popped the clutch. The van kicked like a Red River ox and returned to the land of the living, leaving us choking in a cloud of black exhaust. We ran alongside to hop in the side door, Saskatoon bound. Beez had promised us that everything would be different once we reached Amigos, a venue known to be welcoming to the alternative music wave that was quickly turning tidal in bigger cities to the south. Maybe we wouldn't get booed, maybe we wouldn't get fired, maybe we wouldn't get spat on.

nine

Touch Me I'm Sick

"**S**PIT ON ME NOW!"

The massive crowd of first-wave grunge rockers mashed inside the Student Union Ballroom at the University of BC throbbed and pulsated like an angry heart. Nardwuar the Human Serviette stalked the stage with a microphone in his hand, dodging painted nickels. He had been trying to bleat out information like a confessor facing a firing squad, but he realized the battle between audience and MC was lost. He stopped at centre stage and gave in completely.

After many years of promoting all-ages shows around Vancouver, this was Nardwuar's biggest gig yet. It starred Mudhoney, the kings of the detonating Seattle grunge scene. By 1990, Mudhoney was one of the top sellers at Sub Pop Records, the most famous independent label in the world since Motown. For both Nardwuar and the Smugglers, the grunge era could be traced back to one spectacular seven-inch vinyl single: Mudhoney, "Touch Me I'm Sick," Sub Pop Records, 1988. It was the perfect slab of garage-punk: fuzzed-out guitars, tortured vocals and a furious beat. The UK music press was equally floored, and collectively propelled Mudhoney into overnight rock star status.

The British audience demanded more. Wanting to know where this murky, savage "grunge" music had come from, they sought out other like-minded bands from the same rain-soaked northwest corner of the United States, and the "Seattle Sound" was born. Groups like Nirvana, Pearl Jam, Soundgarden and Alice in Chains were discovered and made famous, and heavily distorted alternative garage-rock-on-heroin was suddenly world renowned. The wave of attention made Seattle one of the biggest geographic focal points in the history of rock 'n' roll. And here was Nardwuar hosting an all-ages gig with Mudhoney at what was arguably their peak. Also on the bill were Beat Happening, a stripped-down, twee-pop band from Olympia (basically the tonal opposite of Mudhoney), the Evaporators and the Smugglers. It was by far our biggest gig to date. Nardwuar MC'd every one of his events, giving elaborate, trivia-laced, high-energy introductions to every band—which at the Mudhoney show was when everything went wrong.

After much convincing, Nardwuar and I had managed to secure the UBC Student Union Ballroom, a huge hall that could contain a thousand people. To Nardwuar's shock, all one thousand tickets sold out in advance. As always, he had put my home phone number on the poster as the concert's "info line." In the days leading up to the Mudhoney show, our telephone rang off the hook.

When the night of the gig arrived, so did the mayhem. Eager to avoid the aggressive backfire of the skinhead security force from our Gruesomes gig, Nardwuar had assembled a small nerd army of geek-rock volunteers from UBC's CiTR Radio to do security; they were easily identifiable from their cardigans, ghostly pale skin, ironic horn-rimmed glasses, blank expressions and terrible posture. As the doors opened, they were overrun on all sides by punks, alternative kids and fledgling, flannel-clad grunge rockers who flooded onto the campus from far and wide, stuffing the Student Union Ballroom several hundred people over capacity.

At the show prior to the Mudhoney gig, Nardwuar had come up with a bizarre customer loyalty incentive program. Upon entry, every person was handed a brightly spray-painted penny, one side red, the other blue. The idea was that the gig-goer would bring the penny to the next Nardwuar gig, trade it in and be upgraded to a similarly painted nickel. In theory, the change-exchange would keep climbing, from penny to nickel to dime to quarter. I don't think Nardwuar had done much planning beyond that. Some audience members who had received the nickels at the door to the Mudhoney gig chose to whip them as hard as they could at Nardwuar while he was trying to MC. Every time he took to the stage, he was bombarded with his own brightly coloured money.

We felt terrible for our nickel-pelted pal. But standing backstage in our pea jackets, toques and rubber boots, we couldn't help but be distracted by how large and rowdy the audience was. We took to the stage with as much false confidence as we could muster and played loudly and quickly, summoning as much airborne energy as possible.

From the first note the crowd was with us, exploding into a pit of chaotic bodies slamming against each other like an ocean riptide. The Smugglers had not only a full-blown "mosh pit" but also stage-divers. Girls and guys alike would hoist themselves up onto the stage as we played, then run through the band to take a flying leap into the sea of frothing bodies. As if by code, outstretched hands in the crowd would reach up to catch the stage-diver, who would then gleefully stretch out all four limbs and surf on top of the crowd for a minute or so before being swallowed safely back into the throng. The more the audience came unglued, the harder we rocked. The final cymbal crash of our set rang out to a roar of approval the likes of which we had never experienced. It was intoxicating.

Unfortunately, the next band didn't fare as well. Beat Happening was about as lo-fi and stripped-down as a band could be. They were the original American indie rock twee-pop band, a sort of minimalist cross between the Shaggs and the Cramps: a shy female drummer; an unassuming, rigid guitarist; and a kooky lead singer named Calvin Johnson who dressed and looked like River Phoenix in *Stand by Me*. He showed off flamboyant, fey and amazingly fluid sixties-style dance moves, and had a flat, deep baritone voice that made him sound like a heavily sedated Johnny Cash.

Calvin Johnson, lead singer of Beat Happening, performing in front of a volatile and hate-filled crowd at the University of British Columbia while opening for Mudhoney. Calvin, who had a voice like Johnny Cash on valium, would soon host one of the most galvanizing music festivals in the history of independent music, which *SPIN Magazine* called "the true Woodstock of the 1990s." NICK THOMAS PHOTO

Regardless of the audience's extreme disapproval of Beat Happening's twangy indie-pop with its dark overtones and songs about graveyards, redheads and black candy, I thought they were one of the coolest bands going. Calvin Johnson owned and operated K Records in Olympia, Washington, a label with the motto, "Exploding the teenage underground into passionate revolt against the corporate ogre since 1982." K Records would be instrumental in the discovery of bands like Beck, Modest Mouse, Built to Spill, the Microphones, Shonen Knife and many others. Nirvana's lead singer, Kurt Cobain, even had the K logo (a hand-scrawled letter K surrounded by a shield) tattooed on his forearm. But on this night, in front of that crowd, none of those credentials seemed to matter. The booing and catcalling drowned out the band, though they kept playing.

I stood nervously watching from the side stage with Mudhoney's guitarist, Steve Turner. I was stunned at how vicious the audience response was to this seemingly docile band; the softer the song, the angrier the crowd became. Steve told me about Beat Happening opening for the hugely popular straight-edge punk rock purists Fugazi at a show in front of thousands in Los Angeles. The band had received a harsh reaction from that massive audience as well, Steve said, except it wasn't just stinging nickels being thrown around. At that show, there were heavy glass ashtrays on tables throughout the venue. Soon the ashtrays were airborne in the direction of Beat Happening. During their final song, one of the flying ashtrays smacked lead singer Calvin Johnson in the face. It shattered on impact, slicing open Calvin's nose. The band members wanted to stop, but Calvin kept singing, his voice canyon-deep, not missing a lyric.

When the song ended, Steve recounted, blood poured from Calvin's face. He stood up straight, dropped his microphone with a loud thunk and walked to the lip of the stage, expressionless. Silence fell over the formerly seething crowd. Calvin stared out into the audience, blood dripping onto his white T-shirt. Then he stepped off the stage and into the pit. The crowd that had been so ready to kill him moments earlier backed away. No one would go near him. He walked straight up the middle of the packed venue as the crowd parted like Laura Ingalls's hair, letting him walk through unmolested. Bloody Calvin walked straight out the front door and into the LA sunshine. When Steve had finished yelling that story in my ear, I looked out at Calvin Johnson and Beat Happening with new awe and respect. To me, Calvin felt like the living definition of punk rock.

Then it was time for Mudhoney. The mass of punks at the front was frantically waiting to explode to Mudhoney's superfuzz bigmuff power chords. Nardwuar's detailed description of Canadian and United States border relations, somehow connected back to Mudhoney, was not going over well. Finally, cracking with frustration, Nardwuar laid down his saliva dare: "SPIT ON ME NOW!"

Many in the crowd did exactly what Nardwuar commanded of them. A sickening hailstorm of gob, spit and phlegm rained down on our dear friend and promoter. Nardwuar stood on the lip of centre stage in a crucifix pose, his head craned back, his eyes shut tight and mouth agape. The stage lights illuminated the gross shower of bodily fluids that arced from the sinus cavities of hundreds of angry punks as they splattered in, around and all over Nardwuar. It was a horrific twist of reverse psychology. None of us had ever experienced this magnitude of pure filth.

Barbaric cheers rose up from the masses when they realized Nardwuar wasn't making any attempt to dodge the loogees. Rather, he was allowing himself to be drenched, mouth open as wide as possible to accept the deluge. When the storm had finally subsided, a soggy but seemingly unfazed Nardwuar lifted the mic to his mouth and shrieked, "Ladies and gentlemen, please welcome from the land of Big Macs and bombers . . . MUDHONEY!" Mudhoney was forced to walk across a stage covered in Canadian phlegm to get to their guitars. Bassist Matt Lukin snatched up the microphone and yelled, "He said shit on him, not spit on him!" before fittingly launching into the furious song "Here Comes Sickness." For years after that night, whenever the spitting incident was mentioned, Nardwuar's response was the same: "I still have a cold from that."

The Smugglers watched in awe from the side stage as the four members of Mudhoney savagely pounded out hit after hit. If we had thought the audience was steaming for us, they were absolutely boiling over for Mudhoney, turning that human ocean into a tempest of slamming, flying bodies. Their eyes were hidden by shoulder-length, shaggy mop-top haircuts. Their noses poked out from between their bangs as they screamed the lyrics of their songs into the microphones at the front of the stage, everyone else screaming along in unison.

The stage-diving was constant. And since Nardwuar's security force could have passed for the cast of *Ghost World*, there was nothing to stem the tide. If Mudhoney cared, they didn't make mention of it. They were seemingly oblivious to the stream of punks, goths and grungers who took flying leaps off the stage to be caught by the crowd every time. Nick and Paul were so caught up in the mayhem that they decided to join the action: both of them were going to stage-dive for the first time in their lives.

Nick took a peek out at the churning crowd, drew a few deep breaths and bolted into the brightly lit stage, diving past Mudhoney's lead singer, Mark Arm, and into the pit while the band cranked out "Sweet Young Thing Ain't Sweet No More." Sure enough, he was caught safely by the invisible hand of the crowd and surfed it on his back with a huge grin on his face.

Paul shifted his considerable girth from side to side backstage, wringing his hands like a kid about to jump off the pier for the first time. With the rest of us egging him on, he finally went for it, running across the stage screaming with both his arms in the air. He took a flying leap off the stage, limbs flailing. In mid-air he stretched out into a dive like a flying squirrel, so that there would be more of him to be caught by the punk rock brethren waiting to accept him with outstretched arms. Except they didn't.

On occasion, an audience at a rock 'n' roll show will think, move, swell and contract as one living force. They can seemingly make split-second, unanimous decisions like a flock of birds. For whatever reason that night, the crowd unanimously decided not to catch Paul. Instead, they did the opposite, moving en masse to create a hole into which Paul violently belly flopped. It was as if he had swan-dived into an empty pool. He slammed face first onto the unforgiving, dirty hardwood dance floor. Further breaking mosh pit code, no one moved to help to pick him up, and so he remained there, face down, as the grunge pounded on. Slowly, Paul crawled on his hands and knees through the thicket of torn denim to the safety of the dance floor fringe. A few minutes later, we found him slumped in a fetal position in the hallway. As Nick later said, "If Mudhoney hadn't been so loud, I swear we would have heard a splat."

Though totally out of control, Nardwuar's "Whoa Dad! It's Mudhoney!" event had a lasting and pivotal effect. Mudhoney loved the show and by extension loved Nardwuar, an endorsement that went a long way. I made friends with Calvin Johnson from Beat Happening, and he shared with me his mushrooming idea to host an "international pop underground convention" in his hometown of Olympia, Washington. Some of the bands he was bringing to town would need gigs in Vancouver, he said, so he would be in touch. That would completely change the fortunes of the Smugglers before long.

Mudhoney rock out at Nardwuar's biggest all-ages gig to date, November 10, 1990. This was just moments after Nardwuar was covered head to toe in a sickening hailstorm of phlegm from the audience, at his own invitation.
NICK THOMAS PHOTO

ten

Amigos

T HE YELLOWHEAD HIGHWAY was one of the prettiest we had travelled. As we rolled west across the gentle hills of Manitoba, Beez
regaled us with stories about Amigos. Our egos and loins responded
as if we were bound for a rock 'n' roll Neverland. Amigos had only been
open for a year or two, but Beez had played the club several times with
the Sarcastic Mannequins. He had made fast friends with the owners and
slept with several of the waitresses.

The good news about Amigos Cantina in Saskatoon, the "Paris of the
Prairies," had spread far and wide. Imagine this: the owners and staff
treated bands *nicely*. They fed the musicians upon arrival, provided a
working sound system and a competent sound person who had neither
a fanny pack nor a ponytail, gave bands free beer without hassle or hes-
itation, and promoted the shows in advance, plastering the town with
posters. They not only allowed but *encouraged* bands to play original music.

The club also had the reputation of being a wild party spot where
bands could get as cut as the crowd. Amigos provided free band accommodation in an apartment directly above the club. That meant no driving
after the show, which meant every member of the band could party as
hard as they wanted. All of these perks were unheard of for younger touring bands in Canada, so we couldn't wait to taste it for ourselves.

The first surprise came when Beez directed us away from downtown Saskatoon, instead having Dave turn the van down a quiet residential side street. We parked in front of an unassuming building that blended in with the dusty sidewalks. Paul and I hopped out and hurried inside, visions of a western Canadian CBGB slam-dancing in our heads.

Instead of our eyes adjusting to a dark den of sin, we had to shield them from the sunlight streaming in through skylights. The sunbeams illuminated hanging plants and long, communal, linoleum-topped tables and upholstered chairs, filled with normal-looking people cheerfully eating lunch. A co-ed softball team sat at the largest table sharing heaping platters of nachos.

"This is the wrong place. This can't be Amigos," I said with disgust.

"Definitely not," answered Paul. "Look at that colourful chalkboard menu. Rock 'n' roll bars do not have chalkboard menus. This is a Mexican cafeteria, man!" He turned to leave.

"Wait, Paul. Isn't *amigos* a Spanish word?"

We had heard so much about Amigos, a rock 'n' roll oasis in the prairies, that we were shocked to find it filled with hanging plants, chalkboard menus and bright skylights. We were certain we had the wrong place. NICK THOMAS PHOTO

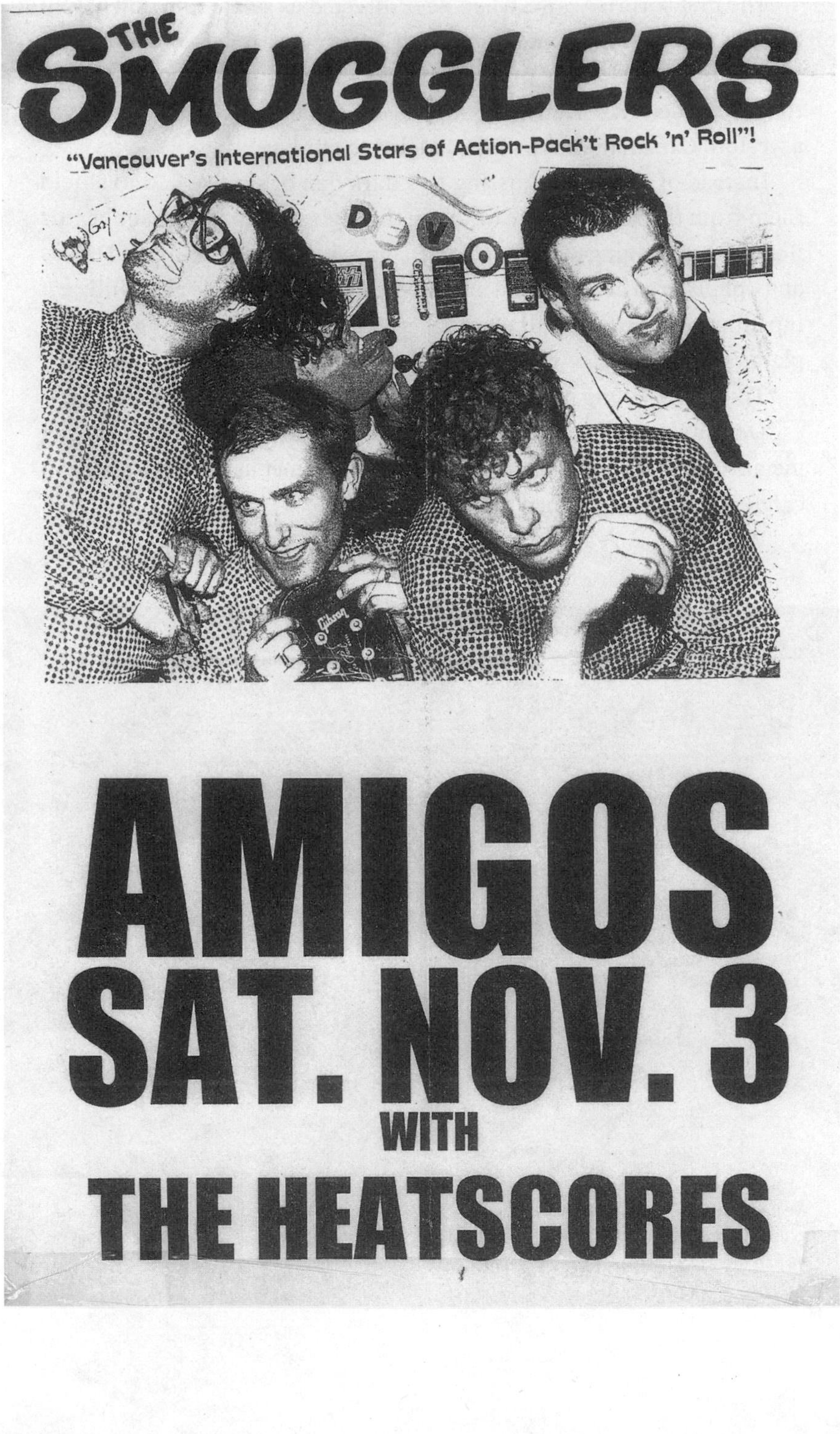

THE SMUGGLERS

"Vancouver's International Stars of Action-Pack't Rock 'n' Roll"!

AMIGOS
SAT. NOV. 3
WITH
THE HEATSCORES

"Oh, shit. So this is it? This is the famous Amigos we've heard so much about?" We were crestfallen and began steeling ourselves for another terrible gig. Behind us, Beez busted through the door with his arms outstretched like a returning king. "AMIGOS!" Waitresses flocked to greet him, wrapping their arms and legs around him as he threw his head back in laughter. "AMIGOS!"

Before we had even unloaded our equipment, we were seated and handed menus. Frothing bottles of Old Vienna lager were plunked down in front of us. Free of charge, we were offered any delectable Mexican dish on the menu. Everyone but Beez was in shock, with an encroaching sense of guilt. It was almost as if we were being treated too well, like we were imposters pretending to be a real band.

When darkness fell, people actually showed up and paid their hard-earned money to see us. The crowd felt more like a bunch of friends. We still stretched our forty-five minutes of material into three hour-long sets, but due to Beez's popularity and the laid-back party vibe of Amigos, the show went over pretty well. So well that the owners of the bar told us we could stay in the upstairs apartment for as long as we wanted, because the next band wasn't due in town for a week. So well even that girls weren't interested just in Beez and Adam but in me as well.

At some point, the party in the bar relocated to the band apartment, our first of countless Amigos all-nighter after-parties. Owner Jim Clarke handed over another cold case of Bohemian Lager before he bid us adieu. "Your agent, Larry Lawrence, never sent me your rider, but I hope this will be enough?" I wasn't even sure what a rider was, but I thanked Jim for having us, and for being so kind to such a young band. Jim saw something in us that night. It wasn't talent—maybe spunk or energy or potential. He stuck with us for years to come, until we could eventually sell out Amigos with a line down the dusty sidewalk. Luckily, thanks to that impending alternative takeover, the days of three sets would soon fall to the wayside, a relic of another time. We never did send Jim a rider, even when we were "big" enough to ask for one. At Amigos, we never felt the need. In some ways, it always felt like coming home to friends.

WE FIGURED OUT pretty quickly what riders were. We also figured out very soon that one of the major backstage perks of opening for bigger bands was *their* rider. Once the headliner hit the stage, it was pretty safe to assume we could enjoy their rider at our sneaky leisure. There was so much waste when it came to riders. Incredible amounts of finger food, deli trays and snacks were thrown out at the end of the night at the bigger shows, so on the rare occasion we landed one of those gigs, Dave and Paul would hang around and bag as much of it as they could, turning it into meals in the van for days.

The term "rider" originally meant requests on top of the agreed financial contract for a gig, conditions "riding" on the contract like a surfer on a wave. Somewhere along the line, riders got written into the contract and guaranteed, just like the money. Riders in rock 'n' roll are legendary, the most famous arguably being Van Halen's request for no brown M&Ms, a stipulation many think is mythology but is actually fact. It was Van Halen's way of testing to see if the promoter was paying attention. If there were still brown M&Ms in the bowl, what other details would the promoter miss? What other parts of the contract were they blowing off or ignoring? Canadian folk hero Stompin' Tom Connors had a drink rider of two twenty-four packs of Moosehead bottled beer. One pack was for his band and crew, the other was for Stompin' Tom exclusively. He drank all or most of it, every night, into the wee hours. Riders also contained food, accommodation and production requests, but for many younger bands it was mostly about the booze, and riders could be a very slippery slope.

Touring musicians must have the only job in the world where, once you reach a certain level of success, you are not only allowed to perform your job drunk (or stoned), but in many cases encouraged to do so. It also must be the only job where, once you attain a certain status (which really isn't that lofty), you can demand your booze rider to be waiting for you on ice upon arrival at your workplace, as early as three o'clock in the afternoon. You hit the stage at ten P.M. Think about it. If you knock back copious amounts of alcohol and get wasted every night of the week in real life, you are most definitely considered an alcoholic and will probably lose your job among other things. On tour, you're considered a fun-lovin' rock 'n' roll road warrior. You are Keith Richards!

Days and nights blend on the road, and no matter what their level of fame or lack thereof, musicians can very easily become alcohol-dependent. We would see many of them, including some in our own band, fall victim to the effects of "free" alcohol. And therein lies the rub: many bands revelling in their supposedly free booze don't realize they're paying for it. Most promoters claim every bottle of beer on the rider as a "hospitality" expense at wildly inflated prices, taking it out of the percentage that would otherwise go to the band: the money that's often known as the "back end." Many bands were essentially paying for their own very expensive backstage party every night. Smaller clubs like Amigos, and notably the Horseshoe Tavern in Toronto, didn't operate this way. The guarantee was always paid, and if there was an overage of cash at the door, you'd get that, too, without the cost of your meals and beer being subtracted. None of that mattered to us yet, since we rarely got anything, but we were always on the lookout for outlandish riders to chow down on. Occasionally, that caught up to us in a very bad way.

The end of another typically boozy night in the upstairs band room at Amigos in Saskatoon. My sleeping bag was so close yet so far. This apartment was the site of several infamous Smugglers incidents, such as "The Slap Heard 'Round Saskatoon" and "I Shit My Pants in Saskatoon." NICK THOMAS PHOTO

eleven

Rock 'n' Roll Pest Control

THE HOODOO GURUS' rider was the largest and most expansive any of us had ever seen. Endless deli trays of meats, fruits and vegetables, sandwiches and salads, cookies and cakes, and muffins and croissants were stretched out on tables from one end of the dressing room to the other. The smorgasbord was bookended by barrels overflowing with glistening imported bottles of Heineken, Foster's and Corona beer, along with bottles of red and white wine, champagne and Jack Daniel's. Our mouths hung open with shock and drool at the opulent sight.

To our extreme excitement, we'd been booked to play a huge party at the University of Manitoba student union ballroom in Winnipeg for "Frosh Week" in early September. The Smugglers would appear first on the bill, which was being headlined by the Hoodoo Gurus, a very popular Australian alt-rock band. In the middle slot were the Young Fresh Fellows from Seattle.

When we arrived at the show, we were in for a Manitoba flood of disappointment: the promoter informed us we had been kicked off the gig. Unbeknownst to him, the fine print of the Hoodoo Gurus' contract specified only one opening act. When the band's road manager saw the poster advertising three bands, he demanded that one be dropped. The promoter's choice was easy: fire the youngest band. We'd still be paid at the end of the night, he told us, but not allowed to play. We were devastated. Our friends in the Young Fresh Fellows thought the situation was ridiculous and decided to take a stand on our behalf.

Of the massive number of bands Seattle churned out, our favourite by far was the Young Fresh Fellows. They were an incredible foursome that combined the best of the northwest garage scene of the 1960s with the dominant up-tempo college alt-rock of the 1980s. They were an introspective, party-rock cross between Paul Revere & the Raiders, R.E.M. and the Replacements. Unlike the Gruesomes, whose image was strictly uniformed to mid-1960s garage rock, the Young Fresh Fellows were ragged and dishevelled, a J.P-Patches-meets-Cheap-Trick thrift-shop rock 'n' roll party. They had been a band since 1980 and had filled the decade with awesome LPs like *Topsy Turvy*, *The Fabulous Sounds of the Pacific Northwest* and *The Men Who Loved Music*, making them college radio staples throughout the States.

On the ill-fated night of the Frosh Week gig in Winnipeg, the Young Fresh Fellows made the kind gesture of inviting us to hop up on stage in the middle of their set. We took them up on it, and they stepped aside, allowing us to blast out two of our songs on their equipment. We managed to bottle the energy of our entire twelve-song set into those two lightning-fast tunes. It was exhilarating, and the audience responded with a roar.

Naturally, with all that time to kill waiting around until the end of the night to get paid, we snuck into the Hoodoo Gurus' dressing room a few times to raid their copious rider. We had yet to spot any members of the Aussie band in their dressing room or in the venue. They arrived from their hotel after the Young Fresh Fellows had wrapped up their set, and were pretty much whisked straight onto the stage. Not being above rider raids either, a couple of the Young Fresh Fellows decided to sneak into the Hoodoo Gurus' dressing room on their own. The Fellows' lead guitarist, Kurt Bloch, was a wild man when sober. When he got drunk on Canadian beer he was downright dangerous. And if Fellows' bassist, Jim Sangster, had the right amount of good-time gas in his tank, he'd occasionally go along for the Kurt Bloch joyride.

We absolutely adored the Seattle band the Young Fresh Fellows. They were everything we wanted to be: great songwriters, awesome performers and best of all, really great people, even though they often got us in a lot of trouble. Left to right: Tad Hutchison (drums), Kurt Bloch (lead guitar), Scott McCaughey (lead vocals, guitar), Jim Sangster (bass).

NICK THOMAS PHOTO

Although we didn't ask them to, Kurt and Jim decided to teach the Hoodoo Gurus a lesson for their egotism. They chugged back every beer they could, then whipped the empty bottles against the cinder block walls of the dressing room. Shards of glass soon covered the nearly untouched deli trays, fruit bowls, sandwiches and salads, along with the Hoodoo Gurus' instrument cases and street clothes. Jim and Kurt then moved on to hurling full bottles, enjoying the sudsy explosions when they hit the wall. They didn't stop until almost every piece of glass in the room was smashed and splintered. Next, in fits of cackling hysteria, they soaked the cold cuts, vegetables, chocolates and Tim Tam cookies with hot piss. After that they overturned every table and chair in the dressing room, flipping the urine-soiled food onto the floor amidst the broken glass and the band's personal effects. Kurt's final strike was to grab the fire extinguisher off the wall and recklessly cover everything in foaming white fire retardant. Once they were satisfied they had trashed the Hoodoo Gurus' dressing room beyond recognition, they turned out the lights and slipped back into the main hall to enjoy the rest of the show, disappearing into the huge crowd.

Somewhere in that same audience, Paul was as thirsty as a goldeye for some more free beer. He slipped backstage and into the Hoodoo Gurus' dressing room to help himself. When he turned on the lights, he gasped at the sight, then started laughing, wondering who had so thoroughly destroyed the place. Like a scavenger in the aftermath of a house fire, he scanned the wreckage, knowing he had to hurry because the band was closing in on the end of their set. At the very moment Paul finally found an intact beer, the Hoodoo Gurus' sizeable Aussie road manager walked into the dressing room.

"CRIKEY! Just what the fuck have you done back 'ere, mate??"

Paul spun around, caught like a raccoon in a trashcan. "Nothin'! I didn't do any of this!"

"Yeah, right, mate, the hell you didn't! Come 'ere, ya waddlin' prick."

The road manager lunged for Paul, grabbing him by the collar of his trench coat. They wrestled with each other, Paul throwing punches and trying to bolt free, but the burly road manager wouldn't let go.

"Get off of me, you Aussie meat-pie shit bag!"

A roar came from the auditorium as the final notes of the Hoodoo Gurus' hit "What's My Scene?" blared out. Within seconds, the sweaty members of the band entered their demolished dressing room. They were outraged at the scene, and soon university security and the promoter were also backstage.

The promoter recognized Paul immediately. "That's one of the Smugglers! The band we dropped from the bill! That's why he did this, to get back at you guys!" The promoter turned to his enforcers. "Security! Get this piece of shit out of here and teach him some Manitoba manners."

Paul tried desperately to break away as two thick security guards in matching black golf shirts dragged him from the room. In a darkened corner of the auditorium, as the Hoodoo Gurus took to the stage for their encore, one of the security guards pinned Paul's arms at his side while the other one slugged him repeatedly in the stomach. When they were done they slammed Paul headfirst through the heavy emergency exit doors and unceremoniously tossed him into the back parking lot. That was where we found him, splayed out like a crash test dummy. Luckily, besides some badly bruised ribs and a battered ego, he wasn't seriously injured, but he was furious.

When the Young Fresh Fellows discovered that Paul and the Smugglers had shouldered the blame for the trashing of the Hoodoo Gurus' dressing room, they apologized, but they also found it hilarious, especially Kurt Bloch. It wouldn't be the last time we were on the receiving end of the Fellows' antics, but we idolized them so much that we never held a grudge. The band would make it up to us in many ways over the years. Lead singer Scott McCaughey released our second and third albums on PopLlama Records, and Kurt would go on to produce our sixth and seventh albums. The Winnipeg promoter withheld our pay, applying it to the damages sustained in the dressing room attack, and he swore we would never play another university event in western Canada. He was good on his word for many years.

We were milling about in the parking lot while the Young Fresh Fellows loaded their van when one of the Hoodoo Gurus emerged from the back doors of the venue. He gave us a glare, then spotted Tad Hutchison's bass drum adorned with the Young Fresh Fellows' logo. The Hoodoo Guru stopped in his Blundstones, staring at the drum. "Did the Young Fresh Fellows play somewhere around here tonight, mate?" he asked.

"Uh, yeah, man," replied Scott McCaughey. "We just opened for you. Tonight. In there." Scott nodded towards the back door of the ballroom.

"What?" answered the Guru. "I love your band! Crikey, I can't believe it. We didn't know, mate!"

Scott and the Hoodoo went on to have an amicable chat. They exchanged a bit of merchandise while I looked on in shock. I couldn't believe how oblivious the Hoodoo Gurus had been at their very own show. I vowed that if the Smugglers ever reached headlining status, we would never be so completely disengaged from our own concerts.

THE SMUGGLERS WOULD ultimately tour our way across Canada countless times. Some of our best shows were in the very venues that had fired us years earlier, though we never played the University of Manitoba again. Thanks to support from our eventual Canadian record label Mint Records and their incredible publicist Yvette Ray, we basked in micro-bursts of fame in places like the fertile all-ages scenes of Vancouver Island, the Okanagan Valley and the Kootenay regions of BC. Farther afield, we found adoration in the Toronto–Kingston–Ottawa–Montreal corridor. Over time, we received a surprising amount of airplay from MuchMusic for our cheap videos, which were directed by Glen Winter, the guy in the Elvis costume who had shut out the lights at the Town Pump. Maybe it helped that we cast Terry David Mulligan, the MuchMusic vj and Vancouver media celebrity, in two of them.

Eventually, we could even sell out the clubs across the country as we grew in popularity. In Toronto, we struck up a long-term friendship with Jeff Cohen and Craig Laskey at the legendary Horseshoe Tavern, which led to an infamous gig where we inadvertently stole Canadian tongue-rocker Danko Jones' pants. That cross-continent trouser tale became a Smug-glers song entitled, fittingly, "Danko Jones' Pants." A string of incredible New Year's Eve gigs at the Horseshoe in the late 1990s and early 2000s would define our career in Toronto for years. Our opening bands at the Horseshoe included everyone from the Sadies to Death from Above 1979.

In the Maritimes, we became all the rage in the unlikely hub of Monc-ton, New Brunswick. The Moncton scene, represented by bands like Eric's Trip, the Monoxides and Bad Luck 13, loved to party as much as we did, and we had some great times after our gigs. Along the outstretched Cana-dian highway, we made fine friends in like-minded bands like Chixdiggit, Pluto, Superconductor, Zumpano, NoMeansNo/the Hanson Brothers, the Leather Uppers, Maow, Thrush Hermit, Duotang, Flashlight Brown, Gob, the Planet Smashers, Inspector Fuzz, the Two Tonne Bowlers (featuring future Wolf Parade member Spencer Krug) and many more.

Back-and-forth pranking was commonplace amongst our Canadian tour-mates. We once trekked from east to west with the Stand GT, a band that hailed from the tiny farming community of Glengarry, Ontario. At our final show together, we decided to give our fellow band a taste of home. While they were onstage, we found their keys, snuck outside and "hayed" their van, ripping apart a giant bale of hay we had purchased from a farmer earlier that day and stuffing every last straw in through the windows and skylight. Had we realized just how uncomfortable rolling in the hay actually was, we probably would have held off. Hay and hayseeds got into every nook and cranny of the Stand GT's van—the seats, the floor mats, their sleeping loft and sleeping bags, and even into their clothing. The band would find painfully sharp strands of hay in their van for years following the incident, and they cursed us every time they did. They were able to take some enjoyment in the fact that we had paid the farmer twenty dollars for the bale, which according to the farm boys in the Stand GT was actually worth about fifty cents.

And we still got blamed for pranks we didn't pull. We met acclaimed Halifax rockers Sloan when our bands played venues right next door to each other on the same night; their show was packed, ours was empty. Most members of Sloan were friendly and approachable, but I clashed immediately with their acerbic bassist, Chris Murphy. Chris had caught a bit of our show in the big empty room and teased us for it ("Great crowd, guys"), and he thought our rubber boots were dumb ("Those look really, really terrible"). He also remarked it was the first time he had ever seen a band end every song with "Cha cha cha." (It wasn't *every* song; maybe . . . ten?) I suppose we had the last laugh that night. Someone let off a stink bomb while Sloan was performing, temporarily clearing the room in the middle of their set. Chris blamed us.

Once the Smugglers began to roam beyond Canada's borders, we were always grateful to get home and play shows amongst friends in the appreciative and understanding land of the maple leaf. The only problem with our country was its epic size. You just had to do the math: the drive between Vancouver and Calgary in good weather was twelve hours, with a giant, jagged, *Game of Thrones*–like wall of stone, snow and ice, otherwise

We once had the pleasure of touring across Canada with a hard-working, hard-rocking farm boy band called the Stand GT, from tiny Glengarry, Ontario. On one of the last nights of the tour, while they were onstage, we snuck outside and paid homage to their farming roots by filling their van with hay, also known as "haying." NICK THOMAS PHOTO

known as the Rocky Mountains, standing in the way. Treks across the Great Plains, which we were nicknamed "The Great Drain," were absolutely exhausting: seven hours between Edmonton and Saskatoon, nine hours between Saskatoon and Winnipeg, and eight hours between Winnipeg and Thunder Bay, in addition to losing time zones as we headed east.

The drive between Thunder Bay and Toronto? Don't ask. Montreal to Halifax? Brutal. After traversing Canada in all manner of blizzards and scorch, we figured there had to be a less death-defying route to success. Just three hours south of Vancouver, the grungy Emerald City of Seattle was exploding with a music scene that captured the attention of the world. The Smugglers decided to put our band name to the test. We were determined to throw our toques across the US border any which way we could.

PART
2

BIG MACS AND BOMBERS

twelve

Border Radio

"Fun in the USA"—Grant Lawrence / The Smugglers (1991)

Well it's time to go and say goodbye,
We've had a real good time.
It's time to roll to the next little town,
South of the border now

We're gonna have fun, fun, fun in the USA
Sausalito and San Bernardino,
Pittsburgh and Boston, too
Maryland, Dairyland, Disneyland,
Oh where the fuck is Kalamazoo?

Well it's all here in America,
Cars and girls and electric guitars

We're gonna have fun, fun, fun in the USA

We inched closer and closer to the US checkpoint at the Peace Arch border along with hundreds of other vehicles heading south. When we got within a couple car-lengths of the border, I positioned a book on the dashboard so the title could be easily read through our dirty windshield: *Father Guild Says HOWDY!* On the cover was a smiling, elderly, bespectacled, respectable, gentlemanly, Caucasian and very clearly Christian preacher man giving the friendliest of waves. I reminded Paul and Adam to check their pockets one last time for stray doobies, hash pipes, acid tabs or worse.

The border separating Canada and the United States is just one hour south of the city of Vancouver. Few of the Canadian bands we knew ever dared a crossing, touring back and forth between Victoria and St. John's instead. The US border has always been intimidating for musicians, staffed as it seemingly is from sea to shining sea by a menacing cast of characters whose sole job is not to let you in. Nonetheless, we were resolute to cross that imaginary line into the rock 'n' roll Promised Land.

Our Volkswagen camper van had The Smugglers stencilled on the side doors for touring in Canada, so we had been forced to paint that over. Our name was a terrible choice for a band who wanted to perform internationally, and we were well aware we were up against it: we were attempting to cross the border in the traditional drug wagon for hippies. We did our best to hide the instruments, because we knew border guards tended to rank "musicians" barely a notch above hobos, hippies, environmentalists and terrorists.

Border guards are apparently trained to assume all musicians are booze- and drug-addled reprobates. Some argue that's an unfair cliché, but the Smugglers would admittedly spend plenty of time in future border lineups scrambling to hide or get rid of illegal substances. On more than one occasion, just a few cars from the checkpoint, we'd discover drug paraphernalia in the van: an elaborate bong under the passenger seat, for example, coated with enough hashish resin to throw us in an American prison for years. In plain view of the frightening US border towers, Nick grabbed the bong, ripped open the side door of van, ran across the pristine green grass of Peace Arch Park and threw the contraband over a manicured hedge. We never learned what was on the other side. Someone's yard? A walking trail? No man's land?

Now, however, it was our turn to cross. The light at the border kiosk flickered from red to green. We fell silent as Dave shifted the van into gear. It puttered forward until the driver's side window drew even with the border guard's booth. The guard was crammed into the space, a milk bag of a man. He had a mangy auburn brush cut, suspicious eyes and a thin moustache that looked like every hair was standing on end. He was wearing a short-sleeved white button-down shirt with a gold badge hanging limply off the pocket. His chin flowed like lava from a volcanic red face. At his throat sat a white plastic button.

The guard glared at Dave. Dave met and held his gaze, but said nothing. The guard glanced down at Father Guild's book. He looked through the side window of the van at the others. He raised his purple index finger to his throat button and pressed down.

The guard's "throat button" was in fact an electrolarynx, a medical communication device designed to help those who have lost their voice box. We didn't know any of that at the time. Instead, our thoughts selfishly revolved around just getting across. All we knew was that, if the US border wasn't stressful enough as it was, we were being questioned by someone who sounded like a cross between Darth Vader and a CB radio.

BORDER GUARD: "Where y'all think yer headed?"

DAVE: "Bellingham."

BORDER GUARD: "Where y'all call home?"

DAVE: "Vancouver."

BORDER GUARD: "How many of y'all in this here vehicle?"

DAVE: "Five."

BORDER GUARD: "How y'all might come to know one 'tuther?"

DAVE: "Friends."

BORDER GUARD: "When you comin' back?"

DAVE: "Tomorrow."

The guard paused, glaring at Dave, and glanced again at the book on the dashboard and the guys in the back seat. He slowly raised his finger to his throat button.

BORDER GUARD: "Welcome to 'Merica."

Dave nodded, jammed the van into first gear and rumbled us into Washington State. We remained deadly silent until we were what we hoped was out of earshot. Then we exploded into wild cheers. "WHOOOOOO!!! We made it! Fuck yeah!" Thanks to Dave's steel nerves, most crossings would prove as successful.

Dave always marvelled at how the culture changed the moment we sputtered across the Canada–US border. We were only an hour away from the multicultural melting pot of Vancouver, with its beaches, mountains and sushi, but as soon as we hit the Thrifty Mart in the border town of Blaine, just minutes from the checkpoint, we might as well have been in Biloxi. That Thrifty Mart gas station was essentially a carbon copy of what we'd find roadside throughout the United States. Along with gasoline, it sold fried chicken and wedge potatoes.

At the Blaine Thrifty Mart they called 'em "mojos," but there were myriad regional terms for these heavily battered, deep-fried, oversized chunks of potato: mojos, hohos, jojos, tater mamas, tater papas, tater babies, tater slammers, potato pals, wedge fries, wedgie tots, spuddy buddies, spud chuds. The Blaine gas station also sold handguns, rifles, knives, crossbows, bullets, firecrackers and booze of all kinds, including an entire wall of cold beer. This sure as hell wasn't the Petro-Canada in Moose Jaw. The drinking age in the USA was twenty-one, but Beez had long soared past that, so he bought the beer, we bought the fried chicken and mojos, and the party was on as we rambled down the Interstate 5.

"The old joke is true," spat Paul from the back of the van after a few slurps from his jumbo can of Miller High Life. "American beer is like making love in a canoe. It's fucking close to water!" We had to drink a lot of it to feel anything, so we were forced to stop at several public restrooms on the I-5 before pulling into Bellingham. It was the closest place of any significance across the border that we could play, and so we did, too many times, at a dump called the Up and Up Tavern.

Bellingham is a college town, home to the University of Washington, and we figured out pretty quickly that the audience we wanted to play for lived there between the months of September and May. Play a US college town in the summer, and you might as well set up a stage in the Gobi Desert. But when college is in session, boy howdy do those American students want to binge-party. Because of the wanton alcohol consumption, US college towns tend to be extremely strict when it comes to their bars and their drinking age: no one under twenty-one is admitted, no exceptions, and these rules extend even to the hired bands. That would prove to be a problem for the Smugglers.

thirteen

Some Velvet Sidewalk

W E FOUND OUT about the ID restrictions the tough way the first few times we were booked to play the Up and Up Tavern. We'd get the bum's rush by the bouncers as soon as they found out we were mostly under twenty-one. We sidestepped the problem after a while by securing fake IDs in Vancouver from a skuzzy drug dealer "associate" of our skinhead pal Roger the Dodger. The dealer charged us ten dollars each for laminated cards that looked incredibly unprofessional and were filled with spelling mistakes. We ran a risk by crossing the border with both real *and* fake IDs, but they actually fooled the US bouncers.

The notoriously rough-and-tumble Up and Up purported to be the top-selling bar of Pabst Blue Ribbon in the entire USA, probably because they sold it for fifty cents a can and the place was usually packed with enough drunk and horny college students to make the cast of *Animal House* seem withdrawn. The completely wasted undergrads didn't seem to care about our band, but we played the place anyway, trying to make ever-important inroads into the States. Occasionally we'd get heckled and threatened so badly by the crowd that I developed all sorts of saucy comebacks to have at the ready: "Listen, pal, if it comes to blows, you blow me first, eh?"

Two orangutan bouncers would meet us at the tavern door upon our arrival, their huge hairy arms folded and resting atop their matching beer bellies. After a few gigs they knew our band—they'd seen and been hood-winked by our fake IDs several times—but none of that mattered the one night I forgot my fake ID. The bouncers steadfastly refused to let me set foot in their crusty, beer-soaked, smoke-filled venue. The rest of the band glared at me with extreme and familiar frustration.

As the band's de facto manager, booking agent and publicist, I had so many details to remember that I sometimes neglected my personal logistics, sabotaging what I'd worked so hard to organize. The Smugglers had victoriously navigated an international border to get there, only to be stopped cold at the front door of the venue because of me. The options were limited: the rest of the band could either play without me, their lead singer and audience conduit, or we could cancel the gig.

We were sitting out on the sticky curb of North State Street, feeling defeated by the situation, when the soundman wandered out and contem-platively lit up a Marlboro. "I been thinkin' 'bout y'all's . . . situation," he drawled, flipping his greasy ponytail over his shoulder. State law said I couldn't perform inside the club without ID, he explained. However, there were no laws, that the soundman knew of anyway, that said I couldn't perform *outside* the club. Dave and the soundman headed back inside together. They attached several microphone cords, then ran them from the stage, across the dance floor, behind the bar, down the hallway, out the front door of the club and onto the street, where the rest of us were still sitting.

The soundman handed me the microphone. "Fuckin' . . . start singin', little dude!"

I tentatively spoke into the microphone: "Check, check, one two, one two." I heard my voice booming through the club's main speakers. The rest of the Smugglers burst out laughing and headed inside for sound check.

Could I really perform our entire set from that spot on the sidewalk in Bellingham? I took a nervous look around. Hordes of drunken college students were stumbling around like cavemen in fraternity sweatshirts, and it was only six p.m. What was it going to be like at our set time of ten p.m.? Luckily the stage backed up onto the wall that faced the street.

Though I couldn't actually see my band, I could hear a muffled version of them, and singing from the sidewalk worked somewhat in sound check. I was still undecided, but the rest of the Smugglers convinced me to go through with it. Partly because we didn't have much choice, but they also enjoyed seeing me punished for my own folly. In the name of showbiz, I reluctantly agreed.

A few hours later, it was showtime. The rain had started minutes before and came on hard. The sight of a little guy in oversized glasses, a curly afro, rubber boots, a thick pea jacket and a turtleneck scream- ing sorely out-of-tune garage rock 'n' roll songs into a microphone all by his lonesome proved an irresistible spectacle for the college drunkards. Occasionally a crowd gathered, then moved on with confused looks on their faces. I kept singing. Some of the onlookers threw money at my feet. I kept singing. Midway through the set I dodged a punch. I kept singing.

Later in the set, at the behest of his buddies, a giant jock put me in a prolonged headlock, his forearm tightening against my windpipe as I doubled over. I kept singing. The soggy cigarette butts that littered the sidewalk started to get fuzzy. I kept the mic close to my lips and sang on. The jock's buddies were close by, laughing. I stomped my rubber boot on his white running shoe, but he squeezed harder. The rain continued to pour. The song mercifully ended, and I yelled for help into the micro- phone. Finally I heard the bouncers splashing towards us, barking at the football players. The vice around my neck loosened and air rushed back into my lungs as the bouncers pried me loose. I let the band know I was okay, and we started up another song.

We finished the set to uproariously drunken applause inside. The audience was made fully aware of what was happening and had gotten into it. That night we learned first-hand the ancient showbiz credo "the show must go on." We would employ the rule with very mixed results for the rest of our career. For years afterward, the story of the singer from the Smugglers performing an entire set from the rainy sidewalk on State Street was written up in the "Infamous Moments" section of the Up and Up's "dinner" menu.

Word of our unlikely performance in Bellingham got around, and soon the Smugglers were playing everywhere we could in the Evergreen State: Spokane, Mount Vernon, Olympia, Tacoma and Seattle. We were

successfully shimmying our way across the border almost every weekend, sharing stages with Washington State bands like Girl Trouble, the Posies, the Fastbacks, Joey Kline and the Cropdusters, Stumpy Joe, the Squirrels and our heroes the Young Fresh Fellows. In Bellingham we often played with pop-punk band Stagnant Water, staying with them after the show.

It was in Washington that the Smugglers won our first real diehard American fans and attracted sustained female interest for the first time, girls who would follow us from gig to gig. In Tacoma, we met a wild rock 'n' roll woman named Neko Case. She was already something of a legend, being a member of several local bands and the subject of a really cool Girl Trouble song called "Neko Loves Rock 'n' Roll." Dave immediately hit it off with Neko, and the two began a tumultuous cross-border love affair that lasted many years. Neko Case would eventually move to Vancouver to live with Dave and his family. She was a huge help to us, designing our album covers, gig posters and sets for our videos. Neko punched her way into the local music scene, first as the drummer in cub, an all-female indie sensation, then in the punkabilly band Maow, all while attending art school. After a fiery breakup with Dave on the eve of one of our tours, Neko stuck around Vancouver, starting her successful solo career and joining the New Pornographers.

```
May 1, 1991
The Vogue
Seattle, Washington

We showed up for sound check but it turned
out we didn't even get one. To kill time
before the show, Neko suggested we visit the
Sub Pop Records office, which happened to
be on the eleventh floor of a building right
across the street from the club. Me, Beez
and Neko went up, excited to see where it all
happens. To our surprise, we found Sub Pop's
door wide open, yet there was no one there!
Everybody had left for the day and forgot
```

to lock up! A mass collection of CDs, tapes,
records, T-shirts, computers and posters
lay at our greedy, music-loving fingertips.
NO, we didn't take a thing, even though we
seriously wanted to. Stealing from the most
famous indie label in the world didn't seem
like the best way for us to "break into" the
Seattle scene. On our way out we told the
security guard about the unlocked, theft-
prone doorway to the indie inner sanctum.
Later that night at the show we met Jonathan
Poneman, co-owner of Sub Pop! Weirdly, he had
a black eye. We told him about the open door
to his office and he left the gig right away.

Older punk bands like D.O.A., NoMeansNo and SNFU had always done it, but the Smugglers seemed to be one of the only young Canadian bands dipping down into the USA in an attempt to build an audience. Introducing us at our gigs in Vancouver, Nardwuar loved to shout unproven claims like "The Smugglers have a better draw in Seattle than the Tragically Hip!" On several of those Washington State jaunts we reunited with Calvin Johnson, who was still working on what he promised to be a game-changing music festival.

A shuffling of our ranks occurred when our harmonica player, Adam Woodall, decided to leave the band. His musical interests had always been in a decidedly different freedom rock direction, but a solid indication that he just wasn't getting the onstage look of the Smugglers was when he played a show in Seattle wearing a bright tie-dyed T-shirt and a tiny pair of rolled-up spandex banana hammock shorts, having climbed into the van straight from his bike courier job in Vancouver. We lost a great band member and a very good harmonica player. Because we were paying for his insurance, Adam let us keep using his VW van on weekends. It added yet another wrinkle to the weekly border crossing that the *owner* was no longer actually *in* the van. But the Smugglers persevered.

fourteen

The Kids Are All Square— This Is Hip!

THE SIDEWALKS SHIMMERED in the heat of the west coast American summer. Everywhere we looked, we saw kids like us, something we'd been searching for ever since forming our band, whether we were consciously aware of it or not. Our minority was finally the majority: weirdos, losers, geeks, punks, mods, grungers, surfers and indie rockers. There was no overt aggression or disengaged apathy on display. Everyone here was respectful of one another. They were wearing thrift store blazers, clunky horn-rimmed glasses and faded Converse sneakers, just like us. They sat on the curb in clusters, eagerly reading zines while they tilted their heads to catch the corners of floppy slices of thin-crust pizza. Cute girls were everywhere. Rednecks were nowhere. Recognizable faces emerged from the crowd, leaving the know-it-all indie nerds starstruck: That's Ian MacKaye from Fugazi! That's Buzz Osborne from the Melvins! That's Kathleen Hanna from Bikini Kill! This was the most happening musical event the Smugglers had ever experienced. It made the Mudhoney gig look like a battlefield of wildlings. We had arrived at the International Pop Underground Convention.

Calvin Johnson had fleshed out his idea for the Convention months earlier over the phone from his K Records office in quaint downtown Olympia. Calvin, a dramatist, dreamer, doer and daredevil, explained to me in his gallows timbre that he felt something very special was happening in independent music around the world, that a revolution was about to occur, and that he wanted to celebrate it all by holding a week-long special event in Olympia. He was going to call it "The International Pop Underground Convention" after a series of seven-inch singles released on K Records, featuring indie artists from around the world hand-picked by Calvin and his label partner, Candice Pedersen.

Olympia was a picture-perfect little capital city an hour south of Seattle that seemed trapped in the 1950s. Olympia's downtown could have doubled as the town from *Back to the Future*. Juxtaposed with its sleepy, conservative exterior was a burgeoning counterculture that was coming to a rolling boil in the early nineties: Olympia was the home to Evergreen College, a free-thinking liberal arts school, and to KAOS, the college's even more free-form radio station, which birthed Sub Pop, first as a radio show, then a magazine, then the world-famous Seattle record label. Students from Evergreen would help to create the riot grrrl movement that empowered smart, educated women to do whatever the hell they wanted, including playing in awesome rock bands. Bikini Kill and their ferocious lead singer, Kathleen Hanna, emerged from this scene. Kathleen's also credited with suggesting the "Smells Like Teen Spirit" song title to Nirvana, a band from nearby Aberdeen.

The festival would feature a cross-section of the very best bands from the Pacific Northwest and those Calvin could convince to come in from farther afield. That's where I fit in. Calvin had seen first-hand the kinds of shows we held north of the border, just a few hours away, and the kinds of crowds we could get to show up. If I helped him book some Canadian shows to offset travel costs for the international touring artists, he said he would invite the Smugglers to perform at the Convention. I took him up on the offer and thus entered one of the most stressful and out-of-control periods of my life.

Calvin had figured out that, thanks to the exchange rate, it would be much cheaper for him to fly many of the international bands into Vancouver rather than Seattle, and he hoped I could secure guarantees from Canadian clubs as opposed to the risky door deals offered in the USA.

That meant I was suddenly the first base of operations for bands travelling great distances to the Convention by air or land, including prolific garage punk legend Billy Childish and his band Thee Headcoats from Chatham, England (on whose sound Mudhoney had partially based their "Touch Me I'm Sick" hit single); swaddled, foul-mouthed fuzz rockers the Mummies from San Francisco; the brilliant instrumental trio Shadowy Men on a Shadowy Planet from Toronto; twee-pop wunderkinds the Pastels from Scotland; and the mythical DIY post-hardcore purists Fugazi, along with their natty young political pals Nation of Ulysses, both from Washington, DC.

Nardwuar and I put on shows for most of the bands in the days leading up to the festival. Some were massively successful, like our all-ages show in North Vancouver for Fugazi. Nardwuar called the gig "A Moodyville Moo Moo" (a historical nod to the original "Moodyville" moniker of North Van, a reference lost on roughly 100 percent of the audience). The Evaporators' drummer, Scott, had made giant, gorgeous full-colour posters, and we plastered the city. We held it at a huge hockey rink at the North Vancouver community centre, and the gig's attendance figures dwarfed even Mudhoney's. Our pre-sold ticket count was so stratospheric that the community centre representatives got nervous, forcing us to spend an extra eight hundred dollars on rented porta-potties. Nardwuar swears angrily to this day that not a single extra toilet was used. ("WE got shit on!")

A ticket for the biggest gig in the history of Nardwuar the Human Serviette Presents. Thousands of kids showed up to the North Vancouver community centre to see the iconic post-punk band Fugazi from Washington, DC. DESIGN BY COLIN UPTON

Other gigs were disasters, like our all-ages show featuring Thee Headcoats, Girl Trouble (featuring a go-go dancing Neko Case) and the Mummies, which Nardwuar titled "Ubanghi Stomp!" A bill like that should have been fantastic, but the sparsely attended gig devolved into violence when one of the mods in attendance tried to strangle Nick for allegedly having sex with his girlfriend. Johnny, the rough-and-tumble bassist from Thee Headcoats, stood up for Nick, jumping off the stage and joining in the fray. That sent the few people on the dance floor into a knock-down, bloody-fisted mods-versus-rockers brawl straight out of *Quadrophenia*.

I was responsible for all of these bands' payments, performances, transportation, immigration documents (or lack thereof) and accommodation while they were in Canada. I was a dumb teenager with blind ambition, and in way over my head. But I considered the pay-off for the Smugglers so great that I took it all on. This international array of bands stayed at my family home, one after the other, severely fraying my parents' nerves. Billy Childish and his Headcoats (in their deerstalker Sherlock

While the Smugglers adored British garage punks Billy Childish and Thee Headcoats, going so far as to cover several of their songs, when they came through Vancouver they made my life a living hell. Left to right: Bruce Brand (drums), Billy Childish (guitar, vocals), Johnny "Tub" Johnson (bass). PAUL SLATTERLY PHOTO

Holmes hats) were by far the brashest of the bunch. Dad came very close to fisticuffs with a shirtless Billy in our kitchen, but my mom cooled off the situation by recognizing Billy's East London/Chatham accent, which amazed him.

On the flipside, the straight-edge members of Fugazi were the most polite, going so far as to cook breakfast for my parents. Lead singer Ian MacKaye sat down at my mom's desk to make some phone calls to promoters. When he looked up and saw the sweeping vista of Burrard Inlet, he commented, "Shame about the view." The band also left a nice note. The Pastels from Scotland were heavily jet-lagged, incredibly meek and basically incomprehensible when they did murmur any sort of communication. The garage rockin' Mummies fell somewhere in between, nice guys, but often frustrated that their touring vehicle, a white 1960s station wagon ambulance complete with wailing siren and "THE MUMMIES" painted in black along both sides, repeatedly got them pulled over by suspicious cops in ultra-conservative West Vancouver.

Every time I was ready to give up and tell the international array of bands to get out of my life, I'd pull the dog-eared invitation to the International Pop Underground Convention out of my pocket and read it again. It was like our Willy Wonka golden ticket to rock 'n' roll credibility. Written carefully by Calvin, it was a call-out to all the "hangman hipsters, new mod rockers, side-street walkers, scooter-mounted dream girls, punks, teds, instigators of the Love Rock Explosion, editors of every angry grrrl 'zine, plotters of the youth rebellion, Midwestern librarians and Scottish ski instructors who live by night. No lackeys to the corporate ogre allowed."

Calvin and Candice had invited all types of indie bands, from garage to punk to grunge to indie, including many purveyors of the kind of music Calvin's own band Beat Happening dished: proudly fey, simplistic indie-pop that flew in the face of stadium heavy metal, commercial pop, male-dominated hardcore and classic rock. In Calvin's K Records world, anyone who could strum a guitar or bang on a drum could and should form a band. It didn't matter if you couldn't play or sing—if you tried it was good enough for Calvin, and often good enough for a release on K. Calvin also encouraged women to be in bands, and many of the acts he "signed" to K Records were predominantly female. Thus, a bold and vocal

Dear Lawrence Family
Thanks for the
hospitality.
It is appreciated.
FUGAZI

K

Announces the
International
Pop
Underground
Convention
to be held in
Olympia, Washington
on
August 21-25, 1991

Music, Swimming, Discoing, Eating

new form of feminism played a huge role in the Convention. All of these scenes, ideas and musicians would come together in Olympia during that amazing week, August 21 to 25, 1991. The Smugglers were proud to be among over fifty bands performing, and one of just three Canadian bands at the Convention (the other two, trivia fans, were Mecca Normal and Shadowy Men on a Shadowy Planet).

Calvin's plan worked. It felt like the indie rock nation of the world had descended on Olympia: musicians, fans and media alike. Everyone knew something special was going down. The energy crackled. The weather was perfect. The Smugglers played the second night of the Convention, on a bill with Treepeople from Boise, Idaho (within a year lead singer Doug Martsch would form indie darlings Built to Spill), and Tsunami from Washington, DC. Stepping into the venue we were scheduled to play was a shock. The North Shore Surf Club was dark and cool compared to the hot August afternoon. It took several minutes for our eyes to adjust to the light, and when they did, to our delight, the venue was packed.

In preparation for our performance at the Convention, and likely due to the mounting stress I was under trying to keep so many international bands organized, I had demanded Nick give me a dramatic new haircut a few days beforehand. For years I had tried to grow the perfect bob haircut that Bobby Beaton from the Gruesomes rocked, but my curly hair kept exploding into a massive afro, making me look like an unfortunate cross between Woody Allen and Jimi Hendrix. Earlier that summer, I'd marvelled at the haircut of Johnny Johnson, the ultra-cool bassist from Thee Headcoats. His look was 1950s biker, complete with leather jacket, dirty jeans and black leather motorcycle boots with buckles—topped by a low-cut, non-spiked, old-school military-style mohawk about three inches wide and barely a centimetre tall.

When I finally got Billy Childish and Thee Headcoats out of my family home, I handed Nick a pair of shears. He shaved off the afro, leaving only a low-cut, non-spiked, old-school military-style mohawk about three inches wide and a centimetre tall. As with my attempt at Bobby Beaton's mushroom cut, I came nowhere close to looking as cool as Johnny. My mostly naked skull was lumpy and sickly white. My parents couldn't decide which hairstyle they despised more. But the most embarrassing

~~~~~

This is probably the longest my hair has ever been, in the first year or so of the Smugglers. I was trying and failing to create a perfect Ramones-style bob cut like Bobby Beaton from the Gruesomes. JULIET NICHOLL PHOTO

moment was when we bumped into Thee Headcoats a few days later in Olympia. Billy Childish caught sight of my new mohawk and burst out laughing. When Johnny spotted me a few moments later he stared as if he were looking in a circus mirror where everything appeared shrunken and warped. I slowly turned a royal shade of red.

However, Johnny didn't seem to mind me flagrantly ripping off his haircut. He was grinning in the second row of our show, bobbing his mohawk up and down as we roared through our set, trying not to appear intimidated. Amongst those in the packed audience was Molly Neuman, drummer from Bratmobile and one of the founders of the riot grrrl movement. We didn't know it on that hot August night, but Molly was someone we would work closely with during the most successful period of our band's life.

We also didn't realize that esteemed rock writer Ira Robbins was in the crowd. He was the editor and primary writer for the enormous *Trouser Press Record Guide*, and was on assignment for *Rolling Stone* to cover the Convention. Prominent punk rock reviewer and photographer Kirk "KrK" Dominguez was there, too. He had a column in the hugely influential *Flipside*, the LA-based punk rock bible I adored. Also present were writers from *Sassy*, *Hype*, SPIN, *Cryptic Tymes*, the *Rocket* and *Maximum Rocknroll*. Our high-energy performance in our pea jackets, toques and rubber boots made a positive impression on many of them, as well as on several other folks who would help us inch and then leap forward in the States for years to come.

The week was tightly scheduled, with many other events, including Olympia's long-standing pet parade. Calvin and Candice also organized a cake walk, a lakeside picnic featuring the Melvins and Shadowy Men on a Shadowy Planet and a screening of all five *Planet of the Apes* movies, because, according to the printed program, "everything that America fears the most is exposed and examined in this cathartic series of science fiction films." The guide included a map of Olympia's drinking water fountains and a centre-spread manifesto:

> As the corporate ogre expands its creeping influence on the minds of industrialized youth, the time has come for the International Rockers of the World to convene in celebration of our grand independence. Because this society is sick and in desperate need of a little blood-letting; sand,

sidewalk and punk pop implosion. Because the corporate ogre has infected the creative community with its black plague of indentured servitude. Because we are the gravediggers who have buried the grey spectre of the rock star myth. Because we are the misfits and we will have our day. We won't go away. August 21–25 1991 is the time. Olympia, Washington is the place. A double shot of International Hip Swing is the goal. Barbecues, parades, disco dancing, picnics and wild screaming teenage rock 'n' roll are the means. Revolution is the end. Revolution is the beginning.

There was also the "Love Rock Revolution Girl Style Now" night, shortened to "Girl Night," a lineup of female bands that gained legendary status as a pivotal moment in the feminist music movement: Bikini Kill, 7 Year Bitch, Courtney Love (Lois Maffeo's band, not the person), Bratmobile, Mecca Normal and others performed. The convention's vibe was so great and the nights so warm that it was impossible to be in a bad mood. Even the ever-cantankerous Billy Childish spent most of the time wearing a crooked-toothed grin under his curled, waxed moustache.

The Convention ended with a clap of thunder at the final show of shows by Fugazi at the Capitol Theatre. I'd personally had the greatest week of my life. I even had sex! As for the Smugglers, we felt like part of something larger than anything we had imagined. We were far from the best band that played the International Pop Underground Convention, but we were far from the worst. We were far from the most popular band, but we weren't the least popular either, for once. We were finding our rock legs, connecting with fans and friends and lovers and media from around North America.

It wasn't just us. Everyone in attendance felt like they had experienced something collective and unique. Calvin's prediction of a musical revolution was incredibly prophetic. The only thing he got wrong was that the "corporate ogre" would be just as involved as before. One month later, on September 24, Nirvana released *Nevermind*. The record catapulted grunge, punk and alternative into the mainstream, and sounded a death knell for hair metal and stadium rock as we knew it. It wasn't clear at the time whether the Convention was the beginning or the end of something great. In hindsight, maybe it was both. But thanks to the gathering, California was next for the Smugglers.

fifteen

Losing California

O UR OLD VW van had made many trips down to Washington State and across Canada, but our treks traversing the Rocky Mountains eastward had really taken their toll. The driver's side door wouldn't close by then; it had to be tied down with a bungee cord so it wouldn't swing open when the van made right turns. The side door wouldn't slide open anymore; it fell off onto the ground with a clatter when we cranked the handle from the inside. When Dave shifted gears, the van coughed out an ever-worsening jet-black cloud of noxious exhaust that engulfed and infuriated horn-blaring motorists caught behind us as we sputtered up hills. None of that stopped us from booking a solitary Saturday night show in San Francisco.

Before we left, we had a local mechanic check out the van. What he grunted at us wasn't good: the van's chassis was completely rusted out and could give way at any moment. If we were going to drive it at all, he urged us to avoid highway travel and to refrain from loading the van with any excess weight. With the San Francisco show just days away, we knew that was impossible. In an effort to protect ourselves should the chassis collapse on the highway, we decided to wear helmets for safety.

As we motored slowly south along the spectacular Oregon coast, past pristine beaches and towering natural sand sculptures, trailing mushroom clouds of black smoke, we received a lot of second glances from passing motorists. At the wheel, Dave wore a football helmet. Beez had a World War I Canadian army helmet, drummer Paul had a construction hardhat and Nick and I both wore hockey helmets. We acknowledged the puzzled stares from drivers with friendly waves and "thumbs up" signs. We looked like a cross between the Village People and the cast of *One Flew Over the Cuckoo's Nest*. Or, as Dave dubbed us, the "Value Village People."

Crossing the state line into the Golden State, we were thrilled to be in the land where we'd been told all our lives that dreams come true. To celebrate entering California, "the bar was open." In the back, Nick popped open our cooler to mix up some tasty gin and tonics with slices of lime and take out some cold canned beer. As we rolled down the California coast on spectacular Highway 101, Dave slid in the all-time greatest Beach Boys hits collection, *Endless Summer*, and we sang along at the top of our lungs. It felt awesome to be a band on tour.

Halfway through "California Girls," our serenity was shattered when a classic early-eighties z28 Camaro muscle car roared up alongside in the fast lane. The Beach Boys' chiming harmonies were quickly drowned out by another LA band; Mötley Crüe and their pounding anthem "Girls, Girls, Girls" blasted through the open windows of the Camaro from bass woofers that rattled our windows. Inside we were amazed to see two perfect headbanger specimens. We had no idea banger territory extended this far south. Just like Canadian bangers, these two were skinny, mustachioed and mulleted. Cigarettes hung from their lips like smouldering stalactites. They gave us the stink eye through long strands of greasy hair, highway predators prowling for fresh meat.

"Don't react to them!" yelped Beez, fanning both his hands in a "stop" motion. "Remember Regina!" Heeding his advice for once, we tried our best to ignore them.

The Camaro roared like Smaug every time the dude at the wheel touched his accelerator. The bangers kept pace with our rickety old van, glaring at us as their mullets flapdoodled in the wind. Then the banger riding shotgun, clad in a threadbare Judas Priest tour T-shirt, stuck his arms out the rolled-down window. Just minutes into the Golden State, we were recipients of the rarely used, highly effective and extremely offensive … *double bird.*

Everyone but Beez exploded at the outrage. *How dare they?* Why were we always the object of bangers' scorn? Paul jumped to his feet, swearing like Sam Kinison and screaming obscenities out the window. The Camaro let out a last guttural bluster and took off down the slope of the highway.

"CATCH UP TO THEM, DAVE!" I shrieked, instantly caught up in yet another FUBAR-meets-*Little Miss Sunshine* battle.

"What?" exclaimed Beez from the back seat. "You guys promised!"

Luckily, thanks to the VW van being weighed down like Tenzing Norgay, we picked up speed from sheer gravity on the downgrade. "I think we're gaining on them," said Dave through gritted teeth. The bangers' personalized California licence plate, RU 18 YET, was rapidly coming into focus. Soon we were on their rear bumper. With a flick of the steering wheel, the Camaro was suddenly beside us, then gone.

"Where are they? Where'd they go? I can't see them!" Dave panicked, checking his mirrors. He pulled into the fast lane, and suddenly there they were, right beside my passenger window. The driver-banger had his right hand on the wheel. With his left hand he gave us the finger.

The Camaro roared down an exit ramp, still side by side with us. "They're leaving the highway!" yelled Nick.

It was up to me. I gave my can of beer a wiggle. It was still about half full. Perfect weight. The bangers were directly below us now, on the off ramp. I furiously cranked my window down, undid my seatbelt and leaned out of the passenger window as far as I could. Beez screamed at me to get back in the van. I ignored him as the Camaro ebbed and flowed in the exit lane, toying with us. I cocked my arm and whipped my half-full can of beer at the car.

It didn't come anywhere close to hitting the Camaro. Instead the can flew straight back, spraying the side of our van. It hit the hot asphalt, spinning and foaming. Until they turned on their lights and siren, we didn't know that the California Highway Patrol (CHiPs!) was following us. I flinched as the police cruiser drove right over top of the fizzing beer can. The bangers roared away, their birds still flying high and outstretched, to the triumphant pounding of Mötley Crüe's "Too Fast for Love." Dave brought our van to a stop on the side of the highway. Beez was practically in tears. While the rest of us scrambled to hide the booze and take off our helmets, he whimpered, "What the fuck is the story now?"

The CHIPs officers lectured Dave about dangerous driving and littering. Miraculously, they didn't seem to notice the beer suds dripping down the passenger side of the van or that the foaming can they had driven over was alcohol. One of them pointed to a nearby sign that read "MAXIMUM FINE FOR LITTERING $1,000." After they'd written us up for a couple of much smaller fines, we were miraculously freed to continue on to our "Budget Rock Showcase" in San Francisco. We camped that night at a beach on the edge of the glorious Redwood Forest, drunkenly re-enacting our favourite scenes from *Return of the Jedi* while cursing the banger menace.

TWILIGHT WAS SETTLING on San Francisco when we rolled across the massive expanse of the Golden Gate Bridge the next day. Paul was so excited he kept repeating "San... Fran... cisco" over and over from the back seat while sucking back cans of Olympia. The tops of the downtown skyscrapers protruded from the fog like Himalayan mountain peaks. By the time we took the Market Street exit to find our way to the Chameleon Club, our hearts were pounding. Our usual excited and offensive babble had fallen silent as we rubbernecked in all directions, staring out at our first Big City, USA.

Our San Francisco debut had been arranged with help from the Mummies. We would be playing with the Phantom Surfers and their young friends, a new surf band called Eight Ball Scratch. The entire gig was called a "Budget Rock Showcase," in honour of the lo-fi garage rock subgenre the Mummies had created and fostered. It was a fine bill to be a part of for our inaugural Bay Area performance.

San Francisco felt worlds apart from Vancouver or Seattle. It was faster, dirtier and a whole lot bigger. A mosaic of determined and damaged faces surged into the crosswalks at every red light: black, white, Latino, Asian. We inched our way up and down the streets of San Francisco, bound for the Mission District, a densely populated neighbourhood that looked so predominantly Spanish it felt as if we had rolled into Mexico. Turning onto Valencia Street, we spotted the club fairly easily, mostly because the Mummies' infamous white 1963 Pontiac ambulance was parked out front. We'd soon learn that there was a huge gearhead scene in San Francisco: next to the Mummies' ambulance was a lineup of vintage hot rods, motorcycles and scooters.

Inside, the Chameleon was a blueprint of what we would come to recognize as the classic layout of the American rock 'n' roll bar: a long, thin room painted black with no windows. The front doors opened right onto the club, and the stage was at the opposite end. Running almost the entire length of one side of the room was the bar. There was no lining up politely for a drink as we did in Canada. In the USA, you sidled up to the bar from every possible angle, then tried to catch the bartender's attention by leaning forward and casually holding out cash. A scattering of tables and chairs across from the bar led to an open space in front of the stage: the dance floor.

We were late. The doors were already open and the Chameleon was packed with the California version of the indie-rock types we had met at the International Pop Underground Convention: striped T-shirts, rolled-up jeans and Converse low-top sneakers, a cross between the Beach Boys and the cast of The Born Losers. It was always purgatory to arrive early in a new town and wait hours for the crowd to show up, which they sometimes never did. So it was hugely exciting for the Smugglers to peer through the front doors into the jammed club that night.

While we were hastily unloading the van, two punk kids approached. "Hey, so, uh ... so we're both under twenty-one, but we really, really, really want to see this show. Is there any way you can get us in?" We probably should have considered the trouble we'd already had in California as an omen to steer clear. I could sense Beez bristling at the potential predicament arising from sneaking underage kids into an American bar, especially since half of us were still using fake IDs ourselves. But I couldn't help but see myself in those two desperate music fans.

NARDWUAR'S GIGS HAD always been all-ages. He steadfastly believed that music should be seen and heard by everyone, especially those under the age of nineteen. Liquor boards weren't so inclined. Like every other obstacle we faced in music, when he and I wanted to see a band at a club in Vancouver, we found a way around the rules. My beard, which had worked at the Gruesomes show, wasn't always foolproof. Sometimes we'd done exactly what these two punk kids were doing: asked the band to sneak us in. Most bands wouldn't give us a second glance or were too nervous to take the chance, so we'd had to come up with other, more ridiculous ploys before we finally secured fake IDs.

On one occasion, to see the Cramps at the sold-out Commodore Ballroom, a few of us showed up at the venue during sound check in the late afternoon. Both the front and back doors were unlocked, and the bouncers hadn't shown up for work yet, so we slipped up the back staircase undetected. The Commodore had circular tables with floor-length red tablecloths, so a couple of us hid under the nearest table, hoping to remain undiscovered. Three hours later, when the lights went down and the doors opened, we emerged with cramps of our own, blending in with the crowd. It was pathetic, but it worked. Getting bolder, we pulled the same sound-check trick to see R.E.M. but skipped hiding under the table. Instead, we found a dark corner of the venue and slumped into a booth, acting as if we were exhausted musicians who had been in a tour bus all day long. We hid in plain sight until the doors opened.

Waiting around for hours in empty clubs got old fast, so we also came up with much riskier moves. When legendary British band John Mayall and the Bluesbreakers were playing at the Town Pump, Adam called the box office and pretended to be John Mayall calling from his hotel room, complete with a rough cockney accent, and asked the door person to add a few more names to his guest list: ours. It could have been a complete disaster when we showed up at the club, but our ploy worked.

Our favourite tactic, however, was arriving at a show we weren't playing with guitar cases in hand. Employing Jedi mind tricks and brass balls, we'd walk confidently, with an air of slight annoyance, through the front door and past the bouncers. If we were stopped, we'd state briskly, "I'm playing tonight, man." The guitar case ruse was so ridiculously foolproof that one night in Victoria we became even more emboldened when trying to see the Young Fresh Fellows at Harpo's. We left the actual guitar in our friend's dorm room and filled its case with cold beer. Breezing past the lineup and into the club, we drank "imports" all night long.

THOSE TWO SAN Francisco punk urchins didn't have a guitar case with them, but I couldn't turn them away. We wanted to be in a band that didn't ignore or blow off the underage fans, and we were willing to take the risk involved. We allowed the kids to carry some of Paul's drums into the club, the size of the gear helping to conceal their pimply teenaged faces. They scooted by the doormen undetected and were in. Watching from the van, Beez let out a sigh of relief.

Eventually, we'd sneak underage kids into our bar gigs all over the world. It was Beez who figured if we were going to keep doing it, we needed a better method, so he perfected a manoeuvre in four steps:

1. Beez would enter the club wearing a very bright, easily identifiable jacket, a hat and his trademark horn-rimmed glasses.

2. He would ensure he was noticed by the doorman, entering with some sort of musical equipment so it was obvious he was with the band.

3. Back outside at the van, he would dress the underage kid as himself, in the bright jacket, hat and glasses.

4. The kid would grab a piece of equipment and enter the club dressed as Beez. Once inside, he would hand the costume over to one of us to deliver it back out to Beez. It worked.

Not only were we allowing underage kids the thrill of seeing otherwise unattainable live music, we were also inadvertently making fans for life. I still get thank-you letters and thanks in person from now-grown adults for getting them into their first rock shows. And our opening bands on the Canadian all-ages circuit—groups like Gus, the Two Tonne Bowlers and Atlas Strategic—contained members of future Can-Con indie-gold bands like Wolf Parade, the Unicorns, Black Mountain and Ladyhawk. The Smugglers never heard back from those two punk kids we snuck into our San Francisco gig, but here's hoping they formed Black Rebel Motorcycle Club or something.

Saturday, September 28, 1991
The Chameleon Club
San Francisco, California

This weekend was bloody nuts! The Smugglers drove all the way to San Francisco for ONE gig! But San Francisco was great and so was

the ride down. We saw the Redwood Forest
(including the "Trees of Mystery"), real
California surf, Haight-Ashbury, and even
got pulled over by the cops. We used the
tickets they wrote us to start the fire at
the campsite that night. Anyway, the show
in Frisco was SO cool. It was at this hot
spot called the Chameleon and members of the
audience included Ron Silva, drummer of the
Crawdaddys and the Untamed Youth, Jon Von of
the Mr. T Experience, a handful of Mummies
and a really crazy guy from the Dwarves. The
only problem was we thought we were getting
$300 (which meant we would have broken even
for the drive there and back) but it was $300
TOTAL for the three bands. Paul screamed at
the promoter and threw a pint glass, which
was not cool. Jon Von tried to help, but the
promoter wouldn't budge: $100 US. So weird
because the club was packed! Jon Von thinks
the Phantom Surfers probably got more than
they let on. Beez had to lend us money to
get home. Oh, and Dave and Beez saw racial
violence! After our show, they went to the
twenty-four-hour Safeway for dinner. While
they were shopping, they noticed a skinhead
in the parking lot. Suddenly, about eight
black guys surrounded him. He pulled out
a chain and started swinging. Him and one
of the black guys started fighting and the
black guy threw him through the window of
the Safeway! The black guys scattered and an
ambulance showed up later. It freaked Dave
and Beez out pretty bad. Anyway, the best
part of this trip is we made lots of new
friends and can't wait to do it again!

One of the friendships we solidified at the San Francisco gig was with Trent Ruane, lead singer and organist of the Mummies. He would later hand-pick Beez to tour Europe as the Mummies' bass player, recording a Peel Session for John Peel's legendary BBC Radio show while they were at it, which was later released on vinyl. We stayed the night in San Francisco with Jon Von, the first of many touring sleepovers at his home, which was just down the street from the Chameleon. The next morning, Jon took us on a quick sightseeing detour to Haight-Ashbury, one of the most famous musical intersections in the world, the epicentre of the Flower Power movement of the late sixties.

The Haight-Ashbury of the early 1990s was clinging somewhat desperately to that earlier era, with plenty of head shops, record stores and nightclubs lining the trash-strewn stretch. Homeless hippies shuffled along the street begging for a different kind of change from the kind they had marched for in the sixties. You'd think the VW van would have been in its happy place at Haight-Ashbury, but it sounded worse than ever, belching cauldron-black smoke. We snapped a quick photo and said our goodbyes to Jon, who was stunned by our helmets. We rumbled back to Highway 101 North, having no idea if the van would make it across the Golden Gate Bridge, let alone home.

I was no fan of hippies but couldn't ignore the musical history of the Haight-Ashbury neighbourhood of San Francisco. We had to see it for ourselves.
NICK THOMAS PHOTO

sixteen

More Bounce
to the Ounce

T HE VAN MIRACULOUSLY made it to within hours of the Canadian border, but it was shuddering so badly on the trip it felt like it could rip apart at any moment. Just about everything on the road was passing us. We knew it was bad when somewhere near Everett an ancient Model-T pickup truck putt-putted on by. The old rig had a very large, fully inflated bright-orange Zodiac raft strapped to its flatbed, its nose sticking up over the cab. As the truck zig-zagged a few cars ahead of us, the Zodiac began to flap and bounce. Then, to our collective awe, the raft ripped free from its moorings and flew up into the air like a dragon freed from chains. The orange rubber boat soared several feet over the highway and cars, then came down on its end. It bounced down the Interstate 5 freeway, headed straight for us. "DAVE, WATCH OUT!"

Although Dave did his best, it was a busy day on the northbound freeway and we were trapped in our lane. We screamed and pressed our helmets down over our heads, bracing ourselves for sudden impact. The raft smacked straight into us, totally obscuring our view of the road. While we shrieked, the raft flipped up and over top of us, sliding along our roof with a horrific roar, then came crashing down behind us. Somehow the raft hooked itself onto the rear of the van and we started to drag it down the freeway. An explosion overpowered our screams. Paul dropped his beer. Dave shouted that one of our rear tires had probably blown. With the raft still attached to us, our van started to fishtail. Dave fought the wheel to pull us over.

Once we had finally stopped on the side of the freeway, we ripped off our helmets and spilled out of the van to inspect the damage. The Zodiac had deflated and looked pitiful, like a popped balloon at the end of a birthday party. The damage to the van was surprisingly minimal: all our tires were intact, but the bumper had been wrenched from its moorings and was hanging by a single, rusty bolt.

The Model-T pickup truck had pulled over up ahead. The owner, a skinny old bowlegged cowboy, was awkwardly trotting back to where we were parked, clamping a ten-gallon hat to his head. He appeared to be extremely agitated, yelling something at us over the roar of the freeway. When he got close enough, we could make out what he was saying. "My boat! Is my boat okay?"

"No, your boat is not okay! But luckily we are!" Beez shouted back.

Seeing the Zodiac hanging from the back of our van, as limp as a used condom, he turned to us with a bony index finger outstretched. "You damn hippies busted up my raft!"

"WHAT?" Paul blurted between chugs of his newly cracked beer. "*Busted up your raft?*" The cowboy took a step back. "Your boat almost killed us, you stupid old Slim Pickens asshole! Look at our bumper! Get your boat off our fuckin' van and get back to your antique piece-of-shit truck and get out of here!"

As the cowboy nervously wrenched his raft loose, our rear bumper fell off completely, clanking to the pavement. Nick opened up the back hatch of the van and shoved the bumper inside, while the old cowboy dragged his boat back towards his truck. "Fuck you!" Paul yelled at him for good measure.

We climbed back inside the van and strapped our helmets on, all of us in bewildered shock. Dave turned the key. Nothing. He turned it again. The engine made a weak wheezing sound, then fell silent. Dave pivoted in the driver's seat. "Looks like you're going to have to get out and push it again, chums."

Once we got the van rolling fast enough, Dave slid it into second gear and popped the clutch. The van jolted and whimpered back to life as we ran alongside and hopped in like a bobsled team. From then on, even on straightaways, the van dipped well below the speed limit, coughing along like a chain-smoker in a marathon.

Finally, we were a couple of cars away from the Canadian checkpoint, which meant it was time to remove our helmets and make a quick exchange of our dashboard books: *Father Guild Says Howdy* was removed and *Never Cry Wolf* by Farley Mowat took its place. That title was usually foolproof with the Canadians. Not this time. The customs officer did not appreciate being engulfed in a cloud of burnt oil smoke as we grumbled up to her kiosk. Waving the fumes away from her face, she demanded that we turn off the engine.

"I'm afraid I can't do that, ma'am. It may not start up again," Dave answered as politely as possible.

"Turn it off. NOW."

Dave did as he was told. The van sputtered into momentary silence. A backfire that sounded like a shotgun blast followed, making the guard hunch and duck. Her eyes narrowed as she collected herself and stepped out of the booth.

"Open your door. NOW," she ordered Dave.

"I'm afraid I can't do that, ma'am. It's tied down with this bungee cord, so we don't use this door anymore." She rounded the front of the van to the sliding passenger side door, glaring into the back seat. I rolled down the passenger seat window so Dave could answer, observing our rules: only the driver could speak at border crossings.

"Open this door, NOW," she exclaimed, pointing at the sliding side door.

"I'm afraid we can't do that, ma'am. The side door isn't working too well, either," Dave replied.

Clearly thinking we were giving her the ol' hippie-van druggie runaround, she grabbed hold of the sliding side door's handle. We motioned at her from the inside to stop. "Don't do it!" yelled Nick. Ignoring us, she yanked hard enough that the door popped off. The weight of the door knocked her down, pinning her to the concrete. Her boots stuck out from under the bottom of the door like the scene from *The Wizard of Oz*. Nick quickly jumped out and pulled the door off her, helping her up. She was furious.

After a search of the van yielded nothing but our beat-up amps, instruments and empty beer cans, she climbed back into her booth, breathing heavily, and ordered us to proceed. Dave looked over at her one more time. "I wonder if you wouldn't mind giving us a push?"

In true Canadian fashion, she did, and got doused in a choking exhaust cloud for her trouble. Later that night, after I had dropped everyone off, I was motoring the final kilometre to my parents' house when the exhausted van let out one last, long wheeze, like a dying dog, and lost all power. It wouldn't even jump-start. Luckily, West Vancouver is built on the side of a mountain, so I was able to coast down, all the way to my family home. The van rolled into the driveway, where it came to what would be its final stop after valiantly carrying us far and wide. You could call it good timing.

The Smugglers' clear and present goal was to tour the entire USA, and we had known even before it expired that the VW van was not up for the cross-continental challenge. We were aiming to log some heavy kilometres, following in the tire tracks of our rock 'n' roll heroes. We had to find a new van, and we planned to pay for it with our winnings from YTV.

Our typically tight sleeping arrangements in the Volkswagen van. If we wanted to tour as far as we hoped, we knew we would need a much bigger and better vehicle. DAVID CARSWELL PHOTO

seventeen

I'm an Adult Now

A FEW MONTHS BEFORE the Pop Underground Convention, the Smugglers learned we had won something called a YTV Achievement Award. None of us had any idea what that was. It turned out our pal Nardwuar the Human Serviette had entered our debut single, "Up and Down" b/w "Seattle Bound" (on Nardwuar Records, naturally), for an annual awards show that handed out trophies and cash to Canadian youth excelling in all sorts of categories: sports, business, environmentalism, bravery, music and more. We later discovered that the judges for the music category were none other than Toronto band the Pursuit of Happiness, they of the cool alternative hit "I'm an Adult Now." They had apparently appreciated the fact that our first release was a seven-inch vinyl single with a full-colour cover, complete with detailed liner notes by Nardwuar, in an era when (in Canada anyway) vinyl was on the outs. They loved our ramshackle, high-energy rock 'n' roll music too, and so they chose us as the winners. The national recognition made those around us proud: our friends and, most importantly, our parents. We needed everything we could to legitimize the time and effort we were investing in the band.

Unfortunately the award would signal the end of the rock 'n' roll dash for our irritable drummer, Paul Preminger. Paul was proud of being a

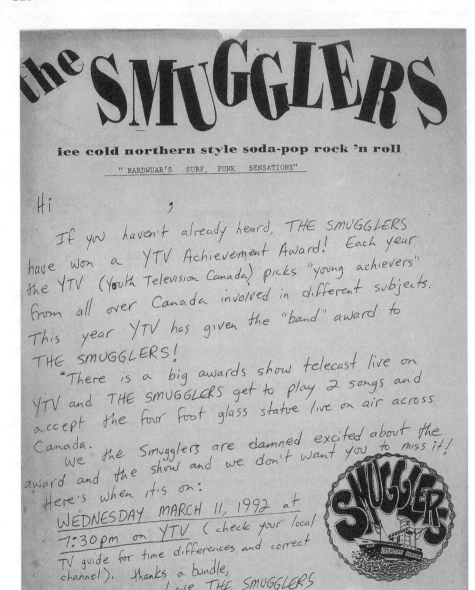

the SMUGGLERS

ice cold northern style soda-pop rock 'n roll

" NARDWUAR'S   SURF,   PUNK   SENSATIONS"

Hi   ,

If you haven't already heard, THE SMUGGLERS have won a YTV Achievement Award! Each year the YTV (Youth Television Canada) picks "young achievers" from all over Canada involved in different subjects. This year YTV has given the "band" award to THE SMUGGLERS!

"There is a big awards show telecast live on YTV and THE SMUGGLERS get to play 2 songs and accept the four foot glass statue live on air across Canada.

We the Smugglers are damned excited about the award and the show and we don't want you to miss it!

Here's when it is on:

WEDNESDAY MARCH 11, 1992 at 7:30 pm on YTV (check your local TV guide for time differences and correct channel). thanks a bundle,
Love THE SMUGGLERS

2874 BELLEVUE AVENUE • WEST VANCOUVER, BC • V7V 1E8 • 604-926-9444
— messages: 604 926 9420, fax: 604 926 9464

The press release for our nationally televised performance on the YTV Achievement Awards, the biggest award the Smugglers would ever win. The event was held at the National Arts Centre in Ottawa and hosted by Alan Thicke. We used the prize money to buy a new van. The press release contains one mistake: the trophy was forty centimetres tall, not four feet tall.

founding member of the Smugglers. He would sit in the van pounding back beer with one hand and holding our first single in the other, flipping it over and re-reading the liner notes aloud, chuckling at Nardwuar's wit. Paul was broke most of the time, so he really cared about having money in his pocket. He thought it horrendous that the Smugglers made so little of it.

Paul came up with ingenious ways of making extra dough in our earliest days on the road. Before we arrived at the venue, he would convince us to swing by the liquor store and dip into the band fund so he could run in and purchase several flats of Black Label beer, promising us a strong return on our investment. In the parking lot of all-ages shows, he would break several laws by popping open the hatch of our vw camper van to sell beer to the kids coming to the show, either single cans or entire six-packs: a kind of alcoholic lemonade stand. Oftentimes Paul would make more money on pre-show beer sales than we got from playing the actual gig.

He also developed terrible stage fright. He had always vomited before shows, in the bathroom or back parking lot of the club. Eventually, the puking made its way onto the stage. We often didn't realize he was back there violently throwing up, because he somehow managed to never miss a beat. After some gigs, there'd be vomit all over his drums, down the front of his pea jacket and on the floor surrounding his drum stool.

Whether it was nerves, lack of cash flow or a need for something better, Paul felt the urge for a solid Plan B. He had always been passionate about food, so he enrolled in a weekend cooking school. Unfortunately the cooking classes clashed not only with the gigs we had booked every weekend all over the Pacific Northwest, but more importantly with the week we'd be spending in Ottawa for the ytv Achievement Awards gala. Sadly for us all, Paul "The Pwem" Preminger, our pukin' pit bull on the drums, left the band. It was a shock, but with so much on the horizon, we didn't have time to mourn his departure. We had no idea just how much Paul would miss being a member of the Smugglers, or the tragic personal depths he would hit after leaving.

With perfect timing, Nardwuar informed me that ex-Vindicators drummer Bryce Dunn had just moved to Vancouver from Calgary. Bryce was pretty much the only guy we got along with from that band. After Paul left, I made the call, and within weeks Bryce "The Dunndertaker" Dunn was on the road with us, playing every weekend around the Pacific

BRYCE DUNN

Bryce Dunn was raised in Calgary, but his dad was an ex-pat from Britain, just like Nick's and Dave's. Bryce's dad made his fortune in Alberta's oil and gas industry (years later he would get a Shell Oil logo tattoo to commemorate his career). Like all of our dads, Bryce's was perplexed by his son's choice to play in a rock 'n' roll band, but he was fairly supportive of the Smugglers. He would invite us over for barbeques at their sprawling family home on the banks of the Bow River whenever the band played Calgary. While we chowed down on burgers on the deck, he'd serenade us, playing classical acoustic guitar. That was more musical talent than any of the other fathers had, but Bryce's dad still thought rock 'n' roll was a dead end, and he never hesitated to cheerfully tell us so.

Bryce was a friendly guy, but an odd duck. His explosive drumming thrilled and tantalized us. His long, straight auburn hair took off like the whirring blades of a helicopter when he drummed, giving him the appearance of Mr. Burns in a Beatles wig. A rake-thin little fellow, he was often hunched over, appearing older than his years, his 1960s thrift-store cardigans and flooded stovepipe slacks completing the look. When Bryce showed up at his first practice with his vintage Ludwig drum set covered in burlap wrap, he blew us away by playing every song beat-perfect and adding all sorts of exciting flourishes, snare rolls and change-up beats. Bryce instantaneously made all our songs better and more danceable. He was a performance unto himself; his head would bop from side to side, his butt jolting off his drum stool with every smash of the cymbals. And yet his face remained relatively stoic, sometimes even angrily so. There was a lot we would learn about Bryce Dunn. I was willing to put up with his unfolding idiosyncrasies, though, because only one thing really mattered: Bryce played rock 'n' roll drums really, really well.

Northwest in various rental vans. He also agreed to perform at the YTV Awards gala. He was the newest member of the Smugglers, whether he liked it or not. It was often hard to tell.

The YTV Youth Achievement Awards flew the Smugglers to Ottawa to perform two songs on the nationally televised awards show held at the National Arts Centre and hosted by Canadian TV star Alan Thicke. Two big musical acts had been booked to bring up the ratings: Crash Test Dummies, a Winnipeg band who had had a Canadian hit with "Superman's Song," and Right Said Fred, a British band with a massive worldwide single (which Dave loved) called "I'm Too Sexy." We were thrilled to be part of the show, but as always seemed be the case with the Smugglers, there was a catch—an obstacle we had to manoeuvre around without anyone catching on.

The YTV Youth Achievement Awards celebrated Canadian *youth*, as in *teenagers*, and were given to kids nineteen years of age and younger. Almost a year earlier, when we learned the prize would be awarded to the Smugglers, our average age was legitimately eighteen. By the time the awards show rolled around—they had informed the winners far in advance, to be sure to have everyone in Ottawa for the show—young Adam had left the band, Nick and I had turned nineteen, Dave was twenty and Beez was a ripe old twenty-nine. Gaining Bryce didn't bring down our average age; he was also in his early twenties, but he had long, omnisexual hair that sometimes made people mistake him for a sickly young girl (with a goatee). To hide their age in Ottawa, we insisted that Beez and Bryce keep their long hair in their faces at all times. Beez was shaving twice a day, but by the end of the week the producers were beginning to wonder why one of the Smugglers was always hanging out with the other winners' moms in the hotel bar, making them shriek with drunken delight at his plethora of dirty jokes.

Our nervousness about our legitimacy aside, the YTV Achievement Awards were quite an extravagant experience. We had brunch with the Governor General of Canada at his home in Rideau Hall with all the other winners, including future Nashville country star Lisa Brokop and Olympics-bound athlete Clara Hughes, who would become the first athlete in history to win multiple medals in both the summer and the winter Olympics. On the televised awards show, our songs went over well (Alan Thicke even pogoed across the stage during "Pebble Beach," a new song that would lead off our debut album), and the Pursuit of Happiness were there to present us with a large trophy. We thanked them, our parents and Nardwuar in our acceptance speech.

The after-party across the river in Hull, Quebec, was such a throwdown that we missed our flight home the next morning. But the piece of the YTV Youth Achievement experience that fulfilled the Smugglers' most immediate need was a winning cheque for three thousand dollars. Since the most we had ever been paid for a gig was around three hundred dollars, we felt like we had won the Irish Sweepstakes. With that money, we bought the all-time perfect touring van.

One of the perks of winning a 1992 YTV Achievement Award for Best Band was being flown to Ottawa to meet the Governor General and have brunch with him at his home at Rideau Hall.
NICK THOMAS PHOTO

↑ Partying at the YTV Achievement Awards with the Pursuit of Happiness, the judges in the band category who selected us to win. They were impressed that we had our 7″ single in an age when vinyl was declared a completely dead format (at least in Canada). NICK THOMAS PHOTO

↑ The after-party of the YTV Achievement Awards was in a late-night bar across the river from Ottawa in what was then called Hull, Quebec. Here's a candid shot of Dave dancing with sports winner Clara Hughes, who would go on to become the only person to ever win multiple medals in both the Winter and Summer Olympic Games. NICK THOMAS PHOTO

← Dave was thrilled that British one-hit-wonder Right Said Fred ("I'm Too Sexy") would also be performing on the YTV Achievement Awards national telecast. Trivia fans: "I'm Too Sexy" made music history when it became only the second debut single by a UK band to reach number one in the States, after the Beatles. Richard Fairbrass (left) poses here with Dave. NICK THOMAS PHOTO

eighteen

L & P's Getaway

W HAT MANY ONLOOKERS don't understand about rock 'n' roll touring is that the van is just as important as any member of the band. Without a van, you don't make it to the gig. If you don't make it to the gigs, you're not really a band. To quote fIREHOSE bassist Mike Watt, "If you're not playing, you're paying." If your van breaks down in the middle of a tour, the vast distances between cities on the itinerary can pile up with nightmarish speed. If you're stuck in some Florida backwater on Friday afternoon, waiting for a new transmission that won't arrive until Monday, when you were already supposed to be in Texas, catching up can be logistically impossible. The Smugglers had been extremely lucky with the old VW, but we needed something larger, tougher and more reliable.

Our friend John Wright played drums for NoMeansNo, a legendary hardcore jazz-punk band from Victoria who had already toured the world. When we played a few shows with NoMeansNo and John's other band, the Hanson Brothers, we grilled him on vans. He was stupefied to hear we had spent our first four years in a VW camper van. He advised us to avoid Dodge and Ford vans: "All they do is break down." He then lowered his voice, leaned in and told us in no uncertain terms to find a GMC van with a "350 engine." John promised it would roll on forever. We had no idea what "350" meant, but we didn't need to know. We just had to find it.

We hunted like John Wayne in *The Searchers* and eventually found our Natalie Wood. It was the ultimate ride meeting all of our qualifications: a 1979 raised-roof GMC 350 Vandura camper van that had options for both gasoline and propane. An elderly couple had previously used the van as an RV, nicknaming it "L & P's Getaway," and it had a huge amount of interior space: it was practically a studio apartment, in which Dave, our tallest member, could stand to his full height. Mounted to the dashboard was an invaluable compass shaped just like R2-D2. Then there was the Trans-Awn 2000, an awning over the side door that could be pulled out and set up over picnic or merchandise tables. We used our cheque from YTV, plus a loan from Dave's sister, to meet the thirty-five-hundred-dollar asking price.

Nick got to work customizing the interior to our exact needs, building not one but two large double beds in the van so that all five of us could sleep (fairly) comfortably. The lower bunk covered a large plywood box in the rear that housed our equipment and merchandise, and he also built a big back seat bench in front of the bunks and installed a luggage rack over the driver's and shotgun seats. Along the inner sides of the van he constructed shelves that held our cassettes, our VHS tapes and our books—including my entire Tintin collection. All of this space provided great hiding places as well, which saved us lots of money on BC Ferries

Our new van, L & P's Getaway, in its full glory with extended awning, somewhere on the California coast en route to San Francisco. Compared to our Volkswagen camper van, this 1979 GMC was an upgrade in just about every way. We bought it with our winnings from the YTV Achievement Awards and outfitted it with two double beds, bench seating and plenty of secure storage for gear. NICK THOMAS PHOTO

whenever we were playing Victoria or Nanaimo. When Dave pulled up to the ticket booth and was asked, "How many in the van?" he would brazenly answer, "Just me today!"

For security, we installed a large steel strongbox and padlock for valuables, including a portable TV/VCR combo on which we played old movies and *Seinfeld* marathons during long drives. To further fortify the van, we bolted two metal brackets to the inside of the back door so we could slide a big wooden bar snugly into them. Then we covered every surface in thick, red shag carpet we found rolled up in the attic above Dave's parents' garage. The carpet was filthy, having been home to a family of raccoons, but we shook it out and used it anyway. We laid thick, foamy mattresses down over the double beds and covered them in sheets and sleeping bags.

Just as we were stapling the last piece of carpet into place, Dave's uncle Taz wandered by to check out our work. Uncle Taz was a blue-collar, working-class Brit on vacation from Dover. In an accent as thick as the shag, out of the corner of his mouth he muttered, "You know what we'd call this back 'ome, eh, Davey Boy? We call this a right good *fuck box* ... whot?" Then he glanced over his shoulder, elbowed Dave again and repeated it louder. "A RIGHT GOOD FUCK BOX ... whot? I shagged a few birds meself in a FUCK BOX just like 'iss one back 'ome, I did! Whot?"

With Uncle Taz's hearty christening, the van was ready to roll. Thanks to contacts mostly supplied by Calvin Johnson and the Young Fresh Fellows, and endless calls to every area code in the lower forty-eight on my parents' home phone, I was able to string together a wing-and-a-prayer tour of the United States. The trek would be in support of our first album on Nardwuar Records: a ten-inch vinyl record entitled *At Marineland*, which we recorded at Egg Studios in Seattle with producer Conrad Uno. Released at the height of CD mania, it was not a seven-inch single, not a standard twelve-inch LP, but a ten-inch album, the likes of which were usually reserved for obscure, vintage jazz seventy-eights. It was another of Nardwuar's highly questionable ideas, but when the full-colour sleeve and the black vinyl came back from the plant, we were hugely excited.

We had built up a modest fan club by then, and our seasonal newsletter with the American tour dates was mailed out to everyone who had signed up, as well as to many American bands we loved who hadn't. We were hoping to alert them to our presence anyway. It was shocking how many members of those bands actually did show up and befriend us because of the unsolicited newsletter mail-outs. We sent all our promo, records and posters on ahead to the clubs, trusting that the packages would be received by the promoters, who would in turn plaster our name around town and get our record played on the local college radio station. We could only hope. None of our parents wanted us to go, but we were determined. On the day we departed for our first six-week US tour, my tough rock 'n' roll façade crumbled like a stale chocolate chip cookie, and I wept in my parents' arms when it was time to say goodbye.

Our first full-continent North American tour in the spring and summer of 1992.

"I CAN'T STEER THIS THING!" Dave fought the wheel of our new-to-us touring van as a sickening screech emerged from the engine, which made me want to puke.

Not now, not yet, I thought to myself. *We still have fifteen thousand kilometres to go.* Our engine sounded like a witch dragging her nails down a chalkboard whilst shrieking with malicious delight.

"Do you think we can make it to Portland?"

"Let's just go for it," Dave grunted.

In the early 1990s, Portland was still twenty years shy of the hipster renaissance that would make it the coolest city in North America. As we screamed across the Burnside Bridge, we saw a gritty, working-class town suffering through the depressing echo of a once-booming lumber industry. Crime and poverty were at the forefront in downtown Portland. We were looking for the X-Ray Cafe, an infamous little all-ages venue in the darkened heart of the action at 210 West Burnside, on the border between Old Town and Chinatown. We arrived hours early, parking the van directly in front of the X-Ray, where the homeless population of Burnside Avenue besieged us.

We were rescued by the café's proprietor, a wild, energized character named Tres Shannon who looked like a cross between Yahoo Serious and Andy Warhol. He came running out of the club and onto the busy sidewalk, shooing people away by name. Tres was a sight to behold. He wore oversized red bug-eye sunglasses, a leopard-print fur pillbox hat atop an untamed nest of sandy blond hair, a 1970s double-breasted, pinstriped white suit jacket, bright pink shorts, yellow hi-top Converse sneakers and no shirt. Once the homeless people had scattered, he threw his skinny arms aloft and shrilled, "WELCOME SMUGGLERS!"

Tres showed us around the tiny, one-room X-Ray Cafe. Its walls were covered in framed velvet paintings and thrift-store-treasures-turned-wall-art, as well as posters advertising upcoming shows by Portland artists like Heatmiser (featuring a young Elliott Smith), Dead Moon, the Dharma Bums, Quasi, and Hazel, the boy-girl noise-pop band signed to Sub Pop we were lucky enough to be playing with that night. Tres assured us there was nothing to fear in the surrounding neighbourhood and insisted we visit Portland's 24 Hour Church of Elvis around the corner in Old Town. On our way, we bumped into two of our biggest fans, Polly and Tunisha from Seattle. They travelled all over the Northwest to see us as the Smugglers' first official "superfans." The two of them came along with us to the 24 Hour Church of Elvis, which had no official connection whatsoever to the King. It was a bizarre storefront full of handmade, coin-operated gadgetry and machinery that pumped out little trinkets, scrolls, fortunes and hand-drawn art. It also offered "weddings" for the cost of a few dollars.

Dave turned to Polly. "Hey, do you want to get married at the 24 Hour Church of Elvis?"

"Sure!" Polly replied.

A few dollars and a few minutes of warbled, recorded Elvis-style voice prompts later, Dave and Polly were pronounced "married" by the machine, and the rest of us cheered our approval. There was no real romance between Polly and Dave that night, or for many years to come, but the 24 Hour Church of Elvis ceremony would prove prophetic.

The show that night was packed and fantastic. Though we would have our ups and downs over the years, attendance-wise, the X-Ray Cafe became the Smugglers' home base in Portland until it closed in the mid-1990s, fittingly on August 16, the same day Elvis died. Tres Shannon went on to be a notable character in Portland, unsuccessfully running for city council and mayor, then very successfully opening Voodoo Doughnut, now a worldwide franchise. The original location was just steps away from where the X-Ray Cafe once ruled Burnside Avenue.

The morning after our show at the X-Ray, we screeched into a sketchy Portland auto shop to get the van checked out. We were barely greeted by the shop's sole mechanic, who looked like he had just escaped from a maximum-security prison and was costumed in coveralls. After hearing about our problem, though, he gave us some advice that would save our asses for years to come: "Whenever your vehicle is makin' a racket, look at the pavement underneath. Chances are somethin' leakin'." He pointed to a puddle of red liquid, into which he dabbed his mucky finger. "It's all about the fluids, man." He tasted our puddle and quickly deduced it to be steering fluid. We weren't even aware that our new van had power steering, but the fluid was dripping like blood from a fresh wound.

After spending fifteen minutes under the hood, the mechanic horked up something nasty, then told us we needed a new power-steering box, which would cost us around five-hundred dollars with labour. His diagnosis crushed us. Tres had paid us one hundred dollars to open for Hazel. We had made seventy-five dollars the night before in Seattle playing with the Fall-Outs. We chose his other alternative: we bought three huge jugs of steering fluid with the questionable plan of pouring it in at every gas stop, or whenever the screech became too loud to bear. (Within a day or so, the fluid would be dripping out at such a rate that we could place an empty pint mug under the van overnight to catch it, then pour it straight back into the steering box the next morning. That kept us on the road.)

Dave had stuffed himself into a greasy gas station phone booth for a call back home while the van was being worked on. We idled beside the phone booth, ready to roll, but when he emerged, his usually jovial face was grim and streaked with tears. Climbing in, he told us the awful news: his close family friend Danny had been shot and killed by police in a botched drug raid. Danny had been target practising with a pellet rifle when the police burst in unannounced through his unlocked door. When he turned around with the pellet gun in his hands, they shot him dead.

We drove south in silence, and as the kilometres stretched out behind us, Dave stowed his grief where none of us could see it. We had the night off, so we camped on a beautiful beach in southern Oregon, unfolding the Trans-Awn 2000 over a picnic table. As the sun set over the Pacific Ocean, we raised a glass in memory of Danny.

Dave would never really find the time or personal space to grieve for the friend he had known all his life, because as we learned over the years to come, real life takes an out-of-sight, out-of-mind back seat on tour. It is all too easy to allow the existential world of touring, where landscapes and cities and situations blur, to take over as you sit snugly in a rolling isolation chamber. Before cell phones, no one could reach you or find you unless you reached out to them, so it seemed simple to avoid problems: just don't call home. The problem was that our parents were desperate to hear from us, especially since we were headed into the smoking embers of a Los Angeles race riot.

ASK DAVE

Q: Who decides which tracks to put on the records?

A: Grant.

Q: Would you like to produce a band?

A: Yes. I'm building a studio in my parents' basement right now with a Lionel Richie theme.

Q: What has been the highlight of the Smugglers career so far?

A: Opening for Right Said Fred.

Q: Do you ever listen to Smugglers records in your spare time?

A: Pass.

Q: What's the strangest gift you've received from a fan?

A: Cock-Ring Ken Doll.

Q: How do you feel about people who want nothing to do with a person just because they are overweight?

A: I like them. (Weird, huh?)

Q: How often do the Smugglers practice?

A: Once or twice a week.

Q: How would you describe yourself?

A: OUTRAGEOUS!

Q: How would you describe Nardwuar?

A: Gentle and sweet.

nineteen

I Wanna Riot

LOS ANGELES REEKED. The stench was a disturbing combination of exhaust fumes, campfire smoke and burning plastic. As we got closer to the city on the mega-freeways of southern California, our anxiety became as choking as the traffic. Forbidding concrete walls grew up around us, cutting off our vantage points. Long-neglected overpasses covered in graffiti and hanging vines loomed overhead as we inched towards the sizzling sprawl of the City of Angels. We could see columns of smoke rising from neighbourhoods on either side of the highway. Sickly palm trees poked over the concrete barriers, leaning forward in defeat. The sun and the heat felt unrelenting, and yet the sky wasn't quite blue. The light was different in Los Angeles. There was a white brightness to it all that made you squint. From a side window, Bryce caught sight of the Hollywood sign high up in the hills.

We wanted to be excited at the pop culture references all around us: exits and signs for the Sunset Strip, Dodger Stadium, Disneyland and the LaBrea Tar Pits. But we were too distracted by the smell. We couldn't decide where the stink was worse, inside the van or out. Inside was an odorous potpourri of stale beer, shoes, rotting fast food, BO and the rising stench of our onstage pea jackets, which uncannily smelled like urine.

It was the first time we had experienced soaring summer-like temperatures in our new shag-a-delic van, which lacked air conditioning and was beginning to feel like a rolling pizza oven, heavy on the garlic. Peeling off our sweat-soaked shirts, we rolled all the windows down, hanging various limbs out into the smoke, fumes and general feeling of dread that hung heavy in the air, like the smog. A week before our arrival, hell had burst open on the streets.

Several LA police officers had been acquitted in the case of the beating of an African-American man named Rodney King. A year earlier, King had been pulled over for allegedly driving recklessly and resisting arrest. A group of police officers beat him with batons and kicked him repeatedly, an incident that was caught on video and played over and over again on TV. When the verdict came down, racial tensions in the city of LA exploded like a Black Flag song. Countless stores and businesses were trashed, burned and looted. It was race against race in every direction. The rioting had lasted for almost a week, and there were mass arrests. At a gas stop, Beez bought a paper. The numbers he read aloud from the *San Francisco Chronicle* were staggering: fifty-three people were dead, over two thousand had been injured and over ten thousand had been arrested. That's what we were rolling into.

Almost all live events had been cancelled both during the riot and for days afterwards, including many small-time rock shows. By the time we arrived in LA, the city was trying to get back on its feet. The club we were playing that night was in Long Beach, an area hit heavily by rioting. We gave the club a call from another gas station. The gig was still on.

We drove down the wide main drag of Long Beach, which led from the freeway to the oceanfront, staring out at the charred, boarded-up remains of many storefronts. The shattered glass covering the sidewalks sparkled like diamonds. Despite the heat, our paranoia made us roll up the windows. The LA citizens we saw up and down that boulevard sat slumped on the curbs and at bus stops in the blazing sun, faces drained of emotion. We were afraid of everybody.

Even with the ominous atmosphere, we were pleased the show at Bogart's was still happening. We were set to open for the Reverend Horton Heat, a heavily hyped three-piece on Sub Pop that mixed faux revival tent Elmer Gantry–style preaching with wild psychobilly. Also on the bill was

El Vez, "the Mexican Elvis" (Robert Lopez from legendary LA punks the Zeros). The place was packed, with many in attendance telling us it was the first time they had been outside their homes since the riots began.

Friday, May 15, 1992
Bogart's, Long Beach, California

When we got to this club, to our surprise, we found it was in a very posh mall on the Long Beach Marina! The bar itself was really big, with adobe walls and marina decor. It looked kinda like Pirates of the Caribbean. The show turned out to be really great! Four hundred people! We sold lots of stuff and met people from *Flipside* magazine and members of Popdefect, the Cadillac Tramps, the Muffs and Long Gone John from Sympathy for the Record Industry, a label I love. One punk I was talking to told me that the LA riots were "the calm before the storm"! He told me he heard that all the gangs (black, Latino, Asian) were congregating a force to take over the LA police department!

When the riots broke out, we learned, some people couldn't help but recall Charles Manson's "Helter Skelter" predictions: that the black race would rise up against the whites. One of the people we met that night had a direct connection to the Manson Family. By 1992, Long Gone John was already an infamous art and toy collector, as well as the founder and owner of Sympathy for the Record Industry, a boutique LA label that put out records by many of our favourite bands: the Muffs, Rocket from the Crypt, Billy Childish, the Pooh Sticks and, many years later, the first few albums by the White Stripes. John was a formidable presence with shaggy, long hair and a goatee, dressed in decorated black leather and faded denim like a member of a 1960s Sunset Strip motorcycle gang. He told us stories after the show of LA through the decades—and his macabre link to the Manson Family.

When the Manson Family murders ripped apart Los Angeles, Long Gone John was a seventeen-year-old weirdo kid, living in a boys' home in Echo Park after being expelled from various schools. He remembered the summer of sixty-nine as a crazy time, the media smearing the counter-culture lifestyle as if Manson was everyone's guru and every hippie was poised to go on a killing spree. Long Gone John lived in fear that summer that "straight" vigilantes would start shooting anyone with long hair.

Years later, he told us, after Manson was convicted and in jail, Long Gone John had shared a house near MacArthur Park with several Manson Family women who had been released from prison, including the notorious Lynnette "Squeaky" Fromme (convicted for refusing to testify against Family members directly involved in the Manson murders, then again for a botched assassination attempt on President Gerald Ford) and Brenda McCann (also jailed for an association with a murder). Both were close friends with Long Gone John's girlfriend at the time.

Long Gone John even told us that one of his most prized possessions, among his many, many thousands of artifacts, was a Manson Family jacket he acquired while living with the women. In the late sixties, when LA motorcycle gang culture was exploding, every gang had a jacket with an emblem on the back. Apparently the Manson Family had fancied themselves as a gang of sorts, so patches were created and a handful of cut-off denim jackets were made. John's description of the jacket sent shivers down our spines: the letters that spelled out MANSON FAMILY were hand-cut out of felt and sewn on, framing a woman's face that had swastikas for eyes and an X on the forehead. The jacket was outfitted with many hidden pockets, presumably for weapons and shoplifting.

Long Gone John's LA stories had us buzzing with their tiniest degree of separation between the unknown, the infamous and the terrifying. It was a surreal night, but short-lived. Before we knew it, every Angelino who had seemed so friendly had gone home, leaving us to sleep in the van, tucked away in an alley near the Long Beach marina. We opened all of the van windows just enough to catch the sea breeze.

We woke up covered in thousands upon thousands of flies. They were swarming us: up our noses, in our ears, in our hair and our mouths. The van was thick with them. We kicked open the side door and stumbled out, gagging, spitting and doing stammering barefoot dances of disgust. Looking around, we realized that in the cool darkness of the Long Beach night we had parked beside a row of filthy, overflowing dumpsters belonging to a nearby fish processing plant that were rapidly heating up in the morning sun. There was nothing to do but clear the van of flies by driving away as quickly as we could.

The Smugglers embracing the California lifestyle. Left to right: Nick, Beez, Bryce, Dave, Grant.
TRENT RUANE PHOTO

twenty

'Til the Wheels Fall Off

T HE AMERICAN SOUTHWEST desert was beautiful—something I had only ever seen depicted in *Roadrunner* cartoons and western movies—with towering hoodoo rock formations, spiny cacti of all shapes and sizes and endless stretches of sand and scrub against a wash of blue sky. The cacti were so perfectly Hollywood that Beez expressed the urge to stop the van, get out and try to kick one over. The heat bounced off the steaming asphalt, creating the constant illusion of shimmering water ahead. We slid War's "Low Rider" into the cassette deck and cranked it. When we stopped to pee at the side of the road, the desert sun seared our bare shoulders. Urine sizzled as it hit the light brown dust and evaporated. We had never in our lives experienced heat like that.

We were also the farthest any of us had ever ventured on wheels from Vancouver. We weren't getting paid much, but gas and food were so incredibly cheap that we could survive on rations of eight dollars a day each for meals and sundries. We knew what day it was, but rarely the actual date. A week earlier, Dave had luckily clued in that it was Mother's Day, and we took turns making collect calls to our moms on a pay phone. Bryce stayed in the van. When we got back inside, Beez asked, "Bryce, are you going to call your mom or what, man?" Bryce looked up from his dog-eared copy of *The Electric Kool-Aid Acid Test.* "My mom is dead," he answered. The rest of us fell silent. None of us had known that. None of us had thought to ask. The van resumed its surge forward through the desert; we were headed for the Sun Club in Phoenix, Arizona.

The club was locked and dark when we pulled up. The setting sun had turned the desert sky blood red, casting long, apocalyptic shadows over the wasteland. It looked as if zombies could emerge at any second in the fading light. On the front door Beez discovered a note scrawled in blue ballpoint pen: "SUNDAY NITE: OPEN MIC." We were dejected.

An "open mic night" is a touring band's worst nightmare. Essentially an evening of amateurs, they are designed for anyone who has ever wanted to gather the courage to perform music on a stage. In our minds open mics were one step up from karaoke and an insult to our egos as a professional touring rock band. As we sat in a row on the dusty curb, waiting for the club to open, we passed a king can of Colt 45 malt liquor back and forth. For over an hour, we didn't see a living soul.

Eventually, headlight beams shone in the distance. A pickup truck soon pulled up. A big guy in a grubby, sleeveless Jack Daniel's shirt, torn jorts and cowboy boots walked bow-legged towards the Sun Club. He ignored us, instead yanking on a set of jingly keys attached to a clip on his belt to unlock the door. Beez meekly approached. "Hey, man . . . are you the promoter tonight?"

"Nope!" he answered, still not looking at us, propping the front door open with a rock. "Bartender."

The Sun Club stank like all empty, darkened clubs do on a Sunday: the party from the night before. Everything inside was painted black. Overhead pipes plastered with band stickers dripped mystery liquids that formed shiny pools on the grimy, checkered dance floor. The raised stage was covered by a tattered, once-purple carpet that was littered with empty beer bottles and cigarette butts and spotted with black smears of once-pink chewing gum spat from the mouths of a thousand nameless musicians. This would be our home for the night should we choose to stay.

The bartender continued to ignore us as we reluctantly loaded in our equipment. I approached him and asked a few logistical questions.

"When do the doors open?"

"They are open."

"What is the cover charge?"

"No cover."

"When is the sound check?"

"No soundman on Sunday nights."

"How does the band get paid?"

"Pass the hat."

"To whom?"

"To whomever the fuck shows up, Bubba! Y'all shoulda been here last night. Anal Cunt packed the joint and we had a hell of a fuckin' party, man. Y'all definitely shoulda been here last night." It was a refrain we would hear many times over the years.

One person showed up at the Sun Club in Phoenix that lonely Sunday night. His name was Jason. He was a standoffish black kid with flamboyantly baggy neon clothing. His flat-top fade sat in a perfect Grace Jones pillbox, and he carried a cheap, hot pink electric guitar with no case. It appeared he had walked to the club, but we had no idea from where. Jason was there to perform for the open mic. That made seven of us in total.

While four Smugglers discussed in hushed tones whether we should even play, Dave got the PA running so at least Jason could perform. Jason plugged his guitar into one of our amps, then exploded into a blur of motion, pausing only for a burst of falsetto singing into the microphone. His performance was a cross between Prince and the Tasmanian Devil. Beez and Dave were front and centre, loudly cheering him on, which Jason refused to acknowledge. After five deafening songs, he ended his show with a flying leap from the stage, landing in the middle of the dance floor in the splits. Panting and dripping with sweat, he unplugged, then slumped into the shadows of a side booth. It was our turn to play.

Sunday, May 18, 1992
The Sun Club
Phoenix, Arizona

When we made it to Phoenix, we got viciously lost and everyone we asked had never heard of the Sun Club. When we finally found it, we were disgusted to find a little roadside dump in the middle of an industrial wasteland.

As we entered the Sun Club we found no posters of ours at all, even though they were sent, and no indication whatsoever that we were playing. There was even a poster with a bunch of different shows advertised, before and after ours. The bartender allowed me to use the phone behind the bar to call the promoter, who was watching TV at home. She said she didn't put us on the poster because she didn't think we'd draw a crowd. The total amount of paid gig-goers in the Sun Club? Zero. Zilch, nothing! It was so pathetic, I wanted to leave, but Dave and Beez insisted the show must go on. So, the Smugglers broke a new record: the smallest crowd we have ever played to. I mean we've played small shows but NO ONE? So we played to the bartender and a guy named Jason, who was there for Open Mic, but even he left. To top it off, we played horribly, but who cares?

Bryce did. The Sun Club show is a perfect example of how touring is like walking a tightrope in a wind tunnel. It's very hard, anything can happen and you're going to get knocked down a lot. It's also a game of trust, a game of trial and error. The plight to seek out honest promoters who care and good clubs that promote is hard and frustrating, but after all the shitty, no-money gigs, I think it will all be worth it. I hope so, anyway.

We were all down in the dumps about the situation, but Bryce seemed even more so. The bartender had informed him with seemingly malicious intent that it was too bad we weren't sticking around for the following night: none other than L7, the all-female Sub Pop grunge sensation from Seattle, was playing. The bartender told Bryce he expected the place to be packed. Bryce loved L7. He padded across the empty dance floor to our booth. "Guys... could we consider skipping tomorrow night's show in Lubbock so we can stay here and see L7?"

I was stunned that he would put attending another band's show ahead of performing one of ours, affecting the crucial forward movement of our tour. "Absolutely not!" I barked. "We have a twelve-hour drive into Texas, and we have to get going right after this gig."

Bryce looked around. "This *gig*? What gig? There's no one here!"

"Hey," Beez interjected. "You never know who might show up. Let's just play a few songs. We'll make it a practice and perform some tunes for Jason. What the hell, man."

"FUCK THAT AND FUCK YOU!" yelled Bryce, marching back across the dance floor and slamming himself into a booth a few down from Jason.

And so the rest of us played. We performed an emotionally damaging, ramshackle, percussionless set. No one clapped. No one else showed up at the deserted desert venue. It was our most demoralizing show ever, one that would leave a scar on our band's collective mental state.

After the show, Beez announced that tomorrow we would have to ration ourselves down to five dollars a day each for food so we could afford the gas for the twelve hundred kilometres to Lubbock, where we were scheduled to perform in a laundromat. In a rare act of kindness, the bartender cracked open the jukebox and told us we were welcome to the coins collected in there from the night before—about twenty dollars in quarters.

"Hey," chuckled Beez, "at least we'll have some change to wash our clothes tomorrow!"

"You know what, Bubba?" the bartender said to Beez. "You're all right, man. You fuckin' play to NOBODY, and you can laugh about it?" He reached under the bar and pulled out a sweating cold six-pack of Pabst Blue Ribbon. "Here," he said, passing the six-pack to Beez. "You deserve this, man. Have a good ol' drive to Lubbock, and remember, don't mess with Texas."

twenty-one

Road to Glory

THERE WAS NO air conditioning inside the Center of the World Café for our afternoon matinee in Fort Smith. The Arkansas heat inside seemed far worse than it had in Texas or Tennessee: 100 percent humidity and 110-degree temperature outdoors. When kids started to show up, lighting cigarettes and slam-dancing to the opening bands, the conditions inside got worse. By the time we took the stage, the air in the café was a murky haze.

The stifling weather was the most intense we had experienced so far. At least the air in the desert was dry. In Arkansas, it was so muggy we could bat our arms and feel the moisture cling to our skin. The only respite was in gas stations, which blasted air conditioning to such chilling depths that going through the automatic doors felt like stepping from an oven into a walk-in freezer.

In the South, rural Americans would see Bryce's long, mushroom-cut hairdo and constantly think he was a girl, even with the grungy little goatee that extended from his chin. At one gas station, the attendant offered to wash our dirty windshield, but Bryce was already doing it. "Ah!" the gas jockey said cheerily. "I see the little lady beat me to it!" In restaurants, when Bryce ordered his daily club sandwich for lunch, more often than not the server would answer "Yes, ma'am." Bryce would ignore the gender bend-ers, but the rest of us couldn't help but let out a delayed burst of laughter.

```
Thursday, May 21, 1992
Center of The World Café
Fort Smith, Arkansas


This is one of those shows that everyone in
the band wonders about... where the hell is
Fort Smith and what is even there? Well, we
just happen to have a Smugglers Fan Club
Member who lives in Fort Smith: Kevin "KP"
Sampsell, who recently relocated to Arkansas
after becoming a fan of ours in the Pacific
Northwest. He saw our US tour itinerary in
our newsletter and called to say he wanted
to do a gig in Fort Smith! The venue was
an anarchist cafe/warehouse on one of Fort
Smith's main drags. We played with Kevin's
band, Love Jerk, and a popular local hardcore
band called Securicor. Great attendance! By
the time we got on, I thought the kids would
be a) too heat exhausted to stay or b) not
into our surf-pop-garage rock. Fear not, for
they went just as ape-shit for us as they did
for Securicor, if not more so, stagediving,
slamming, screaming and sweating. The whole
place was a wet, sticky, slippery mess of
sweat. Speaking of sweating, even though
it was insanely hot, we still wore our pea
jackets, turtlenecks, toques and rubber boots.
```

Our stage clothing felt so heavy we could barely move our limbs. Still, it was a great show right up until the end. That's when the punks in the front row saw Bryce's eyes roll back in his toqued head. The band didn't realize anything was amiss, because he kept pounding on his drums, but on the last beat of the last song, still clutching both sticks, he toppled over backward as if he had been shot. His drum stool and one of his cymbal stands went with him.

Bryce lay crumpled in the two-foot space between the stage and the back doors of the café. Steam rose from his body like he was a freshly poached egg and his face was as red as a beefsteak tomato. We freaked out. Was he dead? Dave shoved open the back doors leading to the alley, which offered a slight reprieve. Nick shook Bryce by the sopping lapels of his pea jacket, trying to get some sign of life, while Beez came running with a pitcher of ice water from the coffee bar. He ripped off Bryce's soggy toque and dumped the entire pitcher over his head. That finally snapped Bryce out of it. "Fuuuuuuuuuuck."

As Bryce collected himself, the rest of us made a collective decision. It was time to retire the Smugglers' matching misty Northwest dockworker look. In the morning, we'd visit a Value Village and find some lightweight suits.

ASK BRYCE

The Smugglers Questionnaire –
Butterfly Juice Fanzine

Q: If you weren't in the Smugglers, what group would you like to be in?

A: The Rolling Stones circa 1966.

Q: What kind of music do you usually listen to?

A: Screeching Weasel.

Q: Do you intend to write a song for the Smugglers?

A: My girlfriend really wants me to.

Q: How long have you been playing drums?

A: Since I was sixteen.

Q: Are there any Smugglers songs you don't like?

A: YES! Where do I start?

Q: Are there ever any arguments in the Smugglers?

A: Are you kidding? We're one big happy family, he said sarcastically.

Q: Do you sometimes feel you're an outsider in the band?

A: Yes, particularly when my ideas or suggestions go unnoticed, which is all the time.

Q: How does it feel to play live to small audiences?

A: It depends on the show; sometimes it can be great, other times a real letdown.

Q: What is the hardest thing about being a drummer?

A: Taking shit from Grant and the other guys about my gear and the way I play.

Q: Are there any drummers who inspire you?

A: I admire any drummer who plays with 100 percent enthusiasm and entertains the crowd.

Q: What gig was the most memorable?

A: I'll remember a lot of our shows when I look back because we've played with so many great bands I love and admire, but the most memorable one so far was when I puked onstage without missing a beat. The Railway Club with the Subsonics from Atlanta, Georgia.

Q: What do you think you'll be doing in ten years' time?

A: Hopefully something to do with music, but not necessarily with the Smugglers.

twenty-two

Maniac Dragstrip

W E COULDN'T AGREE on whether Memorial Day was the very best or very worst day to visit Washington, DC, but there we were, seemingly just minutes away from the American capital. We weren't particularly interested in American politics; it was just that we were always excited about spotting recognizable structures. Our van rumbled past the Pentagon, over the Potomac River and into the District of Columbia. We'd arrived early enough that we had all afternoon to check out the sights before finding our club.

```
Monday, May 25, 1992
Mountain Lodge #6
Washington, DC

Unfortunately, in our giddy haste spotting
the sites of DC, we took a wrong turn and
ended up driving down a parkway on the wrong
side of the river, heading away from the
monuments. We were all getting really antsy,
```

yelling directions at Dave at the wheel, who
was getting equally frustrated. He missed
another exit. Finally, in disgust, I did a
really dumb thing and chucked the road atlas
at Dave. He flew off the handle and started
screaming at me, calling me a "fucking fool"
and telling me to "grow up fast." Things have
been brewing between me and Dave for too long.

We had been on the road for several weeks, and I felt Dave and Beez were teaming up to challenge me on just about everything, from where we should stay to when we should leave to how we should get there. They often had the opposite opinion from mine, and it was exhausting to bicker. Nick and Bryce wisely mostly stayed out of it, but on our approach to DC everything fell apart.

Heading north up the I-95 after pretty good shows in Memphis, Fort Smith and Chattanooga, as well as another truly disastrous one in Athens, I started to ignore Dave and Beez, to the point that I mentally checked out for long stretches of time in the van. Maybe it was the humidity. Maybe it was all of us being in such close quarters for too long. At a road stop in Roanoke Rapids, North Carolina, Dave grabbed me by the shoulders and shook me, saying, "Grant! It's Dave and Beez! Snap out of it and give us some deets on the upcoming shows!" A month in, and I was already burnt out. I couldn't keep up with the pace of the tour. There never seemed to be any time to call ahead, so I stopped bothering and hoped for the best. Sometimes it worked out. Often times, like in Phoenix and Athens, it didn't.

I was also most often to blame for screwing up directions, and that was happening a lot. Most of the time Dave drove and I navigated, which in major US cities was a high-stress partnership at the best of times. Navigating meant I sat with my head bobbing up and down between a large American road atlas with a different state on every page and the road signs that were rapidly approaching. A wrong turn in a huge American city, with its intricate, cloverleaf mazes of highways and byways, meant an arduous, tense and always time-consuming detour. Often we had to get back to the spot where we made the wrong turn so we could go the opposite way.

About halfway through our first Canadian tour, the guys had figured out that I didn't know my left from my right. I constantly mixed them up. Staring at the road atlas, I would say, "Turn left at the lights," so Dave would dutifully start merging left through traffic. I would look up and yell, "What are you doing?! I said left!"

"This IS left, you moron!" he'd yell back.

Embarrassed, I'd lower my voice and say, "Oh, I meant right, turn right, please!" The van would swerve back through traffic, Dave cursing at me as the sound of blaring car horns rained down on us. Eventually, Nick taught me to form a letter "L" with my left index finger and thumb for "left." I still use the trick to this day.

After missing the turn into Washington, DC, we found an off-ramp and pulled into a gas station miles down the road. "Give me the fucking atlas!" Dave demanded.

"You want the atlas? Take it!" I took the large book, about the size of a special-edition *Life* magazine, and threw it into his face in a flapping mess of pages. Justifiably he started screaming at me. Dave took a glance, then heaved the atlas back at me, fired up the van and roared back onto

Like Colonel Kurtz in *Apocalypse Now*, I slowly went mad the deeper we ventured into the urban jungles of America. I went comatose for long periods of time and became completely obsessed with the fluid levels in our van.

NICK THOMAS PHOTO

the George Washington Memorial Parkway, heading in the direction of the city. I felt something inside of me snap. I undid my seatbelt and flung the passenger door open. I jumped out of our moving van.

I tumbled onto the pavement, tearing my jeans, skinning my knees and the palms of my hands, and knocking the glasses off my face. I jumped up pretty quickly, not wanting the guys to look back and see me in a crumpled heap. My anger was greater than the pain, and I started stomping in what I hoped was the right direction. I had to get away from the four other guys in the band, and this was the irrational way I chose to do it.

After five minutes of plodding along the gravel shoulder of the parkway, with cars rushing by me, I heard a honk. The guys had circled back to pick me up, but I was not ready to rejoin them. When Nick slid open the side door and yelled, "Get in the van!" I did another incredibly stupid thing: I dashed across the parkway like Frogger, causing drivers to slam on their brakes and their horns. I made it across to the median and tried to jump the guardrail, but I didn't clear it. Instead, I slammed my shins against the metal and went crashing face first into the knee-high grass of the strip between north- and south-bound parkway traffic.

The band members glared from the van windows as they watched their lead singer go crazy on the George Washington Memorial Parkway. I defiantly picked myself up again, my shins screaming in pain, and continued eastbound on the median, kicking through the grass. A few minutes later the van roared by me again; this time it didn't stop.

It was a long, dangerous walk into Washington, DC, and no one else stopped to offer me a lift. It took me a couple hours of trudging to get to the edge of town, but I kept it up, wearing down my Converse sneakers until I was finally walking through the streets of Georgetown, the neighbourhood of our venue: a weird little coffee house bar called Mountain Lodge #6, in the heart of the university district. Within a few minutes I spotted the venue, our van and Bryce and Dave on the sidewalk coming towards me. Dave stopped and offered a smile. "So you found the place."

I kept walking, stupidly ignoring his peace offering. It was still early in the afternoon, and I was determined to see the monuments I had seen so many times in movies like *Mr. Smith Goes to Washington*, *No Way Out* and *All the President's Men*. All alone, blisters burning on my feet, I walked among the pillars of America on Memorial Day, touching the foot of the Lincoln Memorial and looking out over the Reflecting Pool with the Washington Monument obelisk at the other end. I ran my fingers along the cool black walls of the Vietnam Veterans Memorial, then staggered past the Senate and Congress buildings and the White House. I even made it to the Smithsonian Museum of American History, marvelling at Fonzie's actual leather jacket, Ted Baxter's blue anchorman blazer from *The Mary Tyler Moore Show* and Archie Bunker's armchair.

I arrived at the club just after dark, thoroughly exhausted. I had walked more than twenty miles over many hours, pretty much my first offstage exercise of the tour. (Onstage was a nightly burn of pure cardio.) Nick and Dave were the most diligent about exercising on tour, constantly doing push-ups and sit-ups at the gas station stops. We were all eating terribly, drinking booze constantly and sitting in the van all day, but those two managed to stay fairly fit. The rest of us were in an almost atrophic state. I would pay for my march on Washington.

Thanks to some great DC connections we had made at the International Pop Underground Convention, several far-cooler-than-we-were punk rockers came to see us at Mountain Lodge #6. That flattered us and made us quickly stow the strife from earlier in the day to save face.

Even though Washington, DC, was world famous for its DIY punk rock scene—Bad Brains, Fugazi, Henry Rollins—it also had a scattering of obscure, sixties-obsessed garage bands, one of which opened for us: Thee Flypped Whigs. When we launched into a hyped-up version of "Shimmy Shake," Thee Whigs' gangly, drunken bass player, dressed in tight white jeans and a black turtleneck, jumped up from his chair at the back and ran full speed through the tiny coffee shop, shoving several of the twenty-five or so people in attendance out of the way. Unfortunately, just as he was about to shimmy shake what his mama gave him, the elfin toe of his Beatle boot caught the leg of a chair at the edge of the dance floor. He stumbled, pinwheeling his skinny arms in an effort to maintain his balance. When his flat-soled boots hit the floor, he slid across it like Bambi on ice. The runaway garage rocker slammed directly into me, taking me out at the legs.

My left knee violently dislocated on impact, just as I was hollering out the second verse. My singing turned to a nauseated scream. Both of us came crashing down onto the stage, the drunk garage rocker on top of me, his arms and legs entangled in the microphone cord, his blond, heavily hair-sprayed Prince Valiant locks in my face. The microphone slammed down loudly onto the wooden stage. But the band played on, as we had trained ourselves to do. As I shoved the guy off, my first thought was that it was my karma for acting like such an idiot earlier that day. I limped out the front door of the venue to writhe in pain on the street while the band played a couple of surf instrumentals. To add insult to injury, I discovered that the coolest musicians in attendance—members of Bikini Kill, Fugazi and Nation of Ulysses—were outside chatting.

The drunken Flypped Whigs' bassist felt so guilty for wrenching my knee apart that he insisted we all stay at his place. It was a dirty townhouse across the river in Arlington, Virginia, with wall-to-wall formerly white shag carpeting that was being soiled as we watched by at least half a dozen "indoor-only" cats. We were so physically and emotionally drained from our long day in DC that we simply bedded down in the reeking shag amongst the spraying cats. Before we passed out, I apologized to Dave and everyone else for being such a jerk and said it wouldn't happen again. I also promised them that with New York and Chicago on the horizon, the best was yet to come.

One of the biggest drawbacks of staying at people's houses on the road was something we referred to as "punk rock pets." Territorial urinating cats were a problem. Dave was mildly allergic, and yet they were somehow always drawn to him. NICK THOMAS PHOTO

twenty-three

Big Mouth

OUR FIRST-EVER GIG in New York City was next up on the tour schedule, and it wasn't just any gig. Besides being an actual booked performance in *New York*, our show was at none other than the birthplace of American punk rock, the mecca of the worldwide alternative music scene and the holy grail of hipsters: CBGB. Our friend Todd Abramson, a promoter in nearby Hoboken, New Jersey, had booked us to play at Maxwell's in Hoboken alongside first-wave British punk rockers the Mekons and had also arranged the coveted CBGB opening slot for former Hüsker Dü drummer Grant Hart and fellow Minneapolis power-pop band the Magnolias. Over the phone, Todd had warned me that CBGB was in the Bowery, a rough, crime-ridden neighbourhood bordered by the East Village, the Lower East Side and Little Italy. As he rattled off the landmark neighbourhoods that I associated with Martin Scorsese movies, my heart raced like the tempo of a Ramones song.

We hadn't even known how to pronounce "Hoboken" when Scott McCaughey from the Young Fresh Fellows first gave us the number for Maxwell's, which was the best club not only in New Jersey but arguably on the entire East Coast. We were greeted at the club by Todd Abramson, a friendly cross between Alfred E. Neuman and Elmer Fudd. The first thing he did, before we had even loaded our equipment inside, was sit us down and feed us. A flamboyant bartender named Louie poured us any drink we wanted. We were waited upon by a saucy, shoot-from-the-hip server named Betty Colatrella. Dave immediately hit it off with her, and by the end of the meal it was arranged that we would be staying at Betty's apartment right above the club.

Of the five of us, only Beez had ever set foot in New York City, so as we crawled north on the sprawling I-95, a slithering anaconda of motor vehicles of all shapes and sizes, we let out a collective gasp when the city's jagged skyline appeared. We pressed our faces against the windows of the van to get a better view of looming Gotham. With quivers in our voices, we shouted out landmarks we had seen on shows like *Diff'rent Strokes* and *The Jeffersons*. "There's the Empire State Building! And the World Trade Center! And the Statue of Liberty!" For whatever reason, maybe thanks to *Planet of the Apes*, we had thought the Statue of Liberty was gigantic, towering over all of New York, and we were surprised to realize how minuscule it was in comparison to the skyscrapers.

The day of our show at CBGB, Todd and Betty gave us a few pointers over lunch at Schnackenberg's Luncheonette in Hoboken, an old-school soda fountain straight out of an *Archie Digest*. Their accents were as thick as the milkshakes.

- Trust no one: everyone in New York is trying to rip you off. It is a city of hustlers and sharks.

- Never leave your van alone unless it's in a gated, chain-linked, barb-wired, outdoor parking lot. Park the van with the back doors up against a wall.

- Use "The Club" on your steering wheel. Put on the emergency brake.

- Don't sleep in the van overnight in New York City, no matter what.

- Money talks.

Dave scarfed the last bite of his bacon sandwich and pushed aside the remnants of his egg cream. "Let's go to New York City."

Thirty steaming minutes later we emerged from the Lincoln Tunnel onto the island of Manhattan. For weeks, New York had sat ominously in

the distance on our tour itinerary. None of us really knew what to expect. Now its steel and concrete surrounded us, blocking out the sky. Whereas Los Angeles was an endless spillage of superhighways lined with dirty palm trees, New York City was dense and grey, rising straight up before us, a towering fortress of buzzing, sleepless humanity.

Our first sight was a car fire. The vehicle appeared to be abandoned, with flames raging out of control, yet no other drivers were stopping or slowing down. "Um," stammered Beez nervously, "don't burning cars explode?" We followed the line of cars into Manhattan, all of them rolling by the car fire like it wasn't there. It felt like a bad omen. One NYC block past the fire, we hit our first red light, our first angry chorus of car horns and our first New York City traffic jam. We were at a complete standstill in the sizzling heat. The air reeked of rotting garbage and exhaust fumes.

"ALL LOCK!" ordered Dave from the driver's seat. It was a signal we had agreed upon back in Canada should we ever be set upon in the wilds of urban USA by marauding bangers, rioters or, like now, New York City zombies. Out of the shimmering waves of heat, a gaggle of humans staggered forward, tattered clothing hanging from their limbs like two-month-old gig posters on a telephone pole. Some barely wore any clothing at all. And they were armed. We sprang into action inside the van, frantically rolling up windows and slamming down door locks. As the bodies got closer, we realized what they were carrying weren't weapons; they were squeegees. Several of them set to work, furiously scrubbing off the dead turnpike bugs and Eastern Seaboard soot. It was only seconds before a dirt-encrusted hand pressed against our side window. Bryce gazed into the face of a gaunt, middle-aged hobo.

Afraid of the possible repercussions of not paying, Beez slapped a wet dollar into Bryce's hand. "Give him that and let's go." Bryce hesitated, then opened the window just enough to slip the bill through like a bank machine. "Green light, hurry up!" urged Dave. The man snatched the bill without expression or thanks, spun on a cracked bare heel and wove back through the blaring traffic like a ghost. We watched him disappear behind a mountain of curbside garbage bags.

It was the first time we had encountered the urban phenomenon of the Squeegee Man, which would emerge from eastern American cities and sweep westward. Homeless punk rockers and anarchists adopted the trend, leading to the highly specific subculture of the "squeegee punk."

Crack cocaine had turned the New York City of the late eighties and early nineties into a war zone, full of gangs and gangsters, petty criminals and organized crime, muggers, shakedown artists, con men, drug dealers, murderers and aggressive tramps. Graffiti was everywhere. Garbage storms blew through the streets like miniature tornadoes, spun up from the winds that wailed down New York's concrete canyons. All you could hear was car horns and people yelling at each other.

With Todd and Betty's tips in mind, we found a caged, outdoor parking lot close to CBGB, tipping the shady attendants extra so we could park the back of the van up against the wall. We wandered a few blocks through Greenwich Village, expecting little rows of taverns, cafes and poetry haunts, but it was an enormous area and didn't resemble any description of the beatnik village we had imagined. We soon found ourselves in the famed Washington Square Park. In one corner, men were hunched over chessboards in rigid silence. In another corner, dogs ran free in a fenced-off area while their owners spoke animatedly using equal parts words and hand gestures. In Canada that would have signalled an argument, but in New York, it was seemingly a pleasant conversation. In the centre of the park, just past the iconic archway, there was a large, open round area. We could hear singing.

Surrounding two folk singers strumming acoustic guitars at the edge of the round was a cross-section of humanity that put the United Nations' General Assembly to shame. The guitarists were singing Beatles songs at the top of their lungs and many passersby had stopped to join in. A gigantic, shirtless body-builder with a huge smile on his face sang baritone to "Please Please Me." An orthodox rabbi was singing as loudly as anyone, arms waving joyfully in the air. Two cops stood in the throng singing and smiling. Little kids were singing. Black people were singing. White people were singing. Asian people were singing. Everyone was smiling and having a great time. Soon we were shoulder to shoulder with the rest of the group, lyrics on our lips and warmth in our hearts.

When we pulled away from the singalong, we were buzzing with confidence. We had bonded with the citizens of New York and were feeling bold enough to split up before meeting at CBGB in time for sound check. I issued a stern reminder of Todd and Betty's warnings. Everyone agreed to remain vigilant. Dave and Beez were planning to meet up with Betty to wander the outdoor bookstalls of Greenwich Village. Bryce sauntered off on his own to find Bleecker Bob's Records. Nick and I walked a couple of blocks over to Broadway.

As we navigated the sticky, trash-strewn, pedestrian-clogged streets, we noticed clusters of people gathered around what appeared to be some kind of card game. When we drew closer, I realized it was the famed street hustle three-card monte, a.k.a. the shell game. There seemed to be a game on just about every corner, with groups of people gathered around as flashes of cash changed hands. "Nick, this is *exactly* the kind of scam Todd warned us about. Let's keep moving," I urged him.

Nick and I headed south past Houston and Canal Street and down into Tribeca, eventually reaching the foot of the Brooklyn Bridge. As we walked, we often noticed people quenching their thirst with an open can or bottle of beer, hidden only by a brown paper sack. The concept of open street drinking thrilled Nick and me, so we popped into a disreputable-looking corner store, flashed our fake IDs and bought two forty-ounce bottles of Colt 45 malt liquor. The beer tasted delicious and packed a wallop, washing away the grit from the hot streets.

All the way back up Broadway, the three-card monte games continued. Having survived in New York City for more than five hours, my confidence and the malt liquor beer collided with my cultural curiosity. "Let's watch one of these games for a couple of minutes," I said to Nick nonchalantly.

"Are you sure?"

"Yeah, we'll just check it out from the sidelines. I want to see how they do it."

We joined the edge of the crowd watching as a woman in a fraying tube top and denim short shorts played. The dealer was the definition of creepy: a skinny rat of man with a greasy black skullet, a wispy moustache, stained blue jeans, dirty white tennis shoes and a yellow undershirt. He insisted the woman produce her cash. She pulled a handful of crumpled bills from her clunky high-heeled shoe, balancing like a tipsy flamingo, and placed the money on the cardboard box.

The dealer flipped the ace of spades face up on the cardboard and pointed a dirt-encrusted finger at it for everyone to see. Then he flipped the other two cards on either side: the king of diamonds and the king of hearts. He turned the cards over again and lined them up so they were spaced about an inch apart.

"Follow the ace, babe," the dealer instructed the contestant. "You locked in?"

"I got it," she answered, not looking up.

Game on! The dealer pushed the cards around using circular motions, rearranging their order on the surface of the cardboard box. He was moving them much more slowly than I had expected. I was surprised to find I had no problem following the ace. After about five moves, the dealer stopped and looked up. The ace was back in the centre position.

"Okay, babe, where's that lucky ace of spades?"

"Uh... I think... it's under... that one?" Her voice trembled with uncertainty as she pointed to the card on the left. From the back row, I scoffed to Nick at how daft the woman was, then took another chug of my Colt 45. Next to me, a guy I hadn't noticed agreed. "Can't believe she missed that. Looks like an easy two hundred clams to me."

"Totally," I answered back.

The dealer flipped over the king of diamonds, then the ace of spades, which sure enough was in the middle position. The woman's money disappeared. Suddenly the dealer was staring intently at me with bloodshot eyes and a wide smile, revealing a mouth full of crooked teeth. "Did you know where the ace was, little man?"

Before I could answer, I felt a hand on my back firmly guiding me forward until I was face to face with the dealer. Other spectators closed in. Nick was no longer beside me. "You wanna play, kid? Just put a hundred dollars on the box, and if you win, I'll match your money. You win two hundred dollars right now. Cash on the box, let's go!" I did what was told, opening my previously concealed money belt. I pulled out five twenty-dollar bills and placed them down.

The dealer moved the cards around on the box, a little faster this time, but again I had no trouble following the ace. I felt a surge of confidence. How proud and happy the rest of the band would be to hear that I beat out a real New York City street hustler at his own game! We'd make more money at three-card monte than we'd earned in merchandise sales in a week! Hopefully, the cash infusion would make up for my Washington, DC, meltdown. The dealer's fingers rested.

"Where's the ace, kid?" I pointed confidently to the correct card. The dealer paused, then slowly flipped it over. I stared down in horror. It was the king of diamonds. With a flick of his sticky fingers he snatched up our hundred dollars and stuffed it into some unseen denim cavity on his body. I swayed on my feet, unable to believe what had just happened.

"Tough break, kid. I tell you what, though," hissed the dealer, glancing from side to side like Honest John from *Pinocchio*. "Second chance. You don't put money down until you're certain, no pressure. Just hold onto your money until you're sure."

"Okay," I answered quietly.

"OKAY!" the dealer yelled back, his teeth gleaming in the sunlight like melting M&Ms. The crowd tightened around me. Where was Nick? The dealer showed me the face cards, then flipped them and moved them around for a New York minute in almost comical slow motion. He looked up at me with one eyebrow cocked.

"You locked in on that ace?"

I fixed on it so hard I felt like I was boring a hole through the card.

"Yes, I am."

"If you're sure, if you're really sure, put two hundred dollars down right now, win back what you lost, and walk away with four hundred bucks. Money down, kid."

At the beginning of the tour, the band barely made enough money to get from town to town. After nearly a month of gigs and scrimping, though, we had managed to sock away just over three hundred dollars in case of emergencies. It was all in the money belt attached to my waist.

I pulled up my shirt, unzipped our money belt and peeled ten more twenty-dollar bills from the wad, leaving just three ten-dollar bills inside. I gingerly placed two hundred dollars on the cardboard box. Sweat poured down my face. Where was my beer? Someone exhaled a purple cloud of cigarette smoke into my face.

I pointed to the correct card. A bead of perspiration rolled off my index finger, forming a dot on the surface of the cardboard box. The dealer flipped it: the king of hearts. Our money disappeared. A fog fell over me.

I learned later that Nick had remained at the outer edge of the game, nervously watching me slip under the spell of the dealer. He was beginning to panic when another man who had been watching the game leaned towards him, speaking in a low tone. "You'd better get your friend out of there."

Nick reached into the crowd, grabbed a handful of my Gas Huffer T-shirt and yanked me backward. Once he had freed me from the throng, he jerked the front of my T-shirt down over the exposed money belt. I was staring back at him in shock when someone barked, "Five-O!"

The crowd dispersed in all directions. With a quick kick of his sneaker, the dealer knocked over the cardboard box, spilling the cards onto the sidewalk, then vanished into the Broadway foot traffic. Nick grabbed me by the shoulder and steered me up the street.

On the grimy-black sidewalk in front of the most famous punk rock club in the world, Nick told the rest of the guys the story while I stood there in a sweat-soaked daze. They were furious. Beez screamed that I could have been arrested for gambling in the street, that I would have to pay every cent back. The band now had thirty dollars between us. Dave leaned over towards me and sniffed. "Are you drunk?!"

Beez with Betty Colatrella, our first friend in New York City, enjoying some Lebanese food in the East Village. Dave first befriended Betty when she was our server at Maxwell's in Hoboken. Then she served as our ambassador to the Big Apple for many years. Cub, another Vancouver band soon to be taken under her wing, would eventually name their first album after her!
NICK THOMAS PHOTO

twenty-four

Don't Pack It In

A S DARKNESS FELL on our mood and the Bowery, the bulbs under the tattered awning of CBGB flickered once, twice, then came alit. Though the club was ground-zero for punk rock, those four famous letters actually stood for "Country, BlueGrass, Blues." The venue had been a honkytonk for a few years in the early 1970s before switching over to the subversive sounds that made it notorious. Below the CBGB logo were smaller letters: OMFUG, which stood for "[and] Other Music For Uplifting Gormandizers." A gormandizer usually means a ravenous eater but in this case owner Hilly Kristal was referring to someone with a voracious appetite for music.

The street and sidewalk in front of the club were littered with reprobates. A nauseating stench of urine and sewage intertwined with the knockdown body odour of sickly punk rockers with spiked mohawks and studded leather jackets. They milled about, hunched over and smoking like a Rancid album cover come to life, trying to hide their excitement at having reached the mecca of their pilgrimage from whatever suppressed small-town shithole they had fled. The pilgrim punks didn't care who was playing. In an ultimate dropkick murphy of irony, some of them didn't even go inside. They were too broke from their journey to pay the cover charge. Hanging out in front of CBGB was punk cred enough.

The Smugglers performing our first-ever show in New York City, which just happened to be at CBGB, the holy mecca of punk rock. We should have enjoyed the gig much more than we did, but tensions were running high after I lost a significant amount of the band's money in a scam a few blocks over.
BETTY COLATRELLA PHOTO

Mocking out in front of CBGB, the site of our first-ever New York City show and many future performances. It was as grimy inside as out, but it consistently drew music fans from around the world looking to see for themselves where punk began.
NICK THOMAS PHOTO

Ratso Rizzo–like hustlers and beggars shuffled up and down the sidewalk selling sob stories, demanding handouts and snapping up fallen change, food scraps and tossed cigarettes. Unloading our van in front of CBGB was chaotic, with many outstretched hands offering to help us load into the club. Bryce engaged in a nasty tug-of-war over a cymbal stand with one young guy who looked like he was ready to bolt if he could just wrench it loose. Bryce won, causing the man to retort, "You're one tough chick!" before slinking off.

Beez eventually used a different tactic and employed one of the tramps, offering him ten dollars to watch our van for us while we were in the club, with the money to be paid upon our safe departure from the Bowery. The man was good as his word: he stood sentry by our van for the rest of the night. It played to Beez's theory that humans are worker bees: most people *want* a job; most everyone wants a purpose. From then on, we'd often hire homeless people to guard the van in the big American cities.

Fully aware of the fact that CBGB was an international destination and a living (if stunningly decrepit) museum, promoters stacked the bill with bands every night. The music started at around seven p.m., blaring straight through until two a.m. We were damn lucky that Todd had landed us a slot around ten p.m., just before the two buzzed-about Minneapolis bands that were the main draw.

It felt surreal to walk from the minuscule, graffiti-covered dressing room onto the shabby CBGB stage that had birthed the problem child that became punk and hosted pioneers like the Ramones, Blondie and Television. The genre would defy the odds and conquer mainstream music culture: platinum records, top-forty radio, stadiums, world tours, Broadway shows and Grammy Awards. And it had started at CBGB, now under our Canadian rubber boots. Not that our thirty-minute set contributed in the slightest to the lore, beyond our own vivid imaginations, but it was still ecstasy. We performed with audacious, breakneck abandon.

The fans and friends we had made in Hoboken the night before joined other New Yorkers and Canadian ex-pats to form a loyal, cheering, hip-shakin' pack atop the squalid checkered dance floor. We didn't blow it, although most of the band weren't speaking to me. After our set, we mingled in our stinky thrift-store suits, soaking up the atmosphere. We met famed critic Ira Robbins, who we learned had come because he had seen our show at the International Pop Underground Convention and who also owned our first album, *At Marineland*. We also met members of some New York rock 'n' roll bands we loved and idolized like the Devil Dogs, the Fleshtones and the A-Bones, and turned many audience members into friends that remain so to this day.

The Smugglers would be lucky enough to return to New York City many times. We played bars and clubs like Coney Island High, the Continental Divide, ABC No Rio and Brownies as well as returns to CBGB. We gained a loyal, passionate NYC following that rivalled our fan base anywhere else in the world. We eventually brushed leather elbows with heroes and legends like Joey Ramone, Lemmy, Handsome Dick Manitoba, Joan Jett and Iggy Pop.

Thanks to Mayor Rudy Giuliani, the concrete jungle was rapidly being tamed. By the time of our last visit, CBGB, Coney Island High, the Continental and even Joey Ramone himself were gone. After thirty-three years in business, CBGB eventually closed over a rent dispute and within a few years was replaced by a high-end men's fashion store. The famed CBGB awning was donated to the Rock & Roll Hall of Fame in Cleveland. There's now a CBGB tourist trap restaurant in Newark Airport. The corner of East Second Street and Bowery was officially declared Joey Ramone Place and given its own street sign. It's the most often stolen street sign in New York City.

At the end of our first-ever gig at CBGB, the club's legendarily crusty owner, Hilly Kristal, who had remained in a tiny office beside the front door all night long, paid us $125. Just before handing me the money, he rasped that the club had recorded our show. We could purchase the exclusive recording of "The Smugglers Live at CBGBs" for the small sum of . . . $125. I thanked him for having us but snatched up the cash. Now, of course, I wish we had that tape.

There were a dozen shows left in our first American tour before we finally staggered home. In Albany we played Bogie's, run by Howard Glassman, the world's biggest Young Fresh Fellows fan, one of the greatest pals we'd ever make on the road, and the person to blame for introducing us to Jägermeister. In Minneapolis we played First Avenue, a huge and renowned rock club made famous by hometown hero Prince, who played the venue constantly in his early days and featured the club in many scenes of his film *Purple Rain*, a favourite of Dave's.

In Chicago we played at the famous Lounge Ax nightclub on a stacked bill headlined by the Dwarves, notorious for the violence and nudity that erupted at their shows, onstage and off.

```
Saturday, June 15, 1992
Lounge Ax
Chicago, Illinois


The craziest show of the tour by far?! What
a bill: the Smugglers, the Dharma Bums, the
Supersuckers, the Dwarves! The Dwarves' "set"
was really nutz! Nick took pictures! They
were nude!? I could never do that. Mike Brady
nightmare! And usually bands try to calm
violence down when it breaks out on the dance
floor but the Dwarves practically started it.
Okay, they did start it as far as we could
see. They are basically the EXACT opposite
of Fugazi. Unfortunately, Nick slipped on the
floor at end of the night and cut his knee on
broken glass. He was drunk and didn't mind.
But his camera fell too and we're worried
about the film. We were also nervous hanging
around the Dwarves backstage but they were
funny, especially the lead singer. The Dharma
Bums and Smugglers all stayed at Lounge Ax
owner Sue Miller's place after the show. Lots
of fun and up until almost 5 a.m. Bunk beds!
Sue wasn't too happy how the show ended in
total mayhem just fifteen minutes after
they started, but what did she expect from
the Dwarves, I wonder? That was no Chicago
sock-hop.
```

A year later, we were shocked to hear that the Dwarves' guitarist had been stabbed to death in a bar fight in Philadelphia. Sub Pop sent out a

We played Chicago with the Dwarves, one of the most notorious punk rock bands of all time. Most of their sets lasted just minutes before erupting into naked, bloody violence, just as this one did at Lounge Ax. NICK THOMAS PHOTO

sombre press release confirming the violent end of the guitarist known only as HeWhoCannotBeNamed. The news was reported in media outlets from SPIN to *Rolling Stone*, the SF *Weekly*, the LA *Times*, *Harper's* and *Billboard*. The liner notes on the next Dwarves album included a tribute to their dead guitarist, and gave an address for sending flowers and condolences.

There was only one catch: HeWhoCannotBeNamed wasn't dead. The story was a morbid hoax, a titanic rock 'n' roll swindle pulled off by the band. The staff at Sub Pop, having recently dealt with the actual deaths of various Seattle musicians, was embarrassed and angry. The label tossed the Dwarves from their roster.

Our first US tour had taught us one thing: it was possible. We could do it. We could tour America and not only survive but sell some records, make new fans and (mostly) have a lot of fun while doing it. The van didn't break down and the band didn't break up. (We fixed that steering fluid leak thanks to an honest mechanic and a ten-dollar gasket while we were checking out Mount Rushmore in Rapid City, South Dakota.) We had a patchwork of rock 'n' roll memories that most of us would never forget. All we wanted was to do it again next year, bigger and better. We started planning for that right away.

twenty-five

Go Fish

BACK IN VANCOUVER, we realized our dream of graduating from Nardwuar Records to PopLlama Products, the Seattle label home to the Young Fresh Fellows, the Fastbacks, the Squirrels and Bum, a brilliant power-pop band from Victoria. Owner Conrad Uno also ran Egg Studios, where we did all our recordings. PopLlama released our second album, *Atlanta Whiskey Flats*, somewhat reluctantly; our lyrics regrettably contained so much swearing and teenaged sexist nonsense that Conrad was worried about a backlash. That never happened because the cover was so esoteric—a spot-on rip-off of the obscure Trademark of Quality bootleg series, which only music critics could appreciate—and the record sold in very low numbers. But the label was excited about releasing our first CD, *In the Hall of Fame*, a compilation of songs from our first two albums plus a handful of new tracks that became staples in our live set for years. Neko Case designed the cover. It sold well and received surprisingly good reviews.

I took on some menial tasks at Mint Records, a Vancouver independent label, in exchange for graphic design work on various Smugglers singles. According to label owner Bill Baker, I never left. After a while, Mint employed me as a publicist and booking agent for the bands on their roster.

... For truth in advertising, the record to beat this year has to be the Smugglers' brilliant Beatles-bootleg pastiche *Atlanta Whiskey Flats* (Popllama, LP). The cover is a spot-on takeoff on a mid-Seventies Fab Four contraband release, right down to the title, the typography and the appropriation of the real album's Trademark of Quality labels. The music? A bang-up guitar rumble, Star Club-style barroom bop laced with *Thrasher* magazine attitude. Frankly, the original Beatles boot wasn't this much fun. ...

↓ When we toured across North America with cub, Dave was dating their drummer, Neko Case. Even though we had a "no girlfriends on tour" rule, since Neko was actually in the band we were on tour with, she occasionally hopped in our van between towns. This shot was taken in Albany, New York, after a show at Bogie's.

NICK THOMAS PHOTO

↑ Our first review in *Rolling Stone* by David Fricke, then the music editor, now a senior editor. The review was completely unexpected, especially for what we consider our most esoteric album.

In 1993 the label was experiencing an unexpected explosion of sales thanks to a young band called cub. The lead singer and bassist, Lisa Marr, sassy, smart and usually smoking, had an incredible knack for writing deceptively simple and extremely catchy pop songs, always singing with a smile in her voice. Robynn Iwata, the guitarist, was so painfully shy that for the first few years she performed sitting cross-legged onstage. Their first drummer was a friendly goth named Valeria Fellini, who ran a local candy store. Shortly after the release of cub's second EP, *Hot Dog Day*, Fellini handed over the drumsticks to Neko Case.

Cub's twee-pop timing was perfect. The early 1990s was dominated by dreary, dark and distorted grunge music played mostly by a disenchanted mob of men. Cub provided the musical opposite, a sunny antidote to the male storm clouds, creating a style of music that was eventually branded "cuddlecore." Their first two EPs and their debut full-length album shot to the top of the North American campus radio charts. One of my first jobs

at Mint was to lug their CDs by the crate to the record stores on Seymour
Street. Cub's sound and attitude would prove highly influential for scores
of young indie musicians seeking a new alternative to the new alternative.

Cub wanted to taste the touring circuit first-hand, and they asked if
they could be the opening band for the Smugglers' second North American tour. We were flattered that someone wanted to open for us, but
because we already had plenty of touring under our boots, we fancied
ourselves the experts and cub the novices, and treated them as such.

Once we hit the road, though, we were stunned by the reaction cub
received. Thanks to the band's stratospheric radio play, which was
cracking even mainstream stations and music television, their rabid
fans showed up in droves and bought everything in sight. That led to
some embarrassing nights for the Smugglers, none more so than our gig
together at the Spotted Dog, a lesbian bar in Windsor, Ontario. Because
the Smugglers' merch sales were so low and cub's so high, the five of us
created a conspiracy during our daylong drives to rationalize the lopsid-
edness. We came to the solid conclusion that cub was pushing their merch
over ours—never mind the fact that cub's members often diligently sold
our merchandise for us while we were either performing or off getting
drunk.

While we were onstage in Windsor, Beez thought he had finally caught
cub red-handed. In the middle of one of our songs, he saw a female customer approach the merchandise table and point to a Smugglers shirt
taped to the wall. He witnessed Robynn shake her head, instead pointing
to a cub shirt. The woman bought the cub shirt. Beez stopped the show
mid-song and yelled accusations of merch-pushing into the microphone
at Robynn. Outraged, and sure that our theory had been borne out, I
threw a half-full pint glass in the direction of the merch table. Afterwards,
when we got back to the place we were staying (an unwitting fan's apartment) there was a huge fight between the bands. The Smugglers accused
cub of merchandise favouritism, while cub tried to defend themselves.
Finally Neko got so angry she threatened to beat the hell out of all five of
us, even though she was dating Dave.

When everyone had finally settled down, Mint Records owner Bill
Baker, on tour with us as cub's driver and roadie, explained everything.
The woman in question had asked for a Smugglers shirt in a *size small
women's*. Since it was the grunge era, the only sizes the Smugglers shirts

came in were *extra-large men's*. Of course cub's array of shirts came in myriad sizes for all genders and ages. Crimson embarrassment set in for the Smugglers, and Beez begged for forgiveness.

Ego-crushing incidents aside, the tour proved to be for the most part a rousing and fun experience, and we became friends with cub for life. When the Smugglers and cub dipped into the northeast United States for a series of gigs in and around New York City, cub met our Maxwell's waitress pal and New York City ambassador Betty Colatrella. They all became such good friends that cub named their first album *Betti-Cola* in tribute to Betty.

At the start of our joint tour, Mint Records head honcho Bill Baker was decidedly not a Smugglers fan. It was during this tour that we discovered through idle conversation that it was Bill who had anonymously written the meanest comment card at the Shindig! battle of the bands years earlier. But by the end of the trip, based on either Stockholm syndrome or similar tastes and senses of humour, Bill decided he wanted to release a record for the Smugglers on Mint.

Beez during a happier moment with Robynn Iwata (left) and Lisa Marr, the founding members of cub. We took them on tour to show 'em the ropes and they ended up schooling us just about every night on how to charm a crowd and move mountains of merchandise, so much so that Beez openly accused cub of pushing their stuff over ours. Didn't end well. This photo was NOT taken on that night. NICK THOMAS PHOTO

The Smugglers
Party Party Party Pooper!
7″ EP Promo Sheet

Sheesh! The Smugglers! As I sit before this
Smith-Corona, one-eyed drunk, all I can
think of is how wholeheartedly I've hated
this band for as long as they've existed.
Time was when "The Smugglers" was nothing
more than a shorter way of saying "This band
sucks" for me and everyone I knew. Take note:
I'm talkin' 1992, babe. To me, they were the
epitome of retro: that honkin' harmonica,
the cheesy outfits, the cocksure "vocalist"
crooning in the key of "X", the tambourines—
oh, God, the tambourines. Suffice to say, I
never found it difficult to find the "ASS" in
their nickname the Canadian AmbASSadors of
Rock'n'Roll.

Then came THE TOUR. May of 1993 saw my
stomp back to Pacifica (from Toronto) for
the Smugglers/cub tour across Canada. By
the time we reached Toronto, I had grown to
love these Wellington-wearin', Jägermeister-
swillin' maroons to thee point that each
night I just set right back and cried until
they took the stage. Okay, no, I didn't, but
you get the idea. Imagine: each night the
same amazing songs, the same amazing show,
each Smug' giving 110, no, 111%! 27 shows in
30 glorious wham-bam-thank-you-Grant days,
and the next thing you know, here they are
on Mint!

Bill Baker
February 3, 1994

twenty-six

I'm In Love
with My Knife

W E CONTINUED TO stack up shows, stories and kilometres in the States. Despite the often-frightening backdrop, it was in the southern USA where we found our first consistently growing fan base outside of Canada and the Pacific Northwest. We toured it repeatedly, with varying degrees of boom and bust. One year we had a string of dates booked through the Deep South with an up-and-coming surf-space-rock band called Man or Astro-Man?, playing in towns like Huntsville, Birmingham, Tuscaloosa, Athens and Atlanta.

As we approached Atlanta, we felt the familiar insecurity of venturing into another apocalyptic American mega-city. Atlanta's concrete labyrinths of intertwined roadways curved on top of each other like a gigantic nest of snakes. But we weren't as nervous as we once had been, and if we hadn't played the Point in Atlanta with Man or Astro-Man? and a local band called the Subsonics, we would never have discovered the bustling bohemian neighbourhood of Little Five Points. It has been called the Haight-Ashbury of the East, Venice Beach without the beach and the counterculture centre of the American south. Everywhere we looked we saw record stores, clothing shops, hemp emporiums, pizza joints, bookshops, arcades and clubs. There were freaks and geeks, punks and bikers, goths and hippies in all manner of colourful costumes draped over park benches, curbs, storefronts and bar patios. At the confusing main intersection of Little Five Points, electrical wires criss-crossed each other overhead like pick-up sticks. A massive collection of shoes in all shapes and sizes hung from the power lines by their laces.

An old hippie we met told us the tradition had started as an army ritual: when you wore out your first pair of combat boots, you tossed them up. A stoner told us the shoes indicated a place where drugs were bought and sold. Someone else said it started with bullies stealing the shoes of smaller kids and throwing them up. The Point's soundman told us it was simply street art. I added a Canadian element to the collection, tossing up my completely worn-out black Converse sneakers.

Our band was lucky enough to have gained a big fan in national CBC Radio host David Wisdom, who referred to the Smugglers as "Canada's bounciest band." When David heard we were heading off again on a shoestring budget, he invited me to call in with updates to his late-night music show, *Nightlines*. And so I did, making ridiculous calls from various pay phones across North America and eventually around the world.

In Atlanta I found a phone booth under a giant leafy tree in a square around the corner from the club, which seemed to be the gathering place for anybody who wanted to soak in the neighbourhood's *Carnivale*-like vibe. I stood at the rotary pay phone, which was covered in graffiti and band stickers, describing my field of vision to David Wisdom: jugglers, contortionists, flame swallowers, buskers, hacky sack players, street bums and drug dealers, all in a constant flow of action under the garden of hanging shoes.

Some obnoxious Georgian nudged me on the shoulder in the midst of the live interview. I ignored it, but weirdly, the hand rested on my shoulder and started applying pressure. What was up with these rude people? Couldn't this American idiot wait for their own damn turn? I tried to brush the hand away. Then I realized it was not a hand.

I whipped my head around to see the green and black scales of a very large snake resting on my shoulder, its tubular body as thick as my thigh. I glanced up and saw that most of it was still wrapped around a tree branch directly above the pay phone. I felt an ever-so-slight sensation on my opposite ear. Whipping my head to the other side, I came nose to nose with the blank, serpentine face of a boa constrictor. I felt its body slither heavily across the back of my neck as its face moved directly in front of mine, tongue flicking an inch away from my nose. I freaked out on national radio: "SNAKE! SNAKE! THERE'S A SNAKE WRAPPING ITSELF AROUND ME!!!"

"Pardon me?" David asked, his voice crackling down the phone line. I was frozen in fear but kept talking. "A... very large... snake... has dropped down... from a tree above... and... is WRAPPING ITSELF AROUND MY NECK."

"Great snakes!" David retorted. Being a diehard Tintin fan, I could appreciate that, even when I was about to be choked to death. The snake heaped more of its weight on my shoulders. My knees began to shake. A tall, balding man dressed like a genie rushed up to me. His pointy shoes jingled with every step.

"Bijaboji! There you are!" I turned the phone receiver outward so David Wisdom could hear the authentic southern accent of the genie. "Sorry, man! I took a piss in the bushes, and when I came back my snake basket was empty! Try to relax, man. Bijaboji senses fear, and that's when she's liable to tighten up on you. Hold on while I peel her off." The fourteen-foot snake was removed from my neck, and the audio clip of that phone call became a year-end highlight on *Nightlines* for years to come.

We loved playing with Man or Astro-Man?, but it was the opening band, the Subsonics, who really blew us away. They sounded like Buddy Holly and the Crickets, the Velvet Underground and the Violent Femmes balled together into one screaming fist. As their rattle and shake reverberated off the rafters of the club, we marvelled from our dance-floor view at their lead singer Clay, a near-androgynous praying mantis of a man. Tall and junkie-skinny with a head of exploding red curls, he wore a shiny black two-piece faux-leather suit, red spiked women's heels and a colourful yellow feather boa.

The drummer was equally intriguing—a petite femme fatale named Buffi, a ponytailed Latina who performed in a drop-dead-hot faux-leopard-fur bikini. She wore giant horn-rimmed sunglasses and chewed gum to the beat with her mouth wide open, showing off her perfectly white teeth. In a song fittingly called "I'm In Love with My Knife," Clay whipped out a huge dagger from a hidden sheath somewhere on his body and wildly played slide guitar with it.

After the gig, we hung out with the Subsonics backstage, letting the Georgia sweat dry on our bodies while we quaffed back the few remaining beers we could wrangle from the bar. When the subject of Clay's knife came up, the Subsonics shocked us with casual retellings of their violent daily lives in Atlanta. Clay and Buffi lived and worked in dangerous neighbourhoods, and their alternative wardrobe choices often made them targets for abuse. They faced all sorts of physical threats; muggings, robberies and random fights were commonplace.

To combat this urban menace, the Subsonics were armed like *The A-Team*. The Canadians in the room went into collective shock when Buffi and Clay told us in their southern drawls that besides knives, they carried guns everywhere they went. They pulled them out to prove it. Buffi's firearm of choice was a small, sleek, .25-calibre automatic pistol she had bought from a guy out of the trunk of his car near the Atlanta airport. The weapon was so compact that she could easily stow it in her vintage purse, alongside her keys, switchblade, cherry red lipstick, brass knuckles, leather flask and vial of mace. Clay carried a more powerful 9-mm handgun that he had bought at a pawnshop, no questions asked. He kept it in ready reach, weighing down the right outer pocket of his black leather jacket.

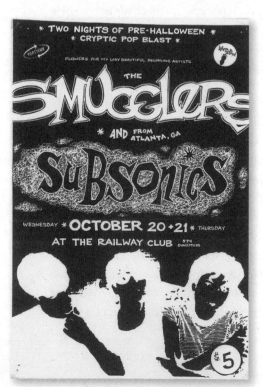

Clay saw that we were a rapt and wide-eyed audience, so he told us with great gothic theatrics that even his gun wasn't enough protection in the South's nastiest inner-city neighbourhoods, which was why he also regularly carried a seven-inch Vietnam War–era Air Force survival knife,

ROBYNN IWATA POSTER

THE SMUGGLERS

A promotional postcard from around 1994, the "pink polka dot shirt era." We found the shirts at a vintage clothing store in Athens, Georgia, and loved how lightweight they were compared to our other onstage outfits of pea jackets and suits. Beez hated these shirts, saying he felt like a "dancing clown" in them. Uh, yeah! RAEANNE HOLOBOFF PHOTO

a switchblade and brass knuckles. The Subsonics were stunned when we explained that we travelled with nary a weapon to our collective name—no guns, knives, not even a hockey stick—and they were suspicious of our stories about the relative safety of big-city Canada.

The Subsonics understood that we were more interested in wardrobe than weaponry, so before we left Georgia they tipped us off to a thrift store in Athens that sold bizarre clothing and sets of matching costumes. Sure enough, the store was packed front to back, floor to ceiling with all sorts of weird get-ups. The crazed hippie proprietor convinced us to purchase five identical bright pink button-up shirts covered in white polka dots. Apparently Pearl Jam had been in the week before and bought a set in yellow. But our pink polka-dot shirts were a look that drove Beez beyond the brink.

twenty-seven

Don't Mess with Texas

HE AIR WAS thick and damp as we crossed the border into Texas. Dave slapped in the cassette of ZZ Top's *Tejas*. Beez had been napping when he suddenly jolted awake. "STOP THE VAN! OUR MONEY IS GONE!" he screamed from our van's rear bed.

Dave's right foot dusted the brake pedal, but he didn't engage, shifting his sneaker back to the accelerator to resume speed. It was the third or fourth time Beez had woken up from a nap screaming something similar. He was in charge of our band's accounting, and ever since the three-card monte debacle, he had also looked after our money belt. He was so paranoid about losing our bankroll (which at maximum only ever held a few hundred dollars) that he wore the belt at all times, even to sleep, day and night. In his nightmare, the moist belt had become unzipped and our money fluttered out the van's open windows like a box of freed butterflies. This time, when he came to his senses, he confessed that he couldn't handle the anxiety anymore. He handed the money belt back to me.

We were bound for a show in Beaumont, tucked along the Texan Gulf Coast. We had heard a new venue called the Fuzzgun was booking non-established, unpopular, independent touring bands with no draw, so naturally we gave them a call. But because I was nose-deep in *Tintin and* the *Calculus Affair* instead of navigating, we missed our exit and ended up in the next town over, where we decided to stop for dinner. Walking around the town against the backdrop of a blood-red sunset, we noticed something *Twilight Zone*–strange that we couldn't quite place our fingers on. We finally figured it out: every single man, woman and child we passed was white. Really white. *Deliverance*-white.

We were accustomed to the array of ethnicities filling American streets: black, white, Latino, Asian, First Nations, South Asian. But not in this town. Nonetheless, we were hungry, so we decided to hit up what appeared from the outside to be a pretty authentic catfish restaurant. The joint had an all-white clientele and an all-white staff. It reeked of deep-fried oil, cigarettes and hairspray.

A pasty, plump waitress arrived in short order to take ours. After she had scribbled down our four variations of catfish and some hush puppies for Beez, Beez cleared his throat. "Um, just one more thing," he said. "What town is this?"

The waitress glared in Beez's direction. "Y'all don't know the name of the town y'all's in?" Beez shook his head nervously. By now, everyone in the restaurant was staring at us.

"Then how the hell did you get here?"

"We took a wrong turn," answered Beez.

"Y'all in Vidor, Texas."

The waitress didn't offer any more information, and we didn't ask. Soon we were nibbling on our greasy catfish, glancing anxiously around at the obese freckled white families who surrounded our booth, still staring at us as they flushed back their catfish with titanic mugs of soda.

That night, before our show in Beaumont, we chatted with the bartender, a boisterous, fun-loving guy who also happened to be black. As soon as he heard the name "Vidor," his friendly demeanour evaporated. Vidor, Texas was a "sundown town," he explained to us through gritted teeth: no black people were allowed on the streets there after dark. The bartender told us that "Bloody Vidor" was an infamous Ku Klux Klan gathering place and the site of the KKK's Texas headquarters. The Klan had held several rallies in Vidor over the years, and had even opened up a KKK gift shop for a short time on Main Street.

"K-K-K-Mart?" Dave quipped.

The bartender shot him a look and continued, telling us stories of racial tension and abuse that caused our overheated Canadian blood to run cold in our veins. "Just last week," said the bartender, "a car full of crackers drove by the only brother in town and some peckerwood from inside hollered that they were going to get a rope to hang the man. He's gettin' the fuck out of there. And that, y'all, is Vidor, Texas." He let his words reverberate ominously in the hazy air of the empty club. Then he straightened up and gave us a grin. "Y'all come back to Texas now, ya hear?"

ONE OF OUR favourite Texas stops turned out to be a club called Taco Land, a little concrete shack in an otherwise deserted industrial zone of San Antonio. Despite the surroundings, Taco Land was a legendary joint that had been in operation since 1965, owned by a squat, no-nonsense

Latino brute with slicked-back hair, a waxed moustache and oversized black sunglasses. Ramiro "Ram" Ayala was a foul-mouthed, gruff curmudgeon who was considered the patron saint of the underground music scene in San Antonio. Taco Land was the first venue in town to regularly allow live punk rock in early 1980s. Oddly, Taco Land didn't sell tacos. Taco Land sold only one thing: beer.

Stepping into Taco Land's dark interior was like entering a Mexican cantina in a Clint Eastwood western. Our first time there, through the shadows, Dave spotted Ram behind the bar in his huge black Ray-Bans and politely asked where we should load in our gear. Ram stopped what he was doing, slammed his calloused, multi-ringed fingers down on the bar and barked, "THROUGH THE FUCKIN' DOOR, YOU DUMB GRINGO PUSSY!" Dave was blown back, *Matrix*-like, by the expletives. We didn't ask Ram any more questions after that.

The Smugglers had an amazing show that sticky Texas night, playing a packed joint filled with dancing Texans. At first, Ram seemed pissed off that his place was hopping, angrily cracking open foaming cans of Lone Star for one dollar each. We managed to get him to warm up a bit by the end of the night. He counted out our money while grumbling that our band was "pretty good for a bunch of Canadian gringo pussies." After getting paid we hung around outside in the warm night under the massive limbs of a two-hundred-year-old oak tree that stood sentinel above Taco Land. We drank cold beer with wide, victorious smiles on our faces.

We would return to play Taco Land a few more times, but sadly, tragedy struck Taco Land and the legendary Ramiro Ayala. Late one night, two shady newcomers hung around until closing time, when they pulled guns on Ram and a few employees, aiming to rob them of the evening's take. True to his nature, Ram barked out a "FUCK YOU" to the robbers while reaching for the sawed-off shotgun he kept behind the bar. One of the gunmen opened fire on Ram, knocking him to the floor, and shot two other employees before fleeing. Ramiro Ayala bled to death on the concrete floor of Taco Land, the bar he had opened forty years earlier. We will always fondly remember the tough-talkin' Ram and our spicy nights of loud rock 'n' roll at Taco Land. Don't mess with Texas.

ASK BEEZ

Q: How long have you been playing guitar?

A: Um... I'm the bassist! I actually started playing guitar in 1977, but you'd never know.

Q: How did you get the nickname "Beez"?

A: I have silly hippie parents who named me "Bees." I changed it to "Beez" to be more punk rock. Maybe I should change it to "Buzz," something the Smugglers have never had.

Q: Do you believe in reincarnation?

A: Yes. I hope this band dies and gets reborn into something people actually like.

Q: What did the other members buy you for your birthday?

A: I got a black toupee and I wear it at every show. You never knew, right??

Q: If you could live anywhere in the world, where would you live?

A: Las Vegas. They play my people's music there.

Q: How would you describe Nardwuar?

A: A sweet and curious man-child with a golden heart.

Q: What bands did you grow up liking?

A: Teenage Head, Eddie Cochran, Van McCoy, Wings.

Q: When did you decide to become the Smugglers' only vegetarian?

A: I stopped eating meat in 1989 when I played at the Macrobiotic Health Food restaurant in Amsterdam on tour with my former band, Sarcastic Mannequins. I don't miss meat and I doubt I'll ever eat it again.

Q: What's the worst gig the Smugglers have ever done?

A: It always seems to be the last gig we've played! But nothing was worse than Phoenix in 1992. NO ONE showed up.

Q: Do you enjoy touring?

A: I love touring because I never get enough of Nick's farts, Grant's rules, Dave's ghost ginch, and Bryce always threatening to quit the tour.

Q: How does it make you feel when people take pictures of you and the Smugglers when you're performing live?

A: I love it. When people take flash photography, the audience and I are in perfect sync. We both have stars in our eyes.

Q: What is your idea of a good time?

A: Getting dropped off at the end of tour. And playing poker, ballroom dancing with my girlfriend, CC, and getting more laughs than Grant at my jokes onstage. And if the jokes are about him, even better.

twenty-eight

Lookout (Here Comes Tomorrow)

THE PURPLE ONION was perched on a steep hill in the North Beach neighbourhood of San Francisco, right across the street from the beatnik literary headquarters of City Lights Books. The subterranean den had been a one-hundred-seat vaudeville and comedy club in the 1950s and '60s, hosting everyone from Woody Allen, Lenny Bruce, Bob Newhart and Phyllis Diller to acts like the Smothers Brothers, the Kingston Trio and the Mamas & the Papas before falling into disrepair. In the 1990s garage rock 'n' roll music had taken over the stage thanks to wild-man promoter Tom Guido. For an average gig, we tried to show up at the venue by five or six p.m. for load-in, followed by a sound check. Then we'd wander off for dinner and pray to the rock gods that when we returned around eight or nine p.m., after doors had opened, there would be something resembling a crowd.

When we arrived at the Purple Onion at six p.m., we found the doors locked tight with no signs of life. After exploring the neighbourhood, we headed back to the club. The other bands were waiting outside the venue, along with a crowd. About thirty minutes later, Tom Guido ran up panting. He looked like a cross between Crispin Glover and all four Monkees. He was flustered, yelling at people to get out of his way so he could get to the front doors. He unlocked them, brushed his bowl-cut bangs out of his eyes, then immediately spun around and started taking people's money for cover. Once everyone was in, he dashed downstairs and opened up the bar, selling anyone who wanted one a beer. Then he ran up onto the stage, flipped a few switches and made some crazed opening announcements into the microphone about mandatory drinking and dancing. He introduced the opening band without any sort of sound check, and they launched into their set.

Even though he seemed to be single-handedly running the club, Tom also danced to each band in the front row. Typically, soundmen ask guitarists to turn their amps down. It's what all soundmen do, blaming the guitarists for being egomaniacs, drowning out the rest of the band and throwing off their precious sound mix. At the Purple Onion, it was the opposite. Tom Guido would leap onto the stage in his Beatle boots, shoving guitarists to get at their amps. He would grab the volume knob on the amp and crank it, jump back down onto the dance floor and do the mashed potato. At first we were stunned by his conduct, but we quickly realized Tom was a one-of-a-kind character that you had to sit back, watch and enjoy. Occasionally, he'd leap back on the stage, grab a mic and bark orders into it: "NO SLAM-DANCING! Only sixties dances!"

Tom had put together a great bill for our show at the Purple Onion: opening bands from Sacramento called the Troublemakers (who wore matching zebra-skin vests) and the Groovie Ghoulies, and a band from San Francisco called the Ne'er Do Wells. As soon as I saw them play, I realized the Smugglers had a startling amount in common with the Ne'er Do Wells. We had heard about the band for the last year or so on the road. Everywhere we went, people asked us, "Hey, have you heard of this band called the Ne'er Do Wells? They're just like you guys!" The same thing was happening to them. Like us, the Ne'er Do Wells frequently wore matching 1960s-era thrift store suits onstage and played urgent up-tempo garage rock 'n' roll. Their drummer was Al Sobrante, a notorious Bay Area punk who was a founding member of Green Day but had quit the band to go to college instead.

Soon after our first show at the Purple Onion, Al Sobrante quit the Ne'er Do Wells too, and the band became the Hi-Fives. The Hi-Fives, and specifically guitarist Chris Imlay, would serve as our ambassadors to their label, Lookout Records, the legendary American pop-punk record company co-founded, owned and operated by Larry Livermore. Larry was a Bay Area icon, having discovered and released records by game-changing groups like Operation Ivy, the Mr. T Experience, Pansy Division and Green Day.

It was Bryce who had introduced us to Lookout Records, through the cassettes he played on our van's stereo. At first, the rest of us didn't like the tinny-sounding pop-punk, but songs by bands like Green Day and Screeching Weasel remained lodged in our heads whether we liked it or not. Soon, on my weekly trips to downtown Vancouver record stores, I found myself adding *anything* on Lookout to my purchase pile. Every release seemed filled with more hooks than a Desolation Sound tackle box.

Dave and I met Larry Livermore at an all-ages show in tiny Manila, California. Larry was standing quietly against the side wall of the hall,

Larry Livermore, co-founder and owner of Lookout Records, and the man with the golden ears. Over the years, Larry discovered and signed San Francisco Bay Area pop-punk bands that would come to define an entire era of music—Green Day, Operation Ivy, the Mr. T Experience, Pansy Division and more—before spreading out across the continent to sign more genre-defining artists like Screeching Weasel and the Queers. We met Larry in 1994, and by 1995 our dream had come true: the Smugglers had joined the Lookout roster, and it would change our lives. NICK THOMAS PHOTO looking somewhat reserved and shy. It surprised me that this slight, seemingly awkward man was largely responsible for unleashing the rapidly mainstreaming pop-punk sound upon the world. For those reasons and others we never stopped discovering, Larry was a fascinating fellow. One of the first things we noticed was that he was considerably older than everyone else at the gig, bands and audience included.

Originally from Detroit, Larry had lived through every era of rock 'n' roll from the 1950s onwards. He listened to doo-wop on his living room radio when he was a kid. He saw the rise of Motown Records up close and in person, and witnessed the birth of obstinate Detroit rock bands like MC5 and the Stooges, groups that were in retrospect considered the precursors to punk. Larry was a greaser in the early sixties, running with gangs and petty criminals, then followed the times into hippie-dom in the late 1960s. At Woodstock he was mesmerized by the Who, taking in their set up close to the stage at sunrise on the last day of the festival. Larry was as high as Roger Daltrey's falsetto, having "hastily gobbled about thirty hits of acid" when the police pulled him over with his hippie pals on the way to the festival.

In the early 1970s Larry was, of all things, an aspiring ballet dancer living in the crime-ridden Alphabet City neighbourhood of New York. On his way to class, he was mugged and beaten for four dollars. One of the muggers held Larry down while the other smashed him in the face with a right hook, breaking his nose and knocking it crooked. The injuries caused Larry to miss a lot of ballet classes, and ultimately to leave the Big Apple for the West Coast. Almost a decade later, he was a northern California glam-punk/new waver. In the small town of San Rafael, he was mugged again, this time by local teenagers, who thought Larry's tiny leather jacket, tight pants and shag haircut were too flamboyant. Once again one of the assailants held him down while the other punched Larry in the face, this time with a vicious left hook. Incredibly, the punch straightened Larry's nose, which had been crooked for nearly ten years.

Larry wandered way off the grid into the "dope-saturated wilderness" atop Spy Rock Mountain in northern California. There he started a magazine called *Lookout* (named after a fire lookout tower on nearby Iron Peak Mountain) and formed a band called the Lookouts (him and some local hippie offspring, including twelve-year-old Tré Cool, who went

We instantly got along with the kindred spirits at Lookout Records. Left to right: Nick, Chris Imlay from the Hi-Fives (who would serve as our all-important envoy to the label), Beez, Cathy Bauer (Lookout's superwoman production manager), and Dave. Here, we were pretending that Chris was handing us the keys to Lookout. GRANT LAWRENCE PHOTO

on to replace drummer Al Sobrante in Green Day). When the Lookouts sought gigs beyond the woods, Larry migrated south to Berkeley, where he helped open the famed all-ages venue 924 Gilman Street. Gilman gave a stage to the East Bay's burgeoning punk scene, specifically bands like the Lookouts, Operation Ivy, Isocracy and the Mr. T Experience. Larry was so inspired by those live performances that he and a friend offered to put out the bands' records.

By the time we met Larry, he was running one of the best independent record labels in the world out of his tiny apartment in Berkeley. Lookout Records saw incredible growth in the mid-nineties, and the label would soon open a second-storey office on University Avenue. Through it all, Larry was a friendly, welcoming, know-it-all, Fagin-like character, the leader of a pop-punk label staffed by people many years his junior. His Oliver Twist was a boy-genius named Chris Appelgren, responsible for a lot of the day-to-day management of the label, along with Larry's Artful Dodger, Patrick Hynes, in charge of much of the accounting. Chris and Patrick also created many of the label's famous record covers and band logos, which were adored by punks the world over. When Green Day exploded, the label added more staff, including Chris Imlay from the Hi-Fives, to do art design. Another was our old friend Molly Neuman, original riot grrrl and Bratmobile drummer, who became the label manager. All of them seemed like amazing people, working at a record label that was reaching a creative zenith. Luckily for us, Larry was kind to the Smugglers from the get-go.

twenty-nine

Selling the Sizzle

THROUGH OUR CONNECTION with Larry, the Smugglers got to play with every Lookout band that came through Vancouver: the Mr. T Experience, Pansy Division, the Queers, the Hi-Fives and Larry Livermore's new band, the Potatomen. Fairly quickly, the deal of my rock 'n' roll dreams was hatched. Larry was looking for solid, trustworthy representation and distribution in Canada, and Mint was always looking for inroads into the States. An agreement was struck. Lookout would release records by cub and the Smugglers in the USA, while Mint would cherry-pick favourites like the Mr. T Experience, Pansy Division and the Groovie Ghoulies to release in Canada. The lead-up to the deal was incredibly fun, including a summer of wild touring with the Hi-Fives in Canada that included, among other things, their bassist, Jess Hilliard, spending almost an entire week in a cow suit. The Smugglers also recorded our first release for Lookout, a split EP with the Hi-Fives called *Summer Games*.

We recorded our next album, *Selling the Sizzle*, with Mass Giorgini at Sonic Iguana Studios in Lafayette, Indiana. Mass had produced some of Lookout's best albums. Up until that point, our band was used to recording very quickly. We'd often go with our first or second takes, and many times the "scratch vocal" (an informal practice in which you sing along

A promotional pic for our breakthrough album *Selling the Sizzle*, released on Mint Records in Canada, Lookout Records in the States and Konkurrent in Europe. For some reason we never used this photo for anything until now. PAUL CLARKE PHOTO

This photo, taken for the publicity around our album *Selling the Sizzle*, became one of the most-used in our "career." It was taken in 1995 but promoters used it on posters for years to come. PAUL CLARKE PHOTO

~~~~~~

to the bed-track recordings of the instruments) wound up as our final vocal take. When it came to lyrics, our third verse was often the same as our first.

Mass did things completely differently. He spent incredible amounts of pre-production time on things we had never seriously considered, like drum tuning, fixing the intonation of our guitars and making me go write third and fourth verses. Once the recording had begun, he forced me to sing my lead vocal takes over and over and over and over again, to the point of pure frustration on my part. Larry Livermore made a surprise drop-in visit to the studio, which, while flattering and exciting, didn't help with my deteriorating confidence. I had never thought I was Bono Vox, but I thought I had a handle on our songs, especially the ones I had written. Working with Mass proved otherwise. My singing voice was mostly as flat as Saskatchewan, though Mass pulled off some amazing magic to reel it in.

The exhausting ten days of recording (the longest we had ever spent in a studio) would result in our highest-selling record. After we wrapped the session, we toured from Indiana to the west coast. When we rolled up to the Bottom of the Hill Club in San Francisco, Chris and Molly from Lookout greeted us as we slid open our van door. We literally handed them the record. In early 1996, *Selling the Sizzle* was released on Lookout Records in the USA, Mint Records in Canada and Konkurrent Records in Europe. It was like we had won the rock 'n' roll lottery: we had *that logo* on the back of our record. (The original, iconic Lookout logo had been redesigned by then, but I insisted that the classic "eyes" brand appear on the back of *Selling the Sizzle*.)

Lookout put the Smugglers on an American winter tour with our old friends the Mr. T Experience (short form MTX), who were enjoying a renaissance in popularity with new members and an excellent new pop-punk album called *Love Is Dead*. The tour began in far-off Portsmouth, New Hampshire, over five thousand kilometres away from Vancouver. When we finally skidded to a stop in the snowy New England town after driving through blizzard after blizzard, the first person we saw, standing on the street corner and looking like a character from a Herman Melville novel in a black peacoat, wool scarf and Greek sailing cap, was Larry Livermore. That's what it was like with Larry. He'd show up unannounced wherever we happened to be.

The show in Portsmouth was amazing, and so was every night that followed. We had never been on a tour where the gigs were sold out night after night. We were flying through boxes of our new CD, LP and T-shirts. From the back of the room, it was nothing but a sea of Lookout Records logos on the T-shirts of the all-ages kids packing the clubs. It was happening, it was freaking us out and our new roadie Ska-T had the perfect vantage point.

Ska-T was known in the underground music scene as "the Canadian King of Ska." In Vancouver, he hosted his own ska show on CiTR Radio, promoted concerts for touring ska bands and helped organize mod scooter runs and ska festivals. The Smugglers were not a ska band in any way, shape or form, but Ska-T had an open mind and a thirst for the open road. Unlike the immaculately clad mod scooter enthusiasts who made up his tribe, Ska-T rocked a black, frayed and falling-apart mod-style flight

Beez (left) with our irrepressible and extremely loyal roadie Ska-T Stewart. Ska-T managed to find the bright side in any situation and was an extremely welcomed burst of energy when he climbed into the van for the first time back in 1996. He looked so similar to Beez that he would often take advantage of it when it came to girls after the shows. NICK THOMAS PHOTO

jacket covered in pins and patches. He often sported five-day stubble and didn't shower all that often. His scooter was at best a jalopy. As a roadie, Ska-T was incredibly kind, loyal and hard-working. His accounting skills gave Beez fits, consisting of scribbled-out sales on scraps of cardboard and the handover of a crumpled ball of cash at the end of the night.

Our merchandise sales began to dwarf our performance guarantees. The merchandise was vital: it kept money in our pockets, the rubber on the road and fans coming back. Every band plugged their merch from the stage; it was becoming part of the noise. Using a slightly different technique, during the show I'd announce, "Hey, it's our roadie Ska-T's birthday tonight! He's at the merchandise area right back there! Everybody turn around and wave to Ska-T!" Ska-T would wave back, showing everyone where the merchandise table was without us obnoxiously plugging it. On alternate nights, we'd insist people stop by the merch stand and buy Ska-T a drink. If they indeed swung by, he would charm them into a sale. By the end of the night, thanks to the "birthday drinks," Ska-T was often completely wasted and covered in lipstick, but he was behind the table for some of our most stratospheric merchandise sales.

Ska-T wore Buddy Holly–style glasses, much like Beez and Dave and me, though Dave and I only wore our glasses offstage. That meant there were now four of us on the road wearing big clunky black glasses. It was a little much for some rural gas station and café employees, who would ask us questions like, "What's the deal with the glasses?" Our multiplied four-eyed look also inspired catcalls. Random people would yell, "Hey, look, it's the Geekenstein twins!" or "I found Waldo!" or "Hey Buddy... Buddy and Buddy!" People would ask us if we were on our way to the chess club, if we were in a Weezer cover band or if we were headed to a Buddy Holly tribute. A few years later I compiled these insults into lyrics for a song entitled "Buddy Holly Convention."

Ska-T became as much a part of the Smugglers as the band members ourselves. As he revealed in the book *Fresh at Twenty: The Oral History of Mint Records,* "I looked so much like Beez that sometimes I would pretend I was him just to get some action. Even his wife on their wedding night, at their wedding, came up to me at one point and got us mixed up." Putting aside his near-constant horniness, Ska-T provided much-needed levity in the Smugglers van. It drove Dave a little skanky that ska tapes were added to the rotation on the stereo, but Ska-T's energy, humour and boundless positivity were a constant reminder that we finally had it pretty good.

On the sold-out Mr. T Experience tour, the Smugglers got tighter and tighter, and with rapturous crowds every night, our confidence grew. We introduced audience icebreakers like dancing and kissing contests into our shows. Once the idea for the dance contest was hatched, we'd pull over to a Value Village every week or so and buy a box full of dusty vintage trophies (bowling, surfing, curling, hockey, hunting, anything) for a couple of bucks. We'd clean them up, peel off the old plaque and glue on a new strip of paper that said DANCE CONTEST WINNER: *I shook my ass the best at the Smugglers show.* The trophies became a mainstay, and we ended up giving out hundreds of them.

WED., FEBRUARY 28
the Mr. T Experience

THE SMUGGLERS THE BREAKUPS
DAILY GRIND
3826 MAIN KCMO ALL AGES 9PM

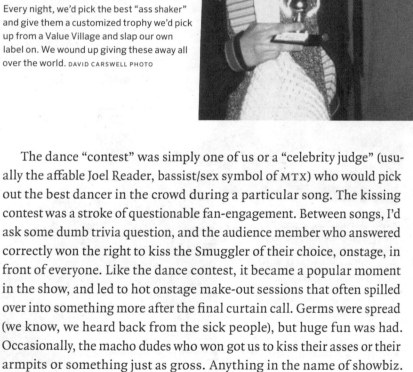

↑ In our constant quest to be entertaining, in the mid-1990s we came up with all sorts of fan engagement ideas, including the "Smugglers Smooch Dollar," which, when exchanged for an actual dollar, could be used to cash in with the Smuggler of your choice for a kiss. We ripped off the design from "Disneyland Dollars."

→ Always looking for new ways to engage with the audience, in around 1996 we introduced dance contests into our shows. Every night, we'd pick the best "ass shaker" and give them a customized trophy we'd pick up from a Value Village and slap our own label on. We wound up giving these away all over the world. DAVID CARSWELL PHOTO

The dance "contest" was simply one of us or a "celebrity judge" (usually the affable Joel Reader, bassist/sex symbol of MTX) who would pick out the best dancer in the crowd during a particular song. The kissing contest was a stroke of questionable fan-engagement. Between songs, I'd ask some dumb trivia question, and the audience member who answered correctly won the right to kiss the Smuggler of their choice, onstage, in front of everyone. Like the dance contest, it became a popular moment in the show, and led to hot onstage make-out sessions that often spilled over into something more after the final curtain call. Germs were spread (we know, we heard back from the sick people), but huge fun was had. Occasionally, the macho dudes who won got us to kiss their asses or their armpits or something just as gross. Anything in the name of showbiz. Once in Montreal, just announcing the kissing contest triggered a woman in white knee-high go-go boots to bound up and run full-speed across the stage. She dive-tackled me to the floor and shoved her tongue down my throat. I milked the moment for all it was worth, convulsing my body on the stage as if her tongue was electrocuting me. The crowd loved it.

In the middle of that Mr. T Experience winter tour, Mint Records let us know that our video for "Especially You" from *Selling the Sizzle* had gone into rotation on MuchMusic in Canada and MTV Europe, and the album was number one on Canadian national campus radio. Lookout informed us it had cracked the top-forty on the US college radio charts. A friend set up our first website, and we heard about fans getting Smugglers tattoos. We had never received so much attention.

↑ Bill Baker and Randy Iwata from Mint Records celebrating after the Smugglers video for "Especially You" entered high rotation on MuchMusic TV in Canada. NEKO CASE PHOTO

→ Joe Kirk, a fan in Philadelphia, has the audacious claim of getting the first-ever permanent Smugglers tattoo. PHOTO COURTESY JOE KIRK; TATTOO DESIGN BY CHRIS APPELGREN

thirty

Night Shift at
the Thrill Factory

THE MR. T Experience tour fabulously wound its way through places like Lawrence, Kansas, where we played an all-ages pinball palace, Rockford, Illinois, where we played an indoor skateboard bowl, and St. Louis, where we met the famed "Beatle Bob," a middle-aged tower of a man who dressed like 1964 John Lennon and maniacally danced to any song that even remotely emulated the 1960s. We were used to young punk rock promoters in each town along the route renting out just about any available space for a gig—laundromats, pet stores, storage lockers, mini-golf courses, warehouses—but our Denver concert was certainly different: it was to be held at the Raven, usually a gay disco for black men.

The Raven was located where many alternative-lifestyle nightclubs were in the cowboy states: in the industrial warehouse district on the outskirts of town. When we pulled up to the nondescript, dusty black box of a club, a far livelier scene across the street distracted us. A group of young punks on skateboards, ill-dressed for the chilly weather, momentarily defied gravity while performing nonchalant tricks off concrete steps and cinder block walls as they killed time, waiting for the gig to start.

For a movement based on non-conformity, it was surprising how prescriptive the American street punk uniform was: threadbare, ripped-up jeans held up by a black leather belt studded with rusting silver spikes. The ankle cuffs of the jeans were shoved into scuffed black combat boots or rolled up over Chuck Taylors. Ragged, often homemade T-shirts boasted band names like Death Sentence, the Swingin' Utters or the Queers. Kids strapped dog-collar choker chains around their necks, and their black leather jackets were adorned with patches and pins of punk rock royalty.

In the skater crowd of testosterone in Denver was one lone female, a tiny tempest in a black leather jacket that was too big for her four-foot-nothing frame. She wore ratty little low-top Converse sneakers, frayed jean shorts that fell just above the knee and a tight white tank top with a German Air Force logo on the front. Her hair was short, spiked and bright purple. When she walked through the skateboarders, they cleared a path.

The show that night was packed with imperfect youth. The staff behind the bar stayed busy serving soft drinks, chips and chocolate bars to the kids on one side of the bar, and booze to those over twenty-one in a roped-off area near the back of the club. It became very obvious very quickly that attendees in the drinking area were simply handing booze over the rope to those underage, if the empty beer bottles rolling around the dance floor, and the growing number of kids puking, were any indication. Our forty-minute, fifteen-song, soaking-wet set flew by.

It was after our performance that the trouble started. The bar staff had kindly given us access to a small VIP balcony overlooking the club that we could use as a changing area. When we clambered into the balcony after our set, we discovered that a dozen or so of the skate punks we had seen across the street had found their way up there and taken over our space as their own private Idaho. Most of them were sitting on our dry street clothes, which contained things like our wallets and watches.

Being Canadian, we initially tried to be as polite as possible, gingerly manoeuvring around the punks to get at our things. But they were obnoxious and defiant. A surly, bleach-blond and buff punker sitting on Beez's clothes looked like a cross between Billy Idol and Moose from the Archie Comics. Beez cordially asked the punk if he and his friends would temporarily vacate the loft so we could change. The behemoth punk refused to get up. I could feel my anger rising, and decided to give them a good ol'

I'm not exactly sure what I was reacting to here, but I was likely ducking from some flying object on a wild night in Denver, when we performed at what was usually a gay disco for African-American gentlemen. The event went right off the hook shortly after we got off stage, possibly due fully or in part to the actions of your Smugglers. JOEL READER PHOTO

Vancouver thundershower. I bent over like a wet dog and shook the sweat out of my hair, spraying it all over them.

.Unfortunately sweat wasn't the only fluid that flew from my body. If you're on a rock tour long enough, you're inevitably fighting off viruses and diseases. I had the standard-issue snotty nose, and our nightly shows tended to open the sinus cavity floodgates. When I shook my head like a soaking Littlest Hobo, a massive snot rocket launched itself from my nostril. It soared across the backstage loft like a slimy comet, landing with a splat on the bare arm of the blond guy's girlfriend. She screamed, which finally got the punks on their feet. The big blond was the angriest, and the situation quickly devolved.

The Mr. T Experience was blaring below and the girl was wailing. Beez stood his ground, demanding that they get the hell out of our balcony or there would be worse bodily fluids to come. He was nose to chest with the big punk. They begrudgingly did leave, but not before they called us a bunch of rock star assholes, along with a string of other obscenities and threats. In the confusion I hadn't realized that I slimed her with the airborne loogie, but when Beez explained that's why everyone was so upset, I was horrified and planned to find the girl and apologize. I never got the chance.

Beez got changed first, so he skipped down the stairs to see how our merchandise was selling. The big blond punk was waiting for him. "You're a fuckin' faggot!" the punk barked at Beez over the music. Beez attempted a double reverse. "Oh yeah? Well, you're kinda cute!" Backfire. The punk recoiled his ham-sized fist and slammed it directly into Beez's face. Beez's nose exploded into a bloody pulp, the punch also snapping his Buddy Holly glasses in half. He collapsed backwards onto the stairs, and his glasses tumbled in pieces into the darkness of the club. The rest of us were still upstairs and missed the whole thing, but the bartenders saw it all.

Two of them hopped over the bar and wrestled the punk to the floor in a flurry of fists, dragging him towards the door. That attracted the punk's skater pals, who entered the fray, which in turn brought on the bouncers. Ska-T witnessed everything from the merchandise stand. He flagged down the tour manager/roadie from the Mr. T Experience, a tough, no-nonsense guy named Paul, who fearlessly lunged through the crowd to find the assailant. That's when those of us still in the backstage loft noticed the growing skirmishes below. We dashed downstairs to find Beez in a bleeding heap.

By the time Paul had pushed his way through the crowd, the bouncers had thrown the main offender into the street. Paul followed, bursting from the front doors of the club right into the arms of a Denver police officer. A dozen cops were about to descend on the club for an unrelated reason: underage drinking. Paul had a few issues with the police, so he thought better of seeking vengeance for Beez. Instead, he took off down the street like Roger Bannister in his Converse All-Stars, disappearing into the Denver night.

The cops stampeded through the front doors of the black gay disco. Their presence escalated the level of punk violence inside. Denver is a cowboy town; I was freaking out that someone would pull out a gun and let hot lead fly, or set the place on fire. We had to scrape up what was left of Beez and get the hell out of there. Just moments before, the dance floor had been your typical mosh pit, no more savage than any other. Now it looked like a cross between *Road House* and the punk episode of *21 Jump*

Street. Fists and boots were flying; kids were screaming at cops; cans, bottles and chairs were airborne. The Mr. T Experience stopped playing mid-song. (Almost nothing will make a punk band stop, so you knew something was seriously wrong.)

In the eye of the fracas, I spotted the tough little skater girl with the bright purple hair. She was climbing up a stack of speakers like a spider monkey. From the top, she took a fearless flying leap as if from a high diving board, leading with her elbows. She landed on a long-haired metal head who had made the dangerous decision to cross the clique tracks to attend a punk show.

We gathered up our bloody bassist and in a five-man box busted through the riot, making a Beez-line for the side door. We grabbed Ska-T along the way and slipped outside, rushing around to the front of the building to our van. It was parked directly outside the front door of the club. After scrambling inside, Dave shouted, "All lock!" We slammed down locks, tightened windows and drew curtains. Dave hopped into the driver's seat, but the police had closed off both ends of the block. Our equipment and merchandise were still inside the disco. We hadn't even been paid yet. We popped open a couple of Coors from the cooler and hunkered down.

The cops eventually forced everyone outside, where a blood-splattered street scrap ensued. Our van was an island in the middle of a storm. We peeked through the curtains, watching the Denver cops single out the worst offenders and herd them like wild mustangs into the gaping double doors of waiting paddy wagons. Eventually, there was just one kid left.

"It's the skater girl!" blurted Bryce. We all tried to get a look. There she was with her purple hair and leather jacket, ferociously defiant in the middle of the debris-strewn street. She was staring down four advancing police officers like some sort of punk avenger. Every time one of them lunged at her, she deftly sidestepped so they were left grabbing air. Finally they cornered her against a cinder-block wall across the street. She tried in vain to climb straight up, like she had with the PA speakers, but the cops nabbed her. It took all four of them to hold her down, but she still wasn't giving up, writhing like a feral cat in all directions. They jogged her towards the paddy wagon, each cop clutching a different flailing limb. A fifth cop opened the doors just wide enough so they could throw her inside like a sixty-pound sack of potatoes, slamming the doors shut behind her. Her face immediately appeared at the grated window, teeth gnashing.

Within an hour, it was all over. Only a few cops remained, and the bartenders and bouncers of the Raven slowly emerged, as did we, desperately needing to pee. Broken glass, beer cans and a few splintered skateboards littered the street. Beez was in a bad way and would be for days. Our van had been rocked a few times by random bodies slamming against it, but it was fine. Paul, the Mr. T Experience roadie, emerged from the shadows. We stood around wondering how the hell that had all happened so quickly. Had Beez started a punk rock riot? Had I?

Bright headlights illuminated the battle zone. A late-model BMW purred into sight and pulled up beside us. The tinted driver's side window slid down to reveal a tanned middle-aged man in a suit. "Is there a music concert here tonight?" he asked cautiously.

"There was, but it's been over for a while now," I answered.

A look of panic crossed his face. "I was told explicitly that the concert would end at midnight. I'm here to pick up my daughter. She has bright purple hair. Have you seen her?"

THE TOUR WITH the Mr. T Experience wrapped up a few days after Denver. We paused our touring just long enough for Beez's nuptials back in Vancouver, then we were straight back out on the road, where Selling the Sizzle would take on a new meaning.

thirty-one

Groovy Underwear

TO GET TO Hoboken, New Jersey, you took the last exit in the Garden State, right before the Lincoln Tunnel, and drove down a narrow underpass. In the late summer, it was overrun with an explosion of vines, creepers and weeds seeping through the tiniest cracks of the stone and concrete walls, Mother Nature slowly taking back what was hers.

We burst back into the sunshine and rolled onto Washington Street, Hoboken's main drag. Citizens moved slowly along the sidewalk, fanning themselves with folded newspapers and hats in the Labour Day weekend heat. As usual, the odour hit us right away. Although Hoboken is famous for being the birthplace of Frank Sinatra, baseball and Maxwell House Coffee (which the club was named after), the town smelled predominantly like a porta-potty at the end of a music festival, something to do with Hoboken's storm drains and sewage combined in the same pipes. On hot summer days the smell hung in the air like a fart in a car. Many Hoboken citizens seemed to consider this the comforting scent of home and took offence if you brought it up, which we did repeatedly.

The hospitality at Maxwell's was incredible compared to many of the venues we played in the United States. We had played there with the Mekons the first time, and while they were rightfully pissed off that we

In our signature rubber boots, rocking the stage at Coney Island High in New York City in 1996 for a Lookout Records showcase that featured such luminaries in the audience as Joey Ramone and Lemmy from Motörhead.

LISA MARR PHOTO

GROUP PHOTO! Members of the Smugglers, the Mr. T Experience, the Groovie Ghoulies, Pansy Division and cub all gather outside Coney Island High. Also pictured: Ronnie Barnett from the Muffs (pointing at face) and Tim "Lint" Armstrong from Rancid (far right). NICK THOMAS PHOTO drank their Rolling Rock beer rider in the Prohibition-era stone basement below the club that served as the backstage, they didn't make too big a stink about it, and we all partied late into the night. A hot-to-trot waitress insisted on initiating us into Maxwell's rock 'n' roll lore by convincing Nick to allow her to rip off his boxer shorts with her teeth. She performed the trick with aplomb, deftly tossing Nick's shredded gonch up alongside many other pairs hanging from the antlers of a stuffed and forlorn buck mounted high above the bar.

By Labour Day weekend 1996, we had played Maxwell's several times. The CMJ Music Marathon, a massive convention in next-door New York, was in full swing. Thousands of bands converged on the yearly event, and we were due to play the Lookout Showcase at Coney Island High amongst a star-studded lineup of the Queers, the Mr. T Experience, Pansy Division, cub and the label's new signees, the Groovie Ghoulies. It turned out to be a huge event, with luminaries like Joey Ramone, Lemmy from Motörhead and Tim "Lint" Armstrong from Rancid in attendance.

The night before that mega-show, we squeezed in a gig across the river at Maxwell's, opening up for Pansy Division and cub. A lot of the places we played were firetraps: small dark rooms with no windows stuffed with people. Fire alarms went off all the time at our gigs, but they were always false alarms. So when we heard the clanging alarm after our set at Maxwell's, I was shocked to hear Dave exclaim, "Dudes, this is real! We gotta get out of here, now! Maxwell's is on fire!"

```
Wednesday, September 4, 1996
Maxwell's
Hoboken, New Jersey

It was great to be back at our favourite club
in America to sell the sizzle, but little did
we know how far Maxwell's was going to take
our performance credo. Shortly after we had
struck our final blazing chord, we retreated
to the upstairs backstage room. While cub
were hurriedly setting up to take advantage
of the heated crowd, a cook came running
```

into the venue, arms in the air, screaming,
"FIRE! FIRE! EVERYWHERE, FIRE!"

Everyone inside the club—musicians and
gig-goers alike—piled out into the side
street as smoke poured out from the kitchen,
into the venue and out the now-broken windows.
Soon fire trucks roared up and were spraying
the fire down, trying to gain control. All
Lisa from cub was able to grab before they
hustled her off stage and out the side door
was her black Fender bass.

In the meantime, your Smugglers had nestled
ourselves upstairs, busy getting changed
and drinking cub's beer rider (this used to
be our friend Betty's apartment but now it's
used as Maxwell's band dressing room). We
heard the really loud, old-fashioned fire
bell ringing out but we didn't budge. Then we
were suddenly engulfed with smoke and heard
sirens. We freaked out, grabbed a couple
more of cub's cold ones, then ran down the
smoke-filled, ancient wooden staircase. I was
clad only in T-shirt, white socks and towel
wrapped around my waist as I joined the rest
of the two hundred disgruntled gig patrons
in the street.

After about forty-five embarrassing
minutes of standing in the street in a towel
and socks, I did a really dumb thing. I
decided the fire had died down enough to
re-enter the building to finish changing.
I slipped under the yellow ribbon when the
firemen weren't looking, dashed up the stairs
and into the backstage room. The room was
still choked in smoke but I managed to get
changed, grab another couple of now-warm

When Maxwell's in Hoboken, New Jersey, caught fire, I was caught changing in the band room. I had to spend a long time in the street in a T-shirt, towel and socks.
CHRIS FREEMAN PHOTO

beers and get back down to the street. As I was dashing out of the building, a fireman spotted me and yelled, "HEY! WHERE'D YOU COME FROM?"

I lamely tried to explain my way out of it, but he was furious, yelling at me in front of everyone. He told me the building was still unsafe and could have easily reignited with me inside. I felt like a complete idiot. Thankfully no one was hurt and we eventually got all of our stuff out unscathed, but all the T-shirts smell like a campfire. On the plus side, cub has learned to never try headlining over us again! Just like when Jerry Lee Lewis found out he had to open for Chuck Berry so he set his piano on fire during the last song!

After the fire, Maxwell's was sadly shuttered for the foreseeable future, making the Smugglers the last band to perform there for many months. Todd Abramson was devastated, though true to his nature he still paid all three bands.

A few nights after the Maxwell's fire, we met up with Lookout's popular New England punk rock band the Queers, embarking together on a six-week American touring odyssey that would pogo us from coast to coast. The Queers were one of our favourite groups from the Lookout stable: an awesome, rough and ready band, blending sixties bubblegum pop with the punk sneer of the Dead Boys and the black leather jacket blitzkrieg bop of the Ramones.

Their lead singer and guitarist was Joe Queer, a cantankerous enigma and pop-punk purist who seemed to either love or hate every moment of touring, depending on the situation. Joe had owned and operated Joe's Place, a restaurant in Portsmouth, New Hampshire, before turning to music full-time. It proved to be a good move: through his snarling, snotty vocals, he could really sing and he penned some anthemic, controversial and self-deprecating tunes. Packed dance floors would erupt into slamming sing-alongs to tunes like "Born to Do Dishes," "Fuck the World (I'm Hanging Out with You Tonight)," "Punk Rock Girls" and "I Met Her at the Rat." Despite their name, the Queers were not a gay group. On the contrary, some of the controversy surrounding the band involved accusations of lyrical misogyny. (The Queers were pretty much the exact opposite of Pansy Division, who claimed to be the world's first openly gay rock band.)

On bass for the Queers was B-Face, a brooding young punk with spiky blond hair and an omnipresent glare who, under his tough exterior, was a surprisingly nice guy. On second guitar was a temporary member, a stocky, friendly dude named Erick. On drums was Hugh O'Neill, one of the best drummers we'd witnessed since Tad Hutchison of the Young Fresh Fellows. Offsetting Joe Queer's onstage growl and B-Face's false malevolence, Hugh often performed with a huge smile plastered across his face, as if there was no place he'd rather be. He had a brash sense of humour and joie de vivre that was infectious to be around.

Both Hugh and Joe battled various substance addictions. During our US tour with them, the Queers were keeping a "clean" backstage—no booze or drugs allowed in their dressing room. Since Adam Woodall and Paul Preminger left the Smugglers, drugs had all but vanished from our day-to-day touring scene, but we definitely loved our beer and any other alcohol we were offered. A clean backstage was a tough order, but the Queers were headlining and we had to respect their wishes. Joe seemed to appreciate the positivity our band brought to the shows, and the Queers enjoyed hearing our road stories. Joe Queer in particular loved playing poker with Beez late into the night after the gigs—and Beez loved taking Joe's money.

After two weeks of pinballing around the northeastern USA with the Queers to packed houses, we finally reached the Great Plains where, just like Joe Queer's mood, hot blue skies could spin into gathering black clouds within minutes. We'd race our vans alongside lightning storms that overtook us with battering hail and rain only to be sunny and dry again within minutes. Fields of towering corn flanked us like armies as we rolled westward convoy-style with the Queers, towards the sunset and the next show. In Minnesota, Land of Ten Thousand Lakes, we were so close to Canada we could taste the wheat field soul in the early fall air.

It felt good to be back in the wide open spaces and out of the Rust Belt, with its tangled cloverleaf highways leading to dirty, exhausted mega cities of industry. We were in recovery mode from massive gigs with the Queers in Cincinnati, Detroit, Philadelphia and Washington, DC. Driving into Minnesota, we were coming off one of our best nights ever, in an unlikely venue called the Concert Café in Green Bay, Wisconsin. Green Bay had become a new Smugglers' hotspot, thanks to "Time Bomb" Tom, a bombastic local promoter who took a shine to the showmanship of our band. We would break many a merchandise record in this rock 'n' roll party town.

The Smugglers were by now practised in the rhythm of touring, most of us eating badly at whatever cookie-cutter fast food dump was within a two-minute trudging radius of the gas station or truck stop we had pulled into. Dave was way ahead of his time on the bottled-water-and-salad thing, and he chastised me for my pit-stop drinks which alternated between beer, Pepsi, beer, Mountain Dew and beer. All of us were tanned and weathered from weeks under the sun, showering only when it was available.

The fans who filled the front rows were singing along to our songs. The merchandise figures Ska-T handed Beez at the end of each sweat-soaked night climbed and climbed. The van was home: we were most comfortable and most content feeling the road underneath our feet, reading and swapping endless music biographies, listening to our homemade cassettes on rotation on the stereo and playing cards, chess or Scrabble. Every once in a while, we'd pull over to cool off in a lake and watch Nick swim like a fish while the rest of us gingerly tiptoed in. We were figuring out how to be a team and how to act as one, on and off the stage. Most of it came down to mutual respect, diplomacy and good humour, something it had taken me many thousands of kilometres to figure out.

As long as we were laughing, we were having a good time. Stories were told and retold, each retelling wilder than the last. Dave still did spot-on impressions of the promoters and band members in our wake, which never failed to crack us up. Beez told us ridiculous stories from different times in his life, like the year he gallivanted around Europe wearing short shorts, cowboy boots, a moustache and a fedora, chased by machine gun–wielding border guards in Morocco and coerced by a gay Italian couple to dress up in a sultan costume and be their live-in boy toy.

Each of us had our duties and our roles to play. Dave proved himself time and again as a tireless warrior with a steering wheel. Beez did the books and made friends with a social rainbow of Americans everywhere we roamed. With a few notable exceptions, he was our ambassador. Bryce was our walking encyclopedia of American underground music, briefing us on the musical style, bios, record label affiliation and background of each band we were playing with. He also remembered the first and last names of every member of every one of those bands.

Nick was our even keel, never too high and never too low, never argumentative or confrontational, and hugely helpful in keeping the despotic leader in me in line. Through thick and thin, Nick was a beacon of hope and good vibes for all of us. He was our shutterbug documentarian too, his camera always in reach. Nick also loaded and unloaded the van at every gig in exactly the same way, with Tetris-like skill. That was even more impressive at the end of the night, when Nick was often as loaded as the van itself. Besides selling merchandise, Ska-T tirelessly lugged our equipment in and out of the venues, and he made sure we never forgot anything, anywhere, thanks to his sweeping "idiot checks." No matter what the weather, he volunteered to sleep in the van in sketchy neighbourhoods to make sure our vehicle stayed safe. He also kept us in constant stitches with his extremely dirty jokes.

I sat exhausted in the passenger seat with the road atlas open on my lap, mostly worrying about making the next show or trying to avoid an argument with Dave or Beez. But whenever I paused long enough to stop fretting about van breakdowns or band breakups, I'd gaze out the window at passing America and remember that we were living our dream.

thirty-two

Bastards of Young

WE WERE SAVING money wherever we could, so we frequently asked from the stage if anyone was willing to let us sleep in their home. The bands we toured with, like the Mr. T Experience and the Queers, always stayed in hotels. They thought we were crazy for putting ourselves out there like that. Sure enough, we ended up staying with so many bona fide nutcases that we were forced to add caveats from the microphone, like no psychopaths, no punk rock pets and no illegal arms dealers. Oftentimes we'd have multiple offers, so we arranged quick, private discussions as to which invitation seemed like the safest bet. We lost a lot of those bets.

Sleeping at the homes of random fans definitely had its extremes. In Green Bay we stayed at a rancher-style house that was completely decked out for Christmas, including a twelve-foot, sparkling Christmas tree surrounded by wrapped gifts in a sunken shag-carpeted living room—in September. According to the teenaged girl who invited us to stay, that's the way her parents kept their home all year long. Okay.

In Bellingham we stayed with a friendly, drunken, end-of-show guy who turned out to be selling contraband guns out of his place. We should have known something was up when we entered his heavily barricaded home. There weren't too many indie music fans whose houses were surrounded by an eight-foot-high barbed wire fence, or whose kitchen and living room walls were decorated with catalogue posters of assault rifles and automatic pistols. He was all too eager to share his collection with us, pulling out handgun after contraband handgun, allowing us to pass them amongst ourselves to feel their weight and power. It scared the hell out of us. Dave refused to touch them.

Punk rock pets were a drag. Certain punks loved taking on pets whether they could look after them or not, extending their anarchist beliefs to their pet care. In Albuquerque, we stayed in a tiny apartment where rabbits hopped about freely. (Beez woke up thinking he had mistakenly gone to bed with an earplug still in from the show the night before, only to realize rabbit shit had somehow wedged into his ear during the night.) We slept in homes with pot-bellied pigs running loose in Oklahoma City, and with territorial asshole cats that purposefully pissed on our clothes and sleeping bags in Fargo. We slept in immediate proximity to punk rock iguanas, llamas, guinea pigs, chickens, fish and, in Spokane, even a horse.

In Memphis, we stayed at the house attached to the famed Shangri-La Records, where I was humped in the face all night long by a horny little black poodle named Bobo. The most common traits amongst punk rock pet owners were their gleeful ignorance about how obnoxious their pets were and their nose-blindness to the stench within their homes. But hey, still, thanks for having us!

One of our wildest nights was in Boston, when we stayed with "Metal Murph." A one-time Queer and member of the Cretins, he came out of the Cambridge night like an answer from a prayer to Satan, supposedly offering us safe haven. Put it this way: our sleeping quarters resembled a cross between the set of Wayne's World and the trash compactor from Star Wars. Then he let on about his idea of an all-night jam. "No way, Murph!" Beez replied. "We're going straight to bed! No jamming!"

Since music was out, Murph and two bickering buddies decided to order up some hookers for us. Ignoring our urgent protests, they called an escort service and made the arrangements. While we waited with nervous anticipation, Murph and his buddies offered us triangular blue pills, which we politely refused. All the more for them, it turned out. They gobbled up all of the "Vitamin K," also known as ketamine, a horse tranquilizer. According to Murph, before it knocked you out, you'd get an aphrodisiac rush that would make Ron Jeremy blush.

The hookers thankfully never materialized, and Metal Murph was now unable to move from his beanbag chair. He managed to call a female friend on speed dial to come over and have sex with us in exchange for Vitamin K. Those of us still awake yelled that we didn't want anything to do with his friend, but within five minutes she had arrived. Nick, who had fallen asleep an hour earlier, woke up to her straddling him. A moment later, a dozen of Murph's friends burst through the basement door in search of a party. Beez was furious, sitting bolt upright in his sleeping bag and yelling at everybody to shut up and get out. They ignored him and partied all around us as we lay on the disgusting carpet in our sleeping bags. Eventually, Beez caved. "Oh, fuck it," he growled. From a sitting position, still in his sleeping bag, he grabbed an acoustic guitar. Soon he was leading everyone in a surreal sunrise singalong of Sugar Ray songs.

Occasionally we'd be lucky enough to stay with extended family in places like Dallas, New York, Winnipeg or Sheffield, or we'd meet someone amazing who would open their home to us and remain friends with the band for years. Many of these folks had tiny apartments in university districts, but sometimes the fan was either really rich or somehow looking after a huge mansion. We would all get our own rooms and our own beds; we could do laundry, eat, drink and swim in the pool. If this lined up with a day off the next day, all the better; we wouldn't budge. Glamorous mansions were an extreme rarity, of course. Most of the time, it was punk rock dives swarming with filthy animals.

IN MINNEAPOLIS WE met a tribe living out a nomadic dream that made our van-touring look positively pedestrian. After our show with the Queers at the 7th St Entry, we were invited to stay at a once-grand, century-old, sprawling home that had devolved into a decrepit punk rock squat. At least twenty transient punks lived there at any given time, spread throughout the many rooms of the four-storey home like roaches. Over the course of our American touring, we had come across a variety of punk rock subcultures: garage rockers in Seattle, riot grrrls in Olympia and DC, surf punks in California, skinheads in Lafayette and mohawked crusties at all-ages shows everywhere. The vagabonds in the Minneapolis mansion were something altogether different.

Tacked to the main wall in their squalid living room was a gigantic map of America, but it was unlike any we had seen. It contained great arching red, blue and green lines that stemmed mostly out of Chicago, like veins from a heart, to all other extremities of the country. We couldn't figure it out until one punk, crumpled in the corner like yesterday's papers, noticed Dave and me staring at it. He introduced himself as Tommy Trouble. "That there's a map of every railway freight route in the goddamn country," he explained in a southern drawl. "Helen Wheels stole it." He nodded towards a woman in a combat jacket covered in spikes who was sinking into an old couch. "We hop trains."

We were staying with a drifter community of modern-day train-hoppers. These were railway punks: guys and girls who climbed aboard freight trains and rode them for free and illegally, all over the continent. Dave and I listened in complete fascination to their current-day stories of hopping into boxcars in the pitch-black night, in freezing winter temperatures or in scorching summer heat.

At first, Helen explained, the railway punks didn't know where the train would take them, or where they had woken up when it finally screeched to a stop. After a few years, they figured out the routes with the help of maps like the one we were staring at. The punks wove stories of falling from trains, being caught by "the bulls" (railway security), not eating for days, climbing into the wrong boxcar and facing violence from other drifters who had already claimed it, and the ultimate feeling of freedom that riding the rails brought them. "Once the train really gets going, once it gets you out of the cesspool of the city railyards, which are terrible places, once you get way out in the open country on those trains, where there's no roads and no people, it's just beautiful scenery and wildlife," extolled Helen excitedly, while snorting some sort of white powder off a grimy coffee table. "It's the greatest way to travel and it's completely free."

It was also a felony. Train-hopping involved trespassing on private federal property and crossing state lines, but more often than not, getting caught resulted not in charges, but a beating or worse instead, Helen added. "The bulls know it's a waste of time to call the cops on us, so they try to teach us a lesson by kicking the shit out of us." As if on cue, another punk emerged from a dark corner of the living room. One whole side of his face looked like an eggplant. Helen pointed a black fingernail at the welt: "A bull's leather blackjack did that."

By listening to hours of outrageous train stories and asking many follow-up questions, we passed some test we weren't aware we were taking. Tommy Trouble put forth an offer: one of the Smugglers could stay in the attic, one of the only private rooms in the mansion. Tommy led the way, first up the once-grand, winding staircase, then up a series of smaller and smaller stairs, until finally, at the top of a fourth rickety set, he opened a door into a room just big enough for a single bed. At the foot of the bed was a television and a top-loader VCR. Stacked around the TV was a selection of porno videotapes. At the head of the bed, on a bedside table, was a TV remote, a box of Kleenex and a large Gatorade bottle half full of a thick, oozing, translucent goo.

Tommy casually explained the bottle was a collection of sorts made by the many different train-hoppers who had stayed in that room over several months. If any of the Smugglers wanted to stay in that room, he explained, that member would be expected to "sign the guest book," as it were, by watching a porno and adding to the collection by masturbating into the Gatorade bottle. Our hosts' dream, for whatever perverse purpose, was to fill the bottle right to the top. Apparently the room at the top of the stairs was known throughout the railway-punk community as "The Jizz Chamber."

Our roadie Ska-T finally broke the silence. "Well, good night, fellas!" And with that, Ska-T stepped into the Jizz Chamber and closed the door behind him.

thirty-three

Not Fade Away

WE WERE ON the outskirts of Clear Lake, Iowa, on a very rare day off from our tour with the Queers, which gave us the chance to continue following Buddy Holly from cradle to grave. On an earlier tour we had played a laundromat in Holly's hometown of Lubbock, Texas, and visited the Buddy Holly statue. What started in Lubbock came crashing down for Buddy Holly in Clear Lake in the early hours of February 3, 1959, barely two years after the release of his first hit single.

Hours earlier he had famously performed at the Surf Ballroom in Clear Lake along with J.P. "The Big Bopper" Richardson and Ritchie Valens, as part of the "Winter Dance Party Tour." The "winter tour" part lived up to the billing: it was a taxing grind of long drives and nightly shows across the frozen Midwest, sometimes in a bus with no heating system. Buddy Holly decided to charter a flight after the Clear Lake show to fly him and his band to the next show in Fargo, North Dakota. That way he could avoid the ten-hour bus ride, catch up on sleep and do his laundry, which he hadn't been able to do since the tour began ten days earlier.

The minuscule plane had four seats, one reserved for the twenty-one-year-old pilot, the other three for Buddy Holly and his band. Buddy's drummer was off the tour, recovering from frostbitten feet incurred on the bus, so the seats would go to Buddy, his guitarist and his bassist. But the Big Bopper, who was completely flu-ridden, convinced Buddy's bassist to give him his seat on the plane. That bassist was none other than future country star Waylon Jennings. Joking around before the flight, Buddy said to Waylon, "I hope your ol' bus freezes up." Waylon was quick to retort, "Yeah, well, I hope your ol' plane crashes." You can imagine how he felt about that offhand remark for decades to come. Ritchie Valens had wanted in on the flight, too. He challenged Buddy's guitarist to a back-stage coin toss for the final seat, which Valens won.

The little plane took off shortly after the gig at 12:55 a.m. in light snow. It didn't get far. Within minutes of takeoff, the plane spiralled into a horrific, full-speed crash in a nearby cornfield, skidding onto the frozen ground at an angle that caused the plane to cartwheel multiple times, ripping apart the fuselage and throwing bodies in all directions. The wreckage came to rest in a wire fence. Everyone was killed. The Big Bopper was twenty-eight, Buddy Holly twenty-two, the pilot twenty-one and Ritchie Valens just seventeen years old. An investigation later concluded the inexperienced pilot had likely misread the instruments in the aircraft and become disoriented in the snow. By the time the bodies were found the next morning, they were frozen stiff in the sub-zero temperatures. The tragedy made headlines around the world, and is often cited as "The Day the Music Died": the end of the first wave of rock 'n' roll.

The Queers had almost as much interest in rock 'n' roll history as we did, so together we not only easily found the spectacular and perfectly preserved art-deco Surf Ballroom in Clear Lake but were able to walk right in through the unlocked front doors and wander around the empty, pristine hall. It was like we had stepped back in time, entering into some sort of sacred space with its rounded ceiling, shiny hardwood dance floor, neatly arranged booths and tiki-themed stage. The Smugglers and the Queers loved to loudly joke around with each other, but while we were in the Surf Ballroom, we remained hushed, all of us imagining the Final Show.

There was an old black pay phone on the wall with a plaque that stated Buddy Holly and Ritchie Valens had used it to make what would be their final phone calls. After a while, a staff member showed up and kicked us out, but not before she asked if we were a Buddy Holly tribute band. Outside the front door of the Surf Ballroom, we posed for a picture beside a musical tombstone-type monument that paid tribute to the three musicians. Then we wanted to find the crash site. Hugh went back and asked the woman who had kicked us out, who sketched out a map on the back of one of our old gig posters. Joe Queer and B-Face weren't interested, so we dropped them off at the hotel and continued.

The Queers' van kicked up clouds of dust in front of us on the gravel road, fishtailing around right-angled corners left, right, then left again. Leafy green cornfields lined both sides of the road, giving us the sense that we were inside a maze and could lose the Queers around any corner. Gravel pelted our front grille like bullets. Abruptly, their van skidded to a stop alongside a six-foot-high cornfield.

Erick leaned out of the driver's side window, waving away the billowing dust. He yelled back to us, "Tune your radio to 650 AM!" We did as instructed. Ritchie Valens's "La Bamba" blasted out of our van's speakers in sync with those in the other van. Both bands cranked their stereos to maximum volume. Hugh jumped out of the van ahead with a huge grin on his face, hands in the air in the devil rock salute. He shouted at us in a Boston accent as thick as a pint of Guinness, "THIS HAS TO BE IT! THE SONG IS A SIGN, MAN! THIS HAS TO BE THE FIELD!" The rest of us piled out.

As we glanced around at the wall of corn, Erick grabbed Hugh's arm and nodded towards the tips of the cornrows. "Hughbie. Is that what I think it is?" Telltale serrated leaves lofted lazily just above the top row of corn, having grown just tall enough to be seen from the road.

"Holy... mother... of... Christ," Hugh whispered. Erick and Hugh disappeared between the stalks of corn. Within seconds, we heard Hugh break into maniacal laughter, followed by "YES! OH, YES! OH, THANK YOU, RITCHIE VALENS! THANK YOU BUDDY FUCKIN' HOLLY! OH FUCK, YES!" The rest of us crashed forward, following the sound of Hugh's voice. We found him on his knees in the dirt in a small clearing, grasping at the stalks of the plants. It took me a few seconds to figure it out.

"What is it, what's going on?" I asked Ska-T.

"This ain't corn, you moron."

"Holy shit," added Nick.

"This is a marijuana grow-op in the middle of an Iowa cornfield," Ska-T declared.

When visiting the Surf Ballroom in Clear Lake, Iowa, we were once again asked if we were a Buddy Holly tribute band.

DAVID CARSWELL PHOTO

"Grab what you can, and let's get the fuck out of Iowa!" yelled Hugh. Erick, Hugh and Ska-T harvested half the grow-op within seconds. Each clutched fistfuls of Midwest Mary Jane. "BACK TO THE VANS! RUN!" shouted Hugh. We ploughed through the cornfield, following the strains of the oldies station still playing in the vans, which had moved on to the Surfaris instrumental "Wipe Out!"—the wild drum fills adding to our urgency. We leapt into the vans and took off, leaving a trail of dust clouds.

When we pulled over to catch our breath at a nearby gas station, the gas jockey told us about a ten-foot-high, eight-foot-wide sculpture of a pair of black Buddy Holly–style glasses installed right by the roadside at the crash site. We definitely had not seen it. No matter. We didn't mention the grow-op to the gas jockey, but we convinced ourselves that the marijuana patch was the right field, and that Ritchie Valens had indeed given us a sign. When we met up with Joe Queer and B-Face back at the hotel, neither of them believed the story.

"This is such bullshit!" shouted B-Face.

"Gimme a break," snarled Joe. "That never happened."

"Oh, really?" answered Hugh. "Then how do you explain this?" B-Face's jaw hung loose and Joe's cat-like eyes widened when Hugh pulled open some dresser drawers to reveal what B-Face later described as "absolutely the biggest bud I have ever seen in my life outside of an issue of *High Times* magazine." There were all sorts of buds and leaves spread out in the drawers on toilet paper, in an effort to dry the marijuana out and keep it away from prying eyes.

"As a rule, I never smoked weed," B-Face told me later. "I hated it. Hated the smell, hated the feeling, but the gods of rock 'n' roll had preordained that I was to partake of that herb, and who am I to argue with the gods? I got stoned out of my skull, and it was great!"

We must have angered the rock gods too, since a wicked storm blew up over Clear Lake that night. We couldn't help but imagine it was much like the one that had downed the plane. The storm gained such velocity that it knocked out power to the town—the one night that the Smugglers had allowed ourselves the luxury of a hotel room. As the rain pounded down outside, flooding the streets, we sat in pitch-black darkness on our only night off on the tour, the sole light being the cherry from the joint containing what we affectionately code-named "Buddy's Bud."

TOURING HAD NEVER been better. During the fun but demanding Queers trek, we found out the Smugglers been offered tours in Japan and Europe. Both Lookout and Mint were eager to follow up on the success of *Selling the Sizzle*. Everything seemed perfect, which is when things tend to even out in rock 'n' roll.

A week after we'd returned to Vancouver, Beez asked me out for dinner at Martini's, our long-time favourite restaurant. As we chowed down on veggie lasagna, he emotionally informed me he was quitting the Smugglers. I was gutted. Ever since he climbed into our crappy VW camper van to brave the blizzards of Saskatchewan, we had depended heavily on Beez, not only as a skilled bass player, backup singer and showman, but as an emissary, negotiator, accountant and, most importantly, a trusted friend and confidant.

Beez had hit a crossroads. He was thirty-four, broke and recently married, and it disturbed him that he was getting older and our fans were getting younger. Beez felt the need to settle down and do something "serious" with his life. The tele-dating company he had started years earlier was rapidly expanding, and domestic life suddenly seemed sexy—at least more attractive than sleeping on floors throughout North America, soaking his clothes with sweat or worse every night, being sick all the time and getting punched in the face in Denver for his trouble. He needed a change of pace, he hated our matching pink polka-dot shirts ("I'm not a dancing clown!") and he thought his needs would clash with full-time membership in the band.

Beez's biggest concern, he explained, was that he would slow the Smugglers down as we were finally finding sustained success. It was impossible for me to ignore the irony in his reasoning, since forcing us to take a break while searching for a replacement bassist would do nothing but slow us down. To his credit, during a negotiation as hot as Martini's baked lasagna, Beez agreed to accompany us on our upcoming trip to Japan, which would turn out to be everything he loved about touring, and an epic six-week tour of Europe, which would be everything he hated.

PART

3

SUSHI
AND
SQUATS

thirty-four

Diode City

I F WE WEREN'T going to get famous through rock 'n' roll, or write a genuine hit song, the Smugglers were at least going to try and see the world. Even flying way under the mainstream radar, there were some pretty great benefits to being in a band. After the records and fans and friends we had made, the greatest perk was the opportunity to visit pockets of the planet we would otherwise likely never have seen, be that Tuscaloosa, Toulouse or Tokyo.

A Canadian ex-pat music promoter living in Tokyo had sent us an email showing interest in bringing the Smugglers to the Land of the Rising Sun. Molly from Lookout was trying to get the Queers over there, and the Smugglers had remained in touch with a very cool, all-women Japanese band called Supersnazz after we had played with them in Vancouver years earlier. After much manoeuvring, a triple bill in the enchanted and mysterious country of our dreams somehow came together in mid-December 1996. A nine-hour flight took us across the Pacific. When we landed in Tokyo we were met by a massive throng of screaming fans. It turned out Michael Jackson was also expected to be arriving in Tokyo at any minute. We passed through the mob unnoticed.

We found the Queers slumped over their guitar and drum cases near the baggage claim. If we thought our jet-setting was exciting, they were in the middle of a world tour, circumnavigating the globe on the strength of punk rock. After they wrapped up their USA fall tour with us a few months earlier, they had gone straight to Europe for six weeks. From there they had flown from Amsterdam to Bangkok for a few days. Now they were in Tokyo for our tour. It was great to be reunited, but they looked like they had the miles of the world gathered under their eyes. We were not quite sure what had happened during those lost few days in Thailand, but drummer Hugh O'Neill was so out of it he resembled a punk rock Ronald Reagan—all pink and deflated, his black, spiky hair hardened over in a two-day crust. A few minutes later, Chris Appelgren from Lookout bounded out to join us. A constant force of boyish energy, Chris had always been fascinated with Japanese pop culture, art and gadgetry. With two Lookout bands headed over, he jumped at the chance to join us in Japan for the tour.

Luckily for all of us, we didn't have to play the night of our arrival. After meeting the tour manager and his driver buddy, we climbed into two vans and began the six-hour drive down the island of Honshu to the city of Nagoya, where our first show was booked for the following night. It was dark by the time we set out, and the drive was a non-stop barrage of brightly lit billboards and neon signs glaring through our dirty windshield. We noticed an odd assortment of North American celebrities splashed across the billboards, advertising products they weren't associated with at home: Michael J. Fox posing with a fishing rod and reel, Kevin Costner with a vacuum cleaner and Tommy Lee Jones with Japan's omnipresent Boss canned coffee. Our eyes were also drawn to the illumination inside many of the cars around us: TV screens built into dashboards, visors and seat backs. Japanese people watched everything from game shows to pornos in their cars.

Our arrival at the shoebox Nagoya hotel began what would be a series of non-stop culture shocks. The lobby was the size of a broom closet. The extremely elderly couple who ran the hotel naturally didn't speak any English; they did a lot of yelling at us in Japanese, complemented with wild, violent gestures. First they forced us to take off our shoes and boots at the front door and put on slippers. Next the elderly man urgently gestured for us to follow him. He led Dave by the hand up a winding staircase while the rest of us followed with guitars and suitcases. Our destination

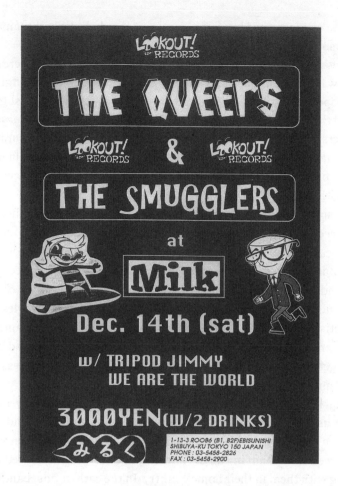

was a windowless room without a stick of furniture. Instead, six thin futons covered every inch of the bamboo-thatched floor. We were each handed a blanket and a small, beanbag-type sack to use as a pillow.

The owner started yelling again, indicating that we weren't to wear our hallway slippers in the bedroom. The bedroom was for bare feet or socks only. The ancient fellow then showed us the communal bathroom at the end of the hall. That was our introduction to the Japanese toilet, a miniature urinal laid on its back and embedded into the floor. To our horror, we were expected to squat over this contraption. The owner ignored me when I asked about a second option with a seat. He was too busy screaming at me for wearing my hall slippers into the bathroom. (At the bathroom door you were expected to switch into a pair of red plastic bathroom-only slippers.)

We were all spared jet lag except for Dave and Chris. They were both wide awake at six a.m. By seven a.m. they had decided to stop fighting it, whispering to those of us awake by then that they were "just going around the corner for a cup of coffee." We considered ourselves seasoned travellers and didn't think anything of it. The rest of us got up hours later and went for a brunch meeting with the tour manager. We were in Japan, and the first restaurant he took us to was Denny's. The meeting came and went with no sign of Dave or Chris.

We spent the day wandering around Nagoya, a massive, heaving city sliced up by grey streets choked with cars and people. The vending machines found on every corner were endlessly fascinating. You could buy just about anything from these machines, right there on the street: beer, wine and hard liquor, cell phones, entire bouquets of flowers, canned coffee, umbrellas, toasted sandwiches, fresh eggs, tubes of Pringles, diarrhea fetish videos and all types of underwear, from bras and panties to boxers and edible briefs. There was still no sighting of Dave and Chris. It was getting late in the afternoon and we were concerned. It was completely unlike Dave to disappear.

Soon it was time to meet up at the hotel, where Supersnazz were waiting for us. It was fantastic to see them again, and a relief to find some Japanese people we could communicate with. It was two years since we had played with them in North America, and we were honoured to be touring with them in their home country. In the early 1990s, bands like Shonen Knife and Supersnazz were at the vanguard of a Japanese invasion of remarkable garage and punk bands into the North American scene. When Supersnazz (who took their name from a Flamin' Groovies album) showed up in Seattle wearing American flag dresses and blasting out their Nippon interpretation of American rock 'n' roll, they became an underground sensation and were quickly signed to Sub Pop Records. Following Shonen Knife and Supersnazz to our shores were other awesome Japanese bands, like Teengenerate (naming themselves after a Dictators song), Jackie and the Cedrics, the 5.6.7.8's, Guitar Wolf and the Lottie Collins, among others. All of them ended up on American labels. Shonen Knife made the most impact early on, finding fans in everyone from Kurt

Members of the Queers, Teengenerate and the Smugglers hanging out backstage at the ironically named Club Gigantic in Tokyo. Left to right: Fifi, Joe Queer, Grant, Fink, Dave, Bryce. We were blown away that the audience in Japan sang along to the songs from our album *Selling the Sizzle*. NICK THOMAS PHOTO

Cobain to John Peel—but it was the 5.6.7.8's who landed an onscreen performance in Quentin Tarantino's *Kill Bill*.

The members of Supersnazz were exceptionally gracious, kind and welcoming. Tomoko, their bassist, was the only member fluent in English, and proved to be a life-saver for us time and time again. The band showed concern when we explained about our lost bandmate and label rep. We loaded up the vans, and away we went to the Diamond Hall—without Dave and Chris.

By 6:45 p.m., nearly twelve hours since we had last seen or heard from Dave, our tour manager was out driving around, searching the streets. We had an emergency band meeting backstage where we agreed that if Dave and Chris didn't show up by seven p.m., I would call the cops. After a pensive fifteen minutes, I left the dressing room to find Tomoko, who said we could use her cell phone. At that precise moment, just one hour before the Smugglers' debut performance in Japan, an exhausted and thoroughly freaked-out Dave and Chris stumbled in through the door-way of the club. Both were near tears. Dave collapsed onto the backstage couch. Nick handed him a tallboy can of Sapporo.

We gathered around as they recounted their adventure. When Dave and Chris left the hotel first thing that morning, they decided to walk around the block, circling the hotel, but they never made it back. What they hadn't realized was that, unlike North America's grid system of squared, right-angle blocks, Japan's streets are laid out at random angles and curves like a giant spiderweb, spiralling out of ancient squares and central plazas, which makes it very easy to get lost. Dave and Chris walked and walked, always thinking they were getting closer, but they never again found the hotel. They didn't know the name of our hotel, the street address or the name of the club we were playing, either. Remembering that the hotel was under a large red neon Sony sign, they spotted one and used it as a landmark, thinking it would lead them back to the hotel. Then they crested the top of a hill and, like a nightmare, there were identical large red neon Sony signs filling the horizon near and far in the expansive Nagoya metropolis.

At the time, English was understood even less in Nagoya than in Tokyo or Osaka, so the cab drivers, pedestrians, bus drivers and even the cops Dave and Chris stopped to ask couldn't help them. All the city signs were in Japanese characters. The only English they saw in twelve hours was major brand names on advertisements. After ten hours of walking aimlessly, they stumbled across a major train station. Downstairs they spotted an international pay phone. When they looked closer, Dave noticed the phone was outfitted with a panel of little flags from around the world, including the Canadian maple leaf.

Dave picked up the phone and pushed the Canadian flag. Within sec-onds, a Canadian operator answered. Dave and Chris burst into cheers. Dave had the operator connect them to Mint Records in Vancouver. By extreme fortune, co-owner Randy Iwata, who happens to be of Japanese heritage, always worked long hours, and was in the Mint Records office at one a.m. Randy accessed my tour files in the office and found a cell phone number for the tour manager, who was still scouring the streets of Nagoya when he got the call. Keeping Dave on one line and the tour manager on the other, Randy conveyed instructions to Chris and Dave for describing their surroundings. The tour manager finally figured out which train station they were at and came to rescue them. The train station where Dave and Chris were found was over twenty miles away from the hotel.

Dave stepped out on stage in Nagoya forty minutes later and thoroughly rocked out. He and Chris slept like the dead back at the hotel that night, completely cured of their jet lag. It was only the first hiccup in a long series of Japanese misadventures.

When Lookout label rep Christopher Appelgren (centre) found out that the Smugglers and the Queers were touring Japan together, he eagerly signed on for the trip. His youthful enthusiasm was infectious, even after he got lost with Dave in Nagoya for twelve hours.
NICK THOMAS PHOTO

thirty-five

Bishy Bishy!

———

IKE THE COUNTRY itself, our Japanese trip was filled with peaks and valleys. The tour manager meant well, but proved to be a disorganized mess. His greatest vice was his cell phone. It rang constantly and he answered it in any situation. When he took calls while at the wheel, he was the poster boy for distracted driving. It was as if the phone call sapped him of all power to operate a motor vehicle, navigate, process thought or contemplate anything beyond his frantic conversation. Driving into Tokyo on the raceway-like Tōmei Expressway, you had to be quick as a macaque to react to exits and turns. Even if we saw a sign looming ahead that basically said "Tokyo this way—nowhere that way," if the tour manager's phone rang, he would juggle it in one hand, desperately trying to answer while Dave and I yelled at him from the back seat. He'd give the Japanese phone hello of *moshi moshi* while flying by the exit.

We had put our trust in the tour manager to guide us into Tokyo, Nagoya, Osaka, Kobe and Kyoto, some of the largest cities in the world, and we were constantly disoriented in the inner city mazes. According to Supersnazz, the venues we were playing were often too big or in the wrong parts of town, and the tour manager couldn't drive worth shit. The Smugglers mostly weathered it all, reminding ourselves that it was because of this hapless tour manager that we were in Japan at all. Despite the daily

234

frustrations, it was still the experience of our lives so far. We were flabbergasted to even be there. One or two shows tanked, but most of them were fantastic, especially in Tokyo.

Joe Queer, the cranky lead singer of the Queers, had a decidedly different take. He had been on tour for months on end, around the world, and he was still fighting to stay sober. And he didn't suffer fools. He was absolutely livid over the ineptitude of the tour manager. Poor routing often had us backtracking up and down the high-speed/high-stress Tōmei Expressway, which many times zipped us right past Narita International Airport. Joe constantly demanded to be dropped off at international departures so he could fly straight home to New Hampshire. B-Face and Hugh did what they could to keep him calm. Eventually they ignored him and joined the party wagon with the Smugglers and Supersnazz, who were having a great time together every night. Joe was friendly and professional at the shows and with the fans, but he often coerced Beez to stay in and play poker with him after the gigs while the rest of us partied all over town.

Driving into downtown Tokyo was a life experience in itself. Endless veins of narrow side streets divided by main thoroughfares stemmed out of massive plazas that dotted the city. We turned onto an artery that led us into one of the most incredible worlds we had ever witnessed. It felt straight out of an Indiana Jones movie. Our van crawled into a narrow alley lined with miniature bars, restaurants, clubs and sushi and noodle counters. The street was made even more constricted by piles of crates and barrels stacked up between doorways. Glowing red lanterns bearing Japanese characters hung from each bar or restaurant, brushing against the van as we passed.

When the tour manager took a turn too sharply, we got wedged up against an omnipresent vending machine. The street was packed with people; pedestrians, cyclists, scooterists and mini-cars surrounded us, all trying to squeeze by every which way but loose. When we finally managed to scrape our van free, the tour manager hit the gas so hard we sideswiped an old man on a bicycle. I opened the window and said one of the only Japanese words I knew: sumimasen, which I hoped meant "excuse me."

The collision caused the tour manager to swerve the van in the opposite direction, straight into a pile of wooden boxes that came crashing down on top of us. Thankfully the old man was okay, and pedestrians helped clear the boxes from our path. From inside the van we smiled and waved thanks, pointing at our tour manager and making the universal "crazy" sign by spinning our index finger next to our temples. The pedestrians smiled and waved back. Communication!

It took two hours of crawling through what was only a two- or three-block space before we made it to the hotel. It was larger than the mom and pop shop we had stayed at in Nagoya, but still miniature, with much of the same slipper shtick. The hotel had beer and whisky vending machines in the lobby and coin-operated TVs in the rooms which, when fed a few yen, played nothing but porn. After exhausting our supply of coins in about half an hour, Dave had only one question he wanted translated: "Is there a change machine in the lobby?"

A bizarre pornographic scene involving a sumo wrestler, his concubine and a glass ball was playing out on the TV when Beez suddenly sat bolt upright on his futon and glanced around. "WHERE'S MY BASS?" Somehow, in the chaos of unloading our guitars and luggage in front of the hotel, Beez's beloved vintage rosewood Gibson SG bass hadn't made it into the room. He and I dashed into the hall, visualizing it sitting just outside the sliding paper door of our hotel room, but the hall was empty. We raced down to the lobby, but none of the staff understood what we were yelling about, and the bass was nowhere to be seen. Running out into the clogged streets, Beez spotted the bass propped upright against the curb where we had unloaded the van over an hour earlier. "MY BASS!" he screeched, popping open the case to find his bass guitar untouched and unharmed.

We couldn't believe the guitar had sat there unmolested for almost ninety minutes in downtown Tokyo, with thousands of people walking by. We found out later that Japan has an extremely low crime rate compared to just about any other major industrialized country in the world. There isn't much demand for used goods in Japan, either, and therefore not much of a black market for stolen used goods. Japan is generally an out-of-the-box brand-new consumerist culture. People often assume an old or used item left by the curbside is garbage. Ex-pat Australians and North Americans in Japan are known to have furnished their apartments with what they had found discarded in alleys: everything from perfectly good couches to last-year's-model TVs. Had we forgotten Beez's bass on a busy street in downtown Vancouver, New York, Chicago, Atlanta, Barcelona or just about anywhere else we had toured, it would have disappeared in seconds, sometimes as quickly as it took to turn your head. Not in Tokyo.

Most of our gigs in Japan had been good, with fine if at times confused audience reception, but the shows in Tokyo felt like a deep-sleep rock 'n' roll dream fantasy come true. They were packed with hundreds of people. Highly enthusiastic kids crammed up against the barricades. To our humbled amazement, the Japanese fans loudly sang along to all the songs we played from *Selling the Sizzle*. The band members looked at each other mid-song in disbelief. We had travelled 7,750 kilometres across the world's largest ocean, over the International Date Line, to a completely unknown land, and we were playing our original songs only to have them sung back to us. I had never felt anything like it. It made many years of music industry bullshit seem worth it, right then and there.

For some disorganized reason, we had to switch hotels each night in Tokyo. Our second abode was known as a "businessman special," or a "capsule hotel." In a long room at the top of a narrow flight of stairs, the Queers and Smugglers were placed in stacked tubes built into the wall. You had to slide in feet first. Upon entry these bunks felt completely claustrophobic, like being in a coffin. The novelty kicked in after a few moments when we realized the sleeping capsules came complete with a miniature flip-down TV and reading light. Once the automatic, *Star Trek*-like doors slid down to seal each of us inside, the tubes provided us with one of our best sleeps of the tour. (The paper walls in most of the other hotels masked nothing.)

In Osaka, we essentially stayed at an old lady's home. It was a cold, grey rooming house with the staircase at such an angle that you had to use your hands to climb up to the rooms, which were freezing and again had the thin strips of translucent paper for doors and walls. The futon-on-the-floor routine was made even worse when a host of cockroaches scattered as the old gal lit the lantern in our room. The Smugglers went with the flow, because it all felt so new and exotic, but we could hear Joe Queer through the paper wall yelling, "I'm goin' to the fuckin' airport first thing in the fuckin' morning, I swear to fuckin' God!" Luckily for the tour, he never did.

Most of our shows started and ended early, which meant the three bands ate dinner together afterwards. We'd follow Supersnazz through astounding neighbourhoods, careful not to fall too far behind and get swallowed by the crowds. Sometimes they led us through gigantic shopping squares like Shibuya in Tokyo, which made Toronto on Saturday night look like Moose Jaw on Sunday morning. TV screens the size of football fields, huge neon signs advertising every Japanese mega-corp imaginable, gigantic 3-D images projected onto buildings—and throbbing hordes of people moving in every direction at once. Within a few minutes, we'd be back in alleyways filled with noodle and sushi counters. No matter where Supersnazz took us, be it massive or minute, there always seemed to be a happy, vibrant pulse to it all.

Thursday, December 19, 1996
Tokyo, Japan

For our final meal of the Japanese tour, Supersnazz took us all to a very traditional and fancy-pants restaurant where we had to once again remove our shoes at the door. We sat on the mats on the floor to eat from foot-high tables in a semi-private booth, separated from the other tables by the omnipresent paper dividing walls. The table was a large square, accommodating all three bands, and the more sake and beer the wait staff brought out, the wilder we got, eventually turning the dinner into an impromptu variety show.

Soon I was on my feet, doing a celebratory dance around the tabletop in my socks. Dave followed my lead, hopping up on the table to do two rousin', foot-stompin', lyric-for-lyric, totally ridiculous John Denver tunes: "Grandma's Feather Bed" and "Thank God I'm a Country Boy." Hugh from the Queers was laughing so hard he started choking, needing Tomoko to bend him over to knock the squid out of his windpipe. That allowed Hugh to get in on the singalong, standing up on the table in his black jeans, black T-shirt, black leather jacket and black spiked hair, to deliver a very loud rendition of "Born in the USA" while the rest of the shocked staff and patrons nervously stared on.

Chris Appelgren from Lookout followed that up with a Fonzie-type Russian folk dance, where he managed to mistakenly kick a full plate of food, a frothing mug of beer and a whole mess of chopsticks directly into the face of poor Kanako, Supersnazz guitarist. She was covered in noodles and booze. When Hugh jumped up to help her, he stumbled and fell backwards through the paper wall divider. He landed on his back directly onto a table filled with food surrounded by a quiet party of Japanese strangers. "Sumimasen, man." Now that we had created a huge mess, damaged the restaurant and offended fellow diners, Chris paid the bill on the Lookout credit card. We left stomping through the restaurant, arm in arm, all joining Hugh in another chorus of "Born in the USA."

Left to right: Drummer Hugh O'Neill from the Queers, Fifi and Fink from Teengenerate, Tomoko from Supersnazz and me backstage in Tokyo. We'd become really great friends with Tomoko and Supersnazz, who were instrumental in bringing us back to Japan years later. NICK THOMAS PHOTO

This is not a laundromat! It is in fact a Japanese "businessman special" hotel. It's just one of the many strange-to-us places the Smugglers and the Queers slept during our tour to Japan in December 1996.
NICK THOMAS PHOTO

We didn't know it then, but that tour was the last time we'd see Hugh O'Neill. The larger-than-life punk rocker with the huge smile bashed the hell out of the drums for the Queers from 1986 until 1998, when he left the band after an unfortunate falling-out with Joe Queer. Hugh had long battled alcohol and drug addiction, but he had been clean for a year when he was diagnosed with inoperable brain cancer in late 1998. Loveable Hugh O'Neill, whom Joe Queer still considers the best drummer he's ever played with, died on January 21, 1999.

The morning after our final celebratory dinner in Japan, we awoke groggy and hungover to the news that both of our vans had been smashed in a hit and run. Our tour manager had parked them illegally overnight on a busy thoroughfare. The poor guy got us lost one more time on the way to the airport, *moshi moshi*-ing all the way on his cell phone. We had to run full speed through the massive Narita International Airport, finally staggering aboard our flight, which they had thankfully delayed for five sweaty, stinking, gasping Canadian musicians.

Aside from the disorganization, Japan was still the tour of a lifetime, and we forged a strong bond with Supersnazz that paved the way for an even better return trip years later. We videotaped parts of the tour for a MuchMusic TV special and edited together our own tour documentary movie, later released on VHS and DVD, entitled *The Smugglers at Japan*. And as usual I kept a tour diary. By now I was posting the tour stories to Mint Records' website, and they had become popular with our fans. I never would have done so, however, had I known that one day the online tour diaries would be cited as a reason for one of the Smugglers to quit the band.

thirty-six

Nobody Can Tell Us

THE SMUGGLERS SAT crowded shoulder to shoulder in the off-white beat-up Mercedes van, glowering through our latest dirty windshield at a dreary parking lot in Münster, Germany. Cold February rain pelted the van in slanted sheets. When we heard we'd be touring Europe for six weeks in a Mercedes-Benz, we had imagined luxury. We didn't realize that Mercedes in Europe were as domesticated as Fords in North America. Our stick-shift Mercedes was a cramped cube van, much smaller than our regular van at home but cumbersome enough to barely fit down Europe's ancient cobblestone streets. Despite its cramped quarters compared to our own van, the Mercedes became our newly trusted home on wheels; it was here we would gather for solidarity, escape and comfort when apprehensive about the show coming up, like we were at that moment.

This wasn't our first time in Europe. A few years earlier, pre-Lookout glory, we had done a week-long trip to Spain to support—ahem—*Wet Pants Club*, our 1994 LP, which was released on a backwoods Spanish label called Radiation Records. Our friends in the Victoria power-pop band Bum had become shockingly huge in Spain, on the strength of their brilliant debut album, *Wanna Smash Sensation*. Bum had completed a few sold-out, rock-star tours of Spain, in one of which Nick filled in on guitar, and he raved to us about the huge gigs, adoring audiences and incredible hospitality. Beez had played bass with the Mummies a year earlier for their European tour, and he also came back with stories of red-carpet hospitality that made the rest of us eager to experience the Continent.

Seen from home, the optics of our Spanish tour were great. Word got out that we were releasing a record in Spain and touring to support it. Rumours abounded that we must be huge over there, just like Bum. We did nothing to squelch the myth. The truth was *Wet Pants Club* was not a smash sensation, and the Smugglers' week-long tour of Spain was mostly a disaster. Save for the amazing final show in Madrid played to three hundred people (which was recorded and later released as our tenth-anniversary live album), our Spanish shows were held in huge halls that were virtually empty.

The draining tour had ground our already fragile pre-Lookout egos into Spanish salt. I had the flu from the outset, so it didn't help that our surly Spanish tour manager/driver was a chain-smoker who went through eight unfiltered cigarettes an hour. When we rolled down the windows of the van seeking fresh air, diesel fumes from Spain's traffic-choked streets wafted in. We were in a constant state of holding our breath when we were in the van, and in a constant state of holding our breath at the oversized venues, waiting to see if anyone would show up.

After a somewhat respectable gig in Barcelona attended by a few dozen Spaniards who gamely bought merchandise, Beez had insisted we all check out the Gaudi church, one of his favourite sites in all of Europe. Within seconds of arriving, he was delighted when a small child offered him a free flower. He leaned down to let her put it in his breast pocket. A few moments later Beez clutched at that pocket, realizing it was where he had put our precious merchandise money. "OUR MONEY! IT'S GONE!" This time it was no nightmare: Beez had been pickpocketed by a six-year-old, losing over three hundred dollars. With memories like those still fresh in our minds, we were nervous when we touched down in Amsterdam for our six-week tour of Europe in 1997.

Amsterdam was like Pinocchio's Pleasure Island with nicer architecture. It was anything goes in that town, and everything seemed to be legal: pot, hash, booze in the streets and sex, sex, sex. We had a wild few nights acclimatizing to the laid-back Dutch way of life. Our shows in the Netherlands and Belgium were surprisingly successful. Then we hit Germany's speed limit–free Autobahn to play the Marquee Club next to the notorious Reeperbahn in Hamburg. The Reeperbahn is a smutty strip where sex, drugs and rock 'n' roll collide with terrific force, making Amsterdam look uptight in comparison. Germans called the area *die sün-digste Meile*, which translated to "the most sinful mile." For the Smugglers and many musicians before us, it was the Beatles who made the Reep-erbahn famous by cutting their musical teeth there in the early 1960s, in clubs like the Top Ten, the Kaiserkeller and the Star-Club. The Beat-les often played ridiculously long sets in Hamburg, up to eight hours in length. John Lennon once said, "I might have been born in Liverpool, but I grew up in Hamburg." We were thrilled to experience it first-hand, and went suitably nuts.

Our roadie, Ska-T, was jacked to find that the Reeperbahn was also the heart of Hamburg's red light district, a peculiar scene where naked women sat in street-level picture windows backlit with red lights. They were like living mannequins, nonchalantly inviting you to have sex with them for money. As a gift for his dedication to our band, we pooled our money, came up with fifty German marks and let Ska-T loose to choose the prostitute of his dreams. It turned out that fifty marks was the equiv-alent of about thirty dollars, and good for little more than a hand job, but that didn't stop Ska-T. He window-shopped up and down the block, even-tually picking one woman. Once in her upstairs lair, her gruff, dismissive attitude and a black velvet painting of Billy Idol killed Ska-T's vibe. He couldn't stand to attention, he told us afterwards, but paid her anyway.

We had a balls-out rock show at the Marquee, partying hard with the locals deep into the night. Leaning over the bar at three a.m., the pro-moter explained to us in slurred, heavily accented English that it was time for us to retire to our sleeping quarters in the basement of the club. He led us down an impossibly tight staircase into a dank stone tunnel that brought us to a windowless, dripping dungeon of a bedroom. Inside were six barracks-like metal-framed bunk beds that looked like they pre-dated the Beatles. On top of them sagged damp mattresses with filthy pillows.

The promoter hung around pulling on a bottle of tequila and telling us stories we only half understood as we anxiously unfurled our sleeping bags. Just before he gave the cord a tug to turn out the single hanging light bulb, he remembered something seemingly very important. He couldn't quite put it into English, so he acted out what he was trying to say. Pointing urgently at the disgusting pillows, he motioned for us to take off our T-shirts and use them as pillowcases. Then he pointed to the pillows again, raised both hands to his head, and made a quick scratching motion in his hair, saying, *"Chee-chee-chee-chee-chee!"* With that he turned out the light, leaving us in pitch-black stone dungeon horror, trying to imagine what his actions could possibly mean. Dave missed it all. Earlier at the bar, he got completely wasted on Jägermeister shots and wandered off. We discovered later he had blacked out for at least six hours and been found in someone's kitchen making himself a cheese sandwich.

In the puddle-filled parking lot in Münster, it didn't help our collective moods that several of us were nursing severe Hamburg hangovers.

Wednesday, February 5, 1997
Gleiss 22, w/ Los Ass-Draggers
Münster, Germany

There we were, sitting outside in our van,
slipping into the pre-show, nothing to do,
feel sorry for ourselves bullshit, condemning
the gig before it even happened for pretty
much no reason. Just a collective bad mood.
I still blame Phoenix '92 whenever this
condition creeps up, some of the other guys
blame Spain. Japan was so great, but Europe
feels like it could crumble at any moment.
Maybe it's because we're on our own on this
tour, without the safety blanket of touring
partners like the Queers or Supersnazz. After
months of package tours, we suddenly feel
very much alone on a huge continent. Bryce
finally went inside to Gleiss 22 to catch
tonight's openers (a cool r'n'r band from
Spain called Los Ass-Draggers), and came

running back to the van to tell us the club
was hopping! To our total surprise, the
show was completely packed with cool kids
that loved punk, pop and rock 'n' roll music.
Seriously, we had one of our best nights ever
as a band, with over-the-top dance contests
(I think a girl with crutches won somehow),
kissing contests and a total of four encores—
our most ever, definitely. By the end we felt
positively Beatles-esque, having played about
sixty songs, every song we knew. We were
totally messed up with exhaustion, soaked in
our sweat and the audience's beer, but we had
a blast. Damn, Europe is actually awesome
so far! Why do we do that pre-gig depressive
shit to ourselves? Things are actually,
truly, finally, really getting better! Beez
better not quit! Nobody better quit! Rock is
great! It's all happening!

Since our first ill-fated Spanish tour, a lot of good things had happened for us in Europe. *Selling the Sizzle* was released on a popular punk and avant-garde label called Konkurrent Records out of Amsterdam, and they were doing a fine job promoting the record. Our video for "Especially You" (the closest thing we ever had to a hit song) was in rotation on MTV Europe. Those two elements, plus the Lookout stamp of approval, made an incredible difference. Despite lingering insecurities we never completely shook, our European shows kept getting bigger, better and weirder. Now on our 1997 tour we had a chance to redeem ourselves in Spain.

thirty-seven

Melee in Madrid

T HE CRUNCH OF metal on metal made me wince as I tried to jam the van into gear. I had just violently rear-ended an unoccupied parked car in downtown Madrid during rush hour. Somehow I'd wedged our Spanish tour manager and myself into a real shit sandwich. Minutes earlier I had been flabbergasted when a car scraped along the side of the van and then sped off. The rest of the band was back at El Sol, a legendary Spanish nightclub that could only be entered through a very narrow alleyway with no parking out front and barely any stopping. We were late, so we unloaded our gear down the club's ornate spiral staircase, then set up for sound check immediately. As the expendable lead singer, it was up to me to brave the steep, congested streets of Madrid to find a parking space for the Mercedes tour van.

After banging into the parked car and swearing loudly, I planned to do what any law-abiding Canadian driver was trained to do: unbuckle my seat belt to inspect the damage, then leave a note with our contact information for insurance purposes. As I was stepping out of the door, Jimmy, our tour manager, grabbed my arm. "Where you go, amigo? Let's get out of here!" He yanked me back into the van. "Start me up, let's go!" I put up a confused argument, but Jimmy convinced me to trust his local knowledge of parking etiquette. I did what I was told, gingerly easing the stick-shift van up the cobblestone slope in reverse.

"Fuck, hombre!" Jimmy shouted at me, exasperated. He leaned over and slammed the heel of his black cowboy boot onto the accelerator. The van roared backwards, smashing into the parked car behind us. My shoulders clenched at the sound of breaking glass. "VAMANOS! What you say in Canada, man? FLOOR IT!" shouted Jimmy, pointing a ringed index finger at Calle de Costanilla de Los Ángeles, a ridiculously precipitous street that dated back to the fifteenth century and was built for horse and buggy. Now it was angrily clogged with twentieth-century automobiles.

When planning this first big European tour, we made the conscious decision not to have a tour manager, based mostly on our negative experiences in Spain a few years earlier and our most recent debacle in Japan. Like most elements of the music industry, we figured we could simply do it better ourselves. Our decision had already paid off: during our first two weeks in Belgium, the Netherlands, England, Germany and France, navigation had gone off without a hitch. We were having fun, as well as saving the money we would have been shelling out for a disorganized kook we didn't know or trust. Dave was mostly at the wheel, and I sat beside him, clutching a very detailed European road atlas. Thanks to the multitude of road signs (some of which we found way too entertaining, like *Ausfahrt*, the German term for "exit"), we got lost a lot less in Europe than we had in Japan or the USA.

In the northern countries like the Netherlands, Belgium and Germany, almost everyone spoke English. In France, our high school French kicked in just enough to get us through (almost) without incident. In one encounter, at the end of a gig in Plassac, a très petite French ville where we had performed at the monthly community dance, Beez repeatedly asked the friendly promoter/town mayor (who spoke not a word of English), for a receipt of payment for the gig. We had been told the French word for "receipt" was "billet," so Beez slathered on what he thought was some French pronunciation and asked him over and over for a "*bee-EH*." After a few minutes of confusion, Beez starting getting frustrated that the guy wasn't getting it, so Beez starting yelling. "*Bee-EH! Bee-EH!* Come on, man, BEE-EH!!!"

Finally, the Frenchman's eyes lit up. "AH HA!" he exclaimed with a

Bryce (left) and Nick spotting some advertising in La Rochelle, France, on our first full European tour. We were trepidatious about our drawing power, but most of the shows were surprisingly great. GRANT LAWRENCE PHOTO

wide smile. "Attendez une minute, mon ami Canadien, s'il vous plaît!" A few minutes later, he returned with a six-pack of Heineken.

Very few people seemed to speak English in Spain, especially outside of Madrid and Barcelona. We were confident we could get by, but Record Runner, the touring company who set up the Spanish leg of shows (and who had somehow agreed to have us back after our first disastrous trip, which they paid for) insisted on a road manager accompanying us.

When we showed up at our first Spanish gig in Vitoria, we were relieved to discover that our Spanish tour manager was Jimmy Garcia. Known throughout the scene as "Rock 'n' Roll Jimmy," he was short, stocky and tough. His black, curly hair was usually slicked back into a pompadour, and he wore a leather jacket, skin-tight jeans and black leather cowboy boots. In contrast to his 1950s greaser exterior, Jimmy was a gentleman: very kind and down to earth. He also had a deep appreciation of rock 'n' roll music and North American pop culture. He explained that he had taught himself how to speak English by watching Marlon Brando movies—which we thought was an odd choice, since Marlon Brando was practically unintelligible in many of his movies.

Jimmy also loved to party. More than in any other country in Europe, as far as we could see, drugs were big in Spain. At almost every club, we were offered heaping piles of cocaine and speed, which was not our scene. We were happy with beer, wine, local liqueurs and the occasional giant doobie for old time's sake. Jimmy stepped up for us, never saying no. He'd quickly roll up a bill and happily snort away. We also met a funny little fellow named Francisco "Franny" Santalices, who didn't smoke, drink or do drugs of any kind but loved rock 'n' roll as much as anyone. Franny released *Señor Pantsdown*, a Spanish seven-inch EP for the Smugglers that came out just before *Selling the Sizzle*, and he and Jimmy both became good friends of ours.

Wednesday, February 12, 1997
El Sol
Madrid, Spain

Ah, Madrid! It was such a pleasure to be back in one of the world's most exciting cities to see our friends... or was it? Unfortunately, it's probably easier to drive the Millennium Falcon through an asteroid field than it is to try and find a parking spot in Madrid. When we finally arrived at the club I was a nervous wreck, certain I'd be arrested at any moment for smashing up various cars while trying to park, but apparently that's just downtown Madrid rush hour at its finest. It certainly freaked me out. Oh yeah, the show was excellent, with a capacity crowd and encores. The night ended at about 6 a.m. after a rock 'n' roll dance party back at the best bar in the entire world, Templo del Gato with Jimmy DJing. Ah, Madrid!

Surprisingly, our van was no worse for wear after the parking incident, though Madrid's traumatic rush hour with Jimmy had a lasting effect on me. The incident resulted in a song that Dave and Nick and I wrote a few weeks later, backstage in Rotterdam. It would be the opening cut on our *Buddy Holly Convention* EP, which we'd release later that year.

Melee in Madrid—Grant Lawrence / The Smugglers (1997)

Jimmy and Grant drivin' all over town
Crashing and banging and messing around
Smashing into cars down cobblestone lanes
Put it in reverse and ram it again
Cops say stop but I say no
Jimmy says, "Floor it" and away we go
Melee in Madrid!

Hookers say, "Hi wanna stop and buy?"
A little later honey, Jimmy zip up your fly!
Won't fit here so slam it into gear
Do the Mercedes Mash while smashing her rear
Hombre says "Caramba!" but I don't want to rumble
Let's get out of here or catch some Spanish Thunder
Melee in Madrid!

Jimmy and Grant driving all over town
Smashing and banging and messing around
But everything's going to be alright
Because we're rockin' in Madrid on a Saturday night!

The gig had actually been on a Wednesday night, but "Saturday" sang better. Despite the traffic madness, we fell in love with Madrid, proving our great show a few years earlier had been—thank the gods—no fluke. Madrid audiences were so amped, so wild and so appreciative of rock 'n' roll that we thought it couldn't get any better for us in Europe. But nothing we had experienced prepared us for the filthy cultural anomaly that was the Italian punk rock squat.

thirty-eight

Forte Prenestino

O
UR LAST GIG in Spain was in a small, picturesque town in the Basque Country. Performing in this region deep in the Pyrenees was fascinating. The Basque Country's fierce demand for independence from the rest of Spain reminded us of the politics in Quebec. We experienced some amazing shows and hospitality, but even Jimmy could barely understand a word anyone said in the local dialects.

Jimmy left us in the Basque Country so he could head back to Madrid and we could continue on to France. The only problem was that the road signs were all in Basque, a very complicated language with seemingly no Latin roots. Finally we asked an elderly Basque gentleman on a street corner. "Francia? Francia?" asked Dave over and over, holding his hands aloft in the international sign for "Help me, I'm confused." Finally the old fellow clued in. "AH! Francia! Si, si." He reached out for our van's sliding side door, opened it up and climbed right into the van with us.

The elderly Basque gentleman then pointed to show Dave where he should drive. Away we went, winding up a mountain road occasionally blocked by lazy herds of sheep the old man urged us to drive right through. After about a half hour, we emerged from the forest on the edge of a mountain, overlooking a patchwork quilt of green farms and vineyards

After a gig in the Basque Country in northern Spain, we couldn't find the road to France. When we stopped to ask this elderly Basque gentleman how to get to "Francia," instead of trying to explain it, he simply got in our van and showed us the way up a mountain pass.
DAVID CARSWELL PHOTO

far below. "FRANCIA!" the old man shouted victoriously, pointing down towards the farms. "Gracias, amigo, gracias!" we said in return. The old man opened up the side door and nimbly stepped out onto the side of the mountain road. Dave looked over at me. "Is he going to be okay?" I looked back at the man's hunched frame as he disappeared around the first corner, heading down the hill, back towards Spain. "I hope so." We've always wondered.

From there we played a deliriously hot Valentine's Day gig in Valence, France. (By some strange fluke, the Smugglers ended up playing in Valence on Valentine's Day on three separate European tours, each concert put on by our French promoter friend Gilles Bonnel.) It was one of the rare shows on the tour where additional bands were performing. Whenever there were more than one or two bands on a bill in Europe, it was automatically called a festival.

We couldn't get used to Europe's border crossings. We rolled over them almost daily but barely noticed. When we entered Germany, we had expected something out of *Gotcha!* Instead, we saw nothing but abandoned guardhouses and didn't even slow down. It was the same thing in Spain. We did pass a guard in a fancy costume when we stopped in Monte Carlo for lunch, but it was the Italian border that turned out to be a highlight of the tour.

Saturday, February 15, 1997
Genova, Italy

We continued to drive along the rugged and gorgeous Côte d'Azur. Soon we crossed into Italy where—surprise—they actually had border guards. They smoke, wear cool leather jackets and look like the cast of *Mean Streets*. Waiting for us just across the border was a small car with a sign in the back window that said, "Welcome Smugglers!" We thought it was great; such a sight at the US border would have the guards drawing guns. Nobody batted an eye here in Italy. The car belonged to our Genova promoter, Andrea, and his brother Sandro, two extremely enthusiastic characters who seemed much more like fans than show promoters. How things are changing. To be welcomed at the border of the country by the promoters, imagine that! We're a long way from Phoenix.

After an over-the-top five-course dinner at a cliff-side restaurant overlooking the sparkling Mediterranean Sea, we followed Andrea and Sandro up and down the winding, steep, seaside hills of Genova (Christopher Columbus's hometown) to what appeared to be a deserted valley. In the depths of this mountain valley, to our raw horror, we

rolled into the polar opposite of lunch in
Monte Carlo: an enormous abandoned warehouse
that had been transformed into a communist
concert hall squat. It was yet another Euro-
shock, but despite our initial fears this
turned out to be an incredible show, our
largest of the tour so far, with over eight
hundred Italians emerging out of nowhere
to pack a long hall the size of an airplane
hangar (actually, the place probably WAS once
an airplane hangar). Thanks to Andrea and
Sandro for a wonderful Italian welcome and a
truly wild time!

Beez (left) and Nick on stage at a massive squat in Genoa, Italy. We were always nervous
about entering these damp, derelict structures and were always amazed at the huge
crowds that seemingly came out of nowhere. ANDREA CARRARO PHOTO

The punk rock gigging scene in Italy was vastly different from anywhere else in the world. In Italy, it was all about the squats. Unlike our
North American image of homeless people temporarily set up in an abandoned building, in Italy a squat was considered a *centro sociale occupato
autogestito*, roughly meaning "self-governing squatted social centre." As
far as we could figure, the squats were a left-wing backlash following the
World War 11–era fascist regime: as long as the squatters claimed some
sort of leftist political stance (socialist, communist, anarchist), the government seemed to leave them alone in previously abandoned buildings
to run highly organized centres of arts and culture, albeit in a somewhat
filthy, rundown state. We played the massive urban squat Leoncavallo in
Milan, along with many others up and down the Boot in Torino, Naples
and the most famous one of all, Forte Prenestino in Rome.

Our battered Mercedes van turned off a busy Roman street and
crunched up a winding gravel driveway through what appeared to be
an overgrown park. The van crested a hill, and there before us lay one
of the most astounding sights of our touring adventures. Dave hit the
squealing brakes to a collective gasp. The apocalyptic eventuality I had
imagined when I saw creeping vines busting through the concrete in the
underpasses of New Jersey seemed to be a reality here in Rome. Before us
loomed a massive stone fort, a castle of sorts, covered in graffiti, homemade banners and vegetation. It was like the set of a *Mad Max* movie come
to life. We had arrived at the gates of Forte Prenestino.

Forte Prenestino and its grounds had originally been part of a net-
work of stone forts surrounding Rome in the late nineteenth century. The
forts were soon abandoned, but the fascists and the Nazis put them to use
again during World War 11. As Rome sprawled, the forts were absorbed
into the urban landscape. In 1976 some of them were designated for
parks and public use. Others, including Forte Prenestino, were locked up
and condemned. On May 1, 1986, Forte Prenestino, located on the eastern
edge of Rome, was broken into and taken over by communist squatters.

Since then the Forte had grown into a massive hub of alternative culture open to the paying public. The squat was completely self-funded. Its
busy schedule was filled with concerts, music festivals, classes of all kinds,
art exhibits, movies, circuses and conferences. Inside the graffiti-covered
walls were extensive gardens, a bookstore, a tavern, a restaurant, a theatre

Our Mercedes touring van crossing the moat of Forte Prenestino, one of the most famous squats in all of Europe. We were lucky enough to play there each time we toured through Rome, to bigger and bigger crowds each time.

NICK THOMAS PHOTO

and other venues of varying sizes. By the time we rolled up, jaws agape, Forte Prenestino had evolved into the largest squat in all of Europe.

We waited a few anxious minutes outside the walls of Forte Prenestino until a bearded, straight-faced Rastafarian slipped through a side door and beckoned us forward. Our van *plunk plunk plunked* across the bridge over a weed-infested moat. The black iron gates of the stone fort slowly rattled upwards. As Dave drove under, we entered a dim stone tunnel. The van bumped along on a cobblestone laneway just wide enough for one car. Mangy skin-and-bones dogs loped alongside, their noses to the ground searching for food. Hippies, punks and gypsies emerged and disappeared into the shadows. As we trundled slowly down the tunnel following the Rastafarian, we passed the lit doorways of what appeared to be shops. Naked, flickering light bulbs hung from the stone ceiling. Even though it was the middle of the afternoon, the lights barely illuminated the tunnel.

Heating was a rarity in most of the old European buildings we played in, and Forte Prenestino was no different. Inside the walls it was damp and frigid, though just beyond the archways we could see palm trees, sunshine and rumbling diesel generators. Except for the hour we were onstage, we were bundled up in coats, hats and gloves.

Sunday, February 16, 1997
Forte Prenestino
Rome, Italy

We had dinner with our Italian agent, Carmelo, in an unheated stone room on communal picnic-style tables. Hygiene or cleanliness didn't seem to be a high priority in the Forte, but the food was really excellent. After dinner, we nervously entered the Forte's massive main hall. We were stunned to turn the corner to find over one thousand partying Italians waiting, and we were the only band playing. Not five minutes before we started, the place was deserted and as spooky as a Scooby-Doo mystery. Out of nowhere, like joyous Roman party centurions from the night, punks, mods, crusties, commies and drunks filled the tunnel, all dancing around to our tunes in this strange, dank, dark castle. It was our best show of this tour! The happy people were packed in and, as far back as we could see, dancing and screaming. A huge Italian soccer team flag weaved its way through the crowd. If we paid the slightest notice to it, the crowd erupted further. It was an awesome night.

One recurring problem we were having throughout the European tour was our famous

international dance contest. Besides the
obvious language barrier, it was becoming
exceedingly difficult to give away the dance
trophies that we shipped in all the way
from Canada. No one, show after show, was
accepting the trophies! They danced like
crazy, and when we selected a winner, they
often refused to come up on stage in a
gesture of some type of European humility.
This particular Roman show was another
first: not only did the winner finally climb
on stage, she grabbed the trophy, broke it
in two and threw it into the crowd with a
defiant "We're all equal" Italian speech that
Carmelo paraphrased for us later. Insulted
but ever-professional, we carried on as if it
was part of the show. I guess it was.

After the gig, we followed some of the
crazy crowd to the bar in the centre tunnel
of the forte for beer, wine and dancing.
Much later, Nick found a crappy, flickering
flashlight, and Ska-T, Nick and I drunkenly
decided to explore deep into the tunnels
beneath the forte to see what weird trinkets
we could dig up (of course the place was
supposed to be haunted). It was truly
frightening. After about ten minutes in the
dark, we were whimpering in fear, holding
on to each other's hands so we wouldn't lose
each other, Nick's flashlight constantly
conked out. All we found down there was
bizarre graffiti and artwork on the walls
(there were art exhibits throughout the
tunnels), and a sleeping bag with a large
lump in it that we were too afraid to inspect.

Certain Smugglers would still suggest the big drawback to playing Forte Prenestino was that the organizers also expected us to sleep at the Forte. The people who ran the place were so nice it made you want to stay there, even though we were housed in a very clammy, cold stone room covered in band graffiti like "Joe Queer was here... AND HATED IT!" Six single beds with saggy, soiled mattresses were lined up along one wall. Although people had supposedly cleaned the room for our arrival, the Forte was so heavily coated in dust and dirt that the room stayed filthy. Getting sick on tour was the worst, but Nick insisted we stay, and Dave backed him up. Beez said he felt his lungs seizing up when we first entered the sleeping barracks, so he blurted out, "Fuck you guys, I'm sleeping in the van."

We slept at Forte Prenestino for two nights. When we finally drove out of the hidden fort in the city of Rome, we were all as sick as the mangy mutts that scoured the place for scraps. Beez got it the worst of anyone (and he was completely pissed off about it), but I'd say it was worth it for one of our greatest gigging experiences.

We would return to Forte Prenestino on every one of the band's subsequent trips to Europe, and without fail the Forte gigs were the best shows of the tour. Also without fail, they left us nursing colds and flu for the rest of the tour. Centuries of dust aside, the vibe was welcoming and wonderful, and the reception we received made us feel like rock stars. Too bad that feeling didn't extend to all European shows, especially a certain Bavarian ski resort no one had ever heard of.

Our barrack-like accommodation at Forte Prenestino, a gigantic communist squat built into a stone fort on the outskirts of Rome. The shows at the Forte were incredible but most of us left with chest colds. NICK THOMAS PHOTO

thirty-nine

Isny

T HE NAME OF one town on our itinerary drew blank stares from
everyone we asked: Isny, Germany. No one, anywhere, had ever heard
of it. We finally found the town's insignificant dot in our road atlas.
To get to Isny from Italy, we climbed up into the snowy mountain passes
and long tunnels of the Alps. We crossed into Switzerland, Austria and
ultimately into southern Germany. When we arrived, we were happy to
discover that Isny was a picturesque skiing village nestled in the forested
hills of Bavaria, a few hours south of Munich. The village had one major
claim to fame: it was home to the crazy King Ludwig of Bavaria's spectacular castle, the fairy-tale like structure Walt Disney used as the model
for the Sleeping Beauty castle in Disneyland. We made sure to visit. That
would be as tranquil as it got in Isny.

Friday, February 21, 1997
The Go-In
Isny, Germany

It took us forever to find this town! The
Go-In is a classic Bavarian A-frame chalet.

Inside, it's clear the place caters to a young
crowd. Many of the walls are covered in photo
collages of people getting completely wasted.
We played to a slightly smallish crowd of
about one hundred, a comedown from the huge
crowds in Italy, but lordy lordy, were they
an insane bunch of danger-punks. These
desperately bored animals felt the inherent
need to destroy everything in their path.
Finished their pint? Smash the mug! Getting
up from the table? Overturn it! Had too much
to drink? Puke on a friend! Don't like the
look of someone's lederhosen? Whack 'em with
a pool cue! By midnight the blood and vomit
flowed as steadily as the Jägermeister.

After the show it just got worse. At
one point I was trying to fend off two
mountaineers who repeatedly tried to snatch
my glasses from my face. Others tried to yank
Beez's passport from his pocket as a souvenir.
While Beez and I were defending ourselves,
Bryce flew by us in a blur of hair and
Converse sneakers. Two mohawk-sporting punks
were hot on his heels, apparently transfixed
by Bryce's trademark mop of hair. They were
convinced it was a wig, so they kept tugging
at it with more and more force. When Bryce
tried to get away, they chased him right out
into the snowy Bavarian forest.

We all managed to get out of there alive,
thankfully, but when Ska-T was caught
tonguing the boss's daughter in the coat-
check closet it didn't help matters. Turns
out most of the kids were on acid?!

Before we escaped, we had to get paid. As we waited, the behaviour of the patrons in the chalet continued to spiral out of control. A nasty ski-punk backed Nick into a far corner of the bar. Beside Nick was one of our big, bright *Selling the Sizzle* tour posters, which happened to feature a bleach blond, sweaty and suited Nick Thomas rocking out on his Les Paul. The glaring punk reached up and ripped the poster off the wall. Never taking his angry eyes off Nick, the punk crumpled the poster into a ball, shoved the entire thing into his mouth and started chewing. Nick stared back incredulously as the punk's jaw moved methodically from side to side. Slowly, the punk started to swallow the poster. He was eventually successful. Still glaring, he opened his mouth wide to show Nick it had been fully devoured. He gave Nick a shove and stomped out of the club. Not a word was exchanged between them.

FOR THE MOST part, Europe lived up to its billing as a sensational place to tour. Outside of England, where the clubs treated us like shit, hospitality was excellent. We were given all the food and drink we could handle every night, always had a place to sleep and made long-lasting friendships with many of the promoters and regional booking agents we met along the way. Despite the widespread knowledge of Europe's riders, which were to die for, we had been given warnings about European touring: stories of lost passports, lost band members, horrible illness, border hassles, terrible shows, van breakdowns, thefts, ransoms, kidnappings and being sent home by immigration upon arrival. Some of our friends' bands had fled the continent mid-tour or broken up permanently as a result of draining Euro-treks.

We scoffed at these road wimps. Melee in Madrid, The Forte Flu and unruly Isny aside, we had cruised through Europe, mostly with no tour manager, no hired driver, just the five Smugglers and Ska-T navigating our way through language after language, culture after culture and gig after gig. Like our first taste of the States, all we wanted to do was turn around and come right back. The tour was so good that maybe, just maybe, Beez would remain in the band.

We weren't immune forever, though. The negative aspects of European tours would one day strike us down like the plague. Years later, on what turned out to be our last Euro-trek, I crash-landed in a hospital in Wales,

ASK NICK

Q: Do you have any phobias?

A: Yes, rats and that guy in the passenger seat with the road atlas and the Tintin comics.

Q: What do you do in your spare time?

A: The Cha Cha... if you know what I mean!

Q: Which is your favourite live band?

A: The Evaporators.

Q: What is your favourite sport?

A: Soccer and sex. And sexy soccer.

Q: What subject did you most enjoy at school?

A: Geology.

Q: What's your favourite B-side?

A: "She's Got Everything" by the Kinks.

Q: What's your favourite Smugglers song?

A: "Flying Buttress of Love."

Q: What is the best thing about being in a band?

A: The travel, the pretty girls and the food for cheap.

Q: Looking back on past mistakes, is there anything you would do differently?

A: I would never have quit piano. Kids, don't quit your piano lessons!

severely dehydrated, exhausted and deliriously yelling about the Queen Mother, which led to our first-ever self-imposed cancellation of Smugglers shows. On that final European tour we would also meet a band that seemed to be a mirror image of the Smugglers. It was like meeting the ghost of our future, but we didn't know it at the time.

Nick and Beez having lunch at the Colosseum on a day off in Rome. We found incredible audiences in Europe, but it could be a grinding, exhausting and sickly place to tour, as we would eventually find out the hard way. GRANT LAWRENCE PHOTO

forty

Bent on Being Bent

T HE EUROPEAN OPUS concluded our marathon touring campaign for *Selling the Sizzle*. We had been on the road for a year, racking up hundreds of shows on three continents. Even though we were finding success overseas, Beez held firm on his decision to quit. What really poured sugar into the gas tank was that once we were safely back in Vancouver, Bryce asked us out to Martini's Restaurant to announce he too was quitting the Smugglers (I've never gone back to Martini's since). His decision stabbed like a broken drumstick to the heart.

Like Beez, Bryce told us he couldn't handle the amount of touring anymore. At the end of each tour, we paid ourselves enough to cover maybe a month or two of rent, but then it was back to our interim day jobs. Bryce didn't always have the luxury of an understanding employer, so he sometimes had to search out a new job after a tour. When pressed, he also blurted out that my too-much-information tour diaries were offending his long-term girlfriend, and she had given him an ultimatum: it was either her or the band. He understandably picked her.

The rhythm section of our band had quit just when it seemed we were hitting the Alps of our career. It felt like it was my fault for breaking the oldest code of touring: "What happens on the road stays on the road." I didn't take Bryce's news well. It made me want to overturn the table covered in baked lasagna. It made me realize that you can work as hard as Cool Hand Luke and still come up short. A band is a group of personalities, all of whom have to buy in; everyone has to come together for a common goal. To my band-always-comes-first way of thinking, it didn't make sense that Beez and Bryce would stick with us through all the grinding, thankless, ego-sucking tours, playing to no one in every honkytonk, laundromat, rental hall and nightclub, and throw in the gig towel once we were finally on a roll.

Whether it was my tell-all tour diaries or my whip-cracking leadership, Beez and Bryce were burnt out. Dave and I were often at odds, and we didn't room together or hang out much on the road. But we were childhood friends and had similar goals. When the chips were down, Dave was at his best, and he never failed to make us laugh. Nick and I were best friends. In other words, both of them put up with me. Beez and I had also become trusted friends, though he often referred to me as a tyrant. Once, out of sheer exhaustion at staying with strangers throughout America, Beez demanded the band get a hotel room on one of our very rare nights off. I eventually relented, but on the condition (after a ten-hour drive) that we load every scrap of our equipment into our hotel room on the outskirts of Pittsburgh for fear of having it stolen. Beez snapped. He chased me down the hotel hallway in a fit of raw emotion, hurling obscenities and his shoes at me. I deserved it, but the gear was loaded in. Our van was never broken into on the road.

Losing Beez and Bryce forced the three of us to have some fairly embarrassing conversations with Lookout and Mint. Both record labels were expecting a conversation about a new album. Instead, they got phone calls from a band in disarray. Bill Baker from Mint was annoyed, but Mint had bigger issues to deal with that spring. Cub, the band that floated the label's boat, had announced they were breaking up on May 15, 1997, exactly five years from the day they had formed, citing irreconcilable differences. Their last tour had been brutal; the band had travelled from the east coast to the west without speaking to one another.

We were in for more bad news when I called Lookout, asking to speak to Larry Livermore to explain the situation and get his advice. The receptionist said, "Larry's gone."

"When will he be back? Could you get him to call me?"

"Um ... would you like ... hold?" A few moments later label manager Molly Neuman hopped on the line and dropped the news: in April 1997 Larry Livermore had abruptly resigned as president, CEO and principal owner of Lookout Records. I was stunned. Everything seemed to be falling apart. Larry, who had some of the best "ears" of any label owner ever, who had co-founded and built Lookout from the ground up, creating a worldwide scene and a trusted brand, had been a mentor, friend and Smugglers booster. Now he had disappeared.

Larry goes into great detail about the reasons for his departure in his book *How to Ru(i)n a Record Label*. Basically, due to internal concerns, he asked to be bought out. That left the rest of the young staff in charge. Those who remained were good friends of ours—Chris Appelgren, Molly Neuman and Cathy Bauer became the leadership core, and they put forth a passionate effort for years. But without Larry, Lookout Records sometimes felt like an out-of-control house party.

After hearing about our departing rhythm section, Molly suggested I convince Bryce and Beez to stick around for a final studio session, recording whatever songs we had for an EP so we wouldn't lose momentum while we put the band back together. The two of them agreed, and we recorded the *Buddy Holly Convention* EP at Dave's newly constructed JC/DC Studio. It was the first of several Smugglers records to be produced by our wild pal Kurt Bloch from the Young Fresh Fellows. Since we recorded *Buddy Holly Convention* after a year of touring, that EP might have captured the Smugglers at our best. I was a good showman, but previous recording sessions had exposed the fault lines in my singing voice. Onstage, I made up for it by being more of a game show host. On this EP, though, everything clicked. I was proud of it, but embittered, too. I couldn't help imagining how awesome a full album could have been had Beez and Bryce stuck with us. Their departure also made me realize that I needed a Plan B of my own. I left Mint Records after landing a job as a researcher at CBC Radio, working for David Wisdom and Leora Kornfeld's new music show, *RadioSonic*. I luckily had a very understanding boss who allowed me to tour.

After much searching, we found a new rhythm section. Our long-time friend John Collins (bassist of On the Go, the Evaporators and the New Pornographers, and the "JC" in JC/DC Studios) would play the bass, and

10TH ANNIVERSARY PARTY!

THE SMUGGLERS

WITH THE Hi-FiVES & THE DONNAS

SEPTEMBER 19

STARFISH ROOM

1055 HOMER

← We charged ten bucks for ten years and didn't sell advance tickets. The tenth-anniversary gig happened kitty-corner to our first-ever show ten years earlier at the Chicago Pizza Works, now a Royal Bank.

→ An ad for our tenth-anniversary album that is still one of my proudest coups in the music industry: this record was released on four different labels in four different countries around the world (Canada, USA, Japan, Spain), which set us up for international touring for years to come.

THE SMUGGLERS
GROWING UP SMUGGLER CD/LP
TEN YEAR ANNIVERSARY LIVE ALBUM

A special 20-song live recording from Spain! Recorded by Imposible Records and Record Runner at El Sol, Madrid. Songs include "Pick 'Em Up Truck," "Hey, Stephanie!," "She Ain't No Egyptian," "Luau!," "Kiss Like A Nun" and others! Extensive liner notes and photos. Produced by Kurt Bloch. COMING IN THE FALL '98

OUT NOW!

a persuasive young turk named Danny Fazio would play drums. We auditioned better drummers, but Danny had a cool factor that was undeniable.

We had fun, if at times frustrating, experiences with John and Danny, touring across the States and Europe. Bryce and Beez proved very difficult to replace. With his black horn-rimmed glasses, affable smile and non-stop onstage energy, Beez had become such a recognizable character that audience members repeatedly shouted, "WHERE'S BEEZ?"

John and Danny lasted about a year. By then, we were staring down the Smugglers' tenth anniversary. Somehow we convinced Beez and Bryce to return for our anniversary show, held at the Starfish Room in Vancouver.

It was a sold-out, weekend-long event that attracted diehard fans from around the world. For Bryce, the show would be a one-off, but Beez had recovered from his midlife crisis. He realized that life as a jet-setting dancing clown wasn't actually all that bad. To our great relief, Beez was back on bass in the Smugglers.

The show also served as our record release party for *Growing Up Smuggler: A Tenth Anniversary Live Album*, recorded at El Sol in Madrid. After a series of faxes and emails in three languages, the record was released on four different labels around the world. *Growing Up Smuggler* acted as a greatest hits of sorts, and it contained detailed liner notes on our first ten years as a band. Heady government touring grants were available if you could prove you had a domestic release in the territory you were touring. With our record being released in four different territories, we looked set for years to come.

In previous years, whenever Bryce couldn't play a show or do a tour, we had leaned on a friend named Graham Watson to fill in on drums. Graham was the very capable drummer in Bum, a band we considered almost like brothers. We had become very good friends with them when we both released albums with PopLlama in 1993. In late 1998 Graham joined the Smugglers full-time, becoming Bryce's official replacement.

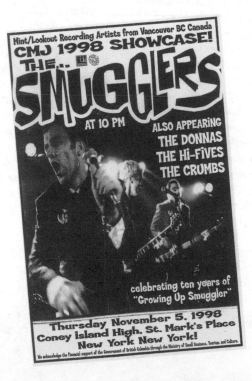

Graham Watson

Graham Watson was the definition of "tall, dark and handsome." At six feet and 160 pounds, he was as lean as his drumsticks. He had grown up in a working-class, devoutly Catholic family in Nanaimo, BC, where despite his height, he was regularly bullied for being a dork. Forced to the fringes, he gravitated away from the mainstream rock of the few bands that toured through Nanaimo in the 1980s (Prism, Trooper, Streetheart) to punk and mod music (the Clash, Generation X, the Jam).

Graham, his brother and a few other friends had formed their own punk band called the Vandals, clueless that there was a much more famous band with the same name from southern California. Graham chose the drums, loving the physicality of the instrument. The Van Isle Vandals rocked out in the DIY Nanaimo punk circuit of house parties and rented-hall shows, and Graham soon learned to love the positive attention he received from being in a band. When Graham was seventeen, his father was diagnosed with a terminal illness, which profoundly affected him. By the time Graham turned twenty-one, his father was gone and booze was a coping mechanism.

In the early 1990s Graham followed a girlfriend down to Victoria. Upon arrival in the Garden City, he broke up with the girlfriend but quickly got ensconced in the local music scene. Hearing about a band called Bum that might be looking for a drummer, he pestered the band members at their day jobs in local record shops until he was finally granted an audition. He blew the members of Bum away and got the gig just weeks before their recording of *Wanna Smash Sensation*. Graham had slid under the wire to perform on a classic power pop record.

When Graham started pounding the beat with the Smugglers, he had been an admirer of our band for years. In his words, he appreciated what he considered was our "firm grasp on the true meaning of rock 'n' roll." What we knew from his earlier jaunts with the Smugglers was that we would get a meticulous, high-energy drummer onstage and on record, as long as he stayed away from booze. Graham was intelligent and gregarious, but he battled the bottle and it often won.

The existential world of rock 'n' roll touring, with its endless free booze, is probably the worst environment for someone with overindulgent tendencies. Graham had his problems with alcohol, but both he and the Smugglers were willing to take the chance it would all work out after we had established some rules. In a backstage argument that almost turned violent after a particularly brutal high-profile show at the Horseshoe Tavern in Toronto, Graham admitted he had been drinking for hours before the show with our opening act, Duotang. Consequently Graham had performed almost the entire concert in a booze-induced blackout. Shortly after that, we struck the deal: no drinking for Graham before or during the show. To help him pull this off while surrounded by hundreds of people drinking to excess, I pledged pre-show sobriety with him for the duration of his time in the Smugglers.

Like anyone joining a band whose core members have been together for years, it took Graham time to fit into our van culture, to get up to speed with our jokes, rapid-fire storytelling and constant roasting of each other. He operated on a somewhat different conversational speed, and would stay silent for long periods, listening to us yammer on. When he did speak, his timbre was extremely deep, slow-paced and loud. It was as if he were wearing a Walkman and speaking to be heard over the music in his headphones. We chalked it up to another case of drummer deafness. (Bryce was basically the same way: a very loud talker, though with a much higher voice.)

Once, when the Smugglers were staying with my relatives in New York City, my aunt Donna asked Graham, "What is your accent?" Graham looked over at her, shrugged and said, "Hoser."

After joining the band full-time, Graham gamely commuted from Victoria to our East Vancouver practice pad, where we finally wrote our follow-up to *Selling the Sizzle*. We released *Rosie* in early 2000. Ambitious plans were hatched to do a "world tour" on our indie-shoestring budget, which was now bolstered by international touring grants. We kicked it off with a sold-out record release party at Vancouver's legendary Commodore Ballroom, playing alongside the latest phenom on Lookout Records and the label's first big success since Larry's departure: the American Teenage Rock 'n' Roll Machine known as the Donnas.

forty-one

Hot Boxin'

THE SMUGGLERS HAD lucked out again. To promote our new album, *Rosie*, in the United States, we were touring with one of the hottest rock 'n' roll bands in the USA. The four women in the Donnas were from Palo Alto, California, all born in 1979. They were in their early years of high school when they formed their first band, the metal-tinged Ragady Anne, which morphed into the equally hard-rocking and brilliantly named Electrocutes. By their senior year they had created the Donnas, each member playing under a "Donna" pseudonym tagged with her last initial. The Donnas played a traditional, Ramones/Runaways style of garage punk filtered through the guise of teenaged girls gone bad, juvenile delinquents singing about having a great time all the time.

The garage rock 'n' roll scene embraced them, and they embarked on their first tour of Japan while still in high school. Much of their bad-girl band image was fostered by a San Francisco rock 'n' roll scenester named Darin Raffaelli, guitarist from Supercharger and owner of Superteem! Records. He co-wrote and released the Donnas' first self-titled record before the band shed their mentor to break out on their own, signing on with Lookout in 1998 for their next album, *American Teenage Rock 'n' Machine*. It could be argued that the record saved Lookout's bacon post-Larry Livermore.

Nick having fun with the Donnas backstage in Detroit. Left to right: Brett Anderson, Allison Robertson, Nick, Torry Castellano.
GRANT LAWRENCE PHOTO

DEVIL DOLLS PRODUCTIONS PRESENTS

THE DONNAS

SMUGGLERS
THE PLUS ONES
FRIDAY MARCH 10TH
SHIM SHAM CLUB
NEW ORLEANS, LA

Soon after the Donnas made their debut on Lookout, we started performing with them frequently in San Francisco and Vancouver. We had heard that, possibly because of their young age and popularity, the Donnas were standoffish and unfriendly, and had a lot of attitude. I'm not sure if it was our disarming Canadian nature, or if the rumours were completely made up, but the Smugglers found them to be friendly, funny and smart, and excellent performers. The engine of the band was Allison Robertson, a.k.a. Donna R, guitarist supreme. Pounding the drums and co-managing the band was Torry Castellano, a.k.a. Donna C. On lead vocals was the tall and exuberant Brett Anderson, a.k.a. Donna A. On bass was the true rebel of the band, the often out-of-control and hilarious Maya Ford, a.k.a. Donna F. One of our lasting memories of

Donna F was seeing her in handcuffs, face down on the hood of a cop car, after resisting arrest for drinking whisky in the streets. The Smugglers were fortunate enough to play many sold-out shows with the Donnas all over North America.

One of our first tours with the Donnas was a week-long stretch in Texas, anchored by the ridiculous, branding-gone-wild South by Southwest Music Festival. Both bands decided to fly in and rent cars to stampede through the Lone Star State. At the car rental counter we discovered the Donnas were too young to legally rent or even drive a rental vehicle, so the Smugglers rented both vans, with various Smugglers taking turns at chauffeuring the Donnas. Beez was old enough to be their dad. When it was his turn to drive them, they insisted on listening exclusively to metal bands at full volume, drowning out his pleas for singalongs to ELO or Wings. Beez was amazed at the Donnas' consistently united front. We weren't proud to admit it, but there were always factions in the Smugglers. The jaunt was a bonding experience and reminded us of the days when we had toured the USA with some of our own members under twenty-one.

One night in Dallas we were seated at a table for ten at Chili's. The Smugglers ordered several outrageous cocktails and nonchalantly slid them across to the Donnas' side of the table. Later, at the hotel, we drunk-dialled their room to ask if they wanted to come to our room to watch a movie. A few minutes later they knocked. "Come on in, door's open!" They found us all naked, tucked in up to our waists in the two double beds watching *Porky's Revenge!* They ran screaming back down the hall to their room.

When the Donnas released their 1999 breakout album, *Get Skintight*, featuring a hot pink cover, they asked us to do a US tour with them. We eagerly agreed. Beez cherry-picked the shows at the Roxy in Los Angeles and the Roxy in New York (with Joan Jett), but six weeks in the USA proved too long for him, so for the rest of the tour we drafted fill-in bassist Jeffy "Pop" McCloy. Jeffy was an eager young Kamloops punk who had one of the largest record collections any of us had ever seen. The opening band on the tour was the Plus Ones, a cute, power-pop indie boy band featuring our pal Joel Reader from MTX on lead vocals and Dan Panic from Screeching Weasel on drums.

The tour proved to be a sold-out smash. Celebrities flocked to see the Donnas. In LA, none other than William Shatner was in the house (he

Our last show in New York City was opening for the legendary Joan Jett and the Blackhearts at a huge venue called the Roxy. That's Jeffy "Pop" McCloy on the left, who filled in for Beez on bass for most of the dates of this tour. ALLISON ROBERTSON PHOTO

was dating Donna A's aunt at the time), along with legendary DJ Rodney Bingenheimer and members of Green Day, the Muffs and the Runaways. In New Orleans famed Runaways producer Kim Fowley made his towering presence known in a glaring red suit and white shoes. In New York the guest list was astounding: Anthrax (there to check out the Donnas), Andrew W.K. (there to check out the Donnas), Lemmy from Motörhead (there to check out the Donnas), Canadian film director Bruce McDonald (there to check out the Donnas) and a guy named Steve (there to check out the Smugglers). The tour was booked before *Get Skintight* started taking off, and consequently some of the shows were in venues that were far too small and got dangerously, well, skintight.

Tuesday, March 21, 2000
Bernie's Distillery
Columbus, Ohio

What our tour itinerary neglected to mention
about this show was the venue's full name:
Bernie's Distillery... and BAGELRY. Hard
booze and bagels in a basement club with a
very low ceiling and a tiny stage, half the
place being a bar and the other half a bagel
joint. It was totally jam-packed and everyone,
bands, staff and audience alike, were soaked
in sweat before a note was played thanks to
the heat of the bagel ovens. For some reason
(maybe hard booze instead of beer?), more
than other nights on this tour, the crowd
went over the top INSANE for the bands. The
Plus Ones barely made it off the stage. We
had a dangerously fab show. It was totally
fun, completely out of control and reckless.
The kids were going ape shit.

Since the stage was only about a half-foot
high if that, the bagelry workers were soon
employed as security to form a human "bagel-
chain," aprons, bagelry shirts, linked arms
and all, facing us across the front to keep
kids from banging into us on the stage. And
those bagel men and ladies worked their asses
off. There was a group of very rambunctious
punks from Dayton, Ohio, who knew the words
to every one of our songs (one of them won
the dance contest) who, pretty innocently,
were inadvertently and constantly elbowing
the owner's wife in the back of the head
as she desperately gripped her co-workers'
wrists to keep the chain alive.

If these bagel security chainers thought
the crowd was wild for us, they had no idea
the magnitude of the Ohio cyclone that hit
them when the Donnas started. It was total
chaos. It became so out of control that
punks kept bursting through the bagel chain,
flying headlong into the Donnas, knocking
them flat on their skin-tight butts. The
constant abuse, beatings and torturous,
swamp-like heat had the bagel chain gang
breaking down, collapsing left and right,
only to be trampled by the boots of the
slamming Ohioans. One audience member tried
to climb onto the stage by monkeying along
the exposed wires in the ceiling. That was
until he grabbed onto a live wire and was
thrown to the floor in a shower of sparks
and vodka. Others climbed up the PA speakers,
toppling them like children's blocks.

The frothing mob eventually lay waste to
what was left of the bagel security chain,
took over the stage and pinned the Donnas
against the back wall so they couldn't even
play any longer. Like a pack of wild dogs,
the Ohio punks surged towards the Donnas,
now completely unprotected by the bagelry
employees, slumped to the side, defeated in
their tattered, booze 'n' blood-splattered
aprons. Eventually the Donnas threw down
their instruments and ran. They raced up the
stairs, onto the street and straight into
their van, hitting "all lock" as soon as they
were all safely inside. It was like a cross
between *A Hard Day's Night* and *The Island of
Doctor Moreau*.

Similar to what we had experienced with cub years earlier in Canada, the Donnas had a rapidly growing fan base of older men referred to in the scene as "G-B-Gs" (girl-band-geeks). After the excited hordes had dispersed, these rumpled fellows would mill around with posters, CDS, LPS and Sharpies in hand, patiently waiting for the Donnas to appear. They often came bearing strange gifts, like the ex-con in Oklahoma City who had just been released from a federal penitentiary. Before he left the Big House, he had stamped out a personalized Oklahoma licence plate for each member of the band.

In Austin a young male fan claimed he had recently won a lifetime supply of Mike and Ike candies in a *Buffy the Vampire Slayer* contest and wanted to share his sweet prize with the Donnas. At the snap of his fingers, the bouncers at Emo's started loading crate after crate of Mike and Ike candies into the backstage. The candies lasted for the rest of the tour and often became projectile weaponry between the vans on the highway. In Chapel Hill, two guys who looked like a cross between Beavis and Butthead and the neighbours from *Rosemary's Baby* hung around in hooded sweatshirts, presenting the Donnas with four large rings embedded with black crystals. The pair hissed that the rings possessed black magic and if worn would help the Donnas rock harder. The rings were later thrown in the toilet.

The Smugglers also introduced/forced the Donnas into our long-standing habit of visiting tourist attractions and historical sites on the road. Although the Donnas generally preferred malls, Japanese candy shops and guitar emporiums, we dragged them to various sites we insisted on checking out. In San Antonio we remembered the Alamo. In Dallas we marched them around Dealey Plaza. In New Orleans we crawled through the French Quarter. By the time we got to Cleveland, they refused to visit the Rock and Roll Hall of Fame with us. Back at the club, we planned to rub in how great the Hall of Fame had been. We never got the chance.

Regardless of the ridiculously extreme heat in the dressing room at Peabody's Down Under, most of the Smugglers and the Donnas were happily engaging in our nightly pre-show dressing room party. The Donnas got two twenty-six-ounce bottles of Jack Daniel's whisky on their rider every night, along with the usual beer, wine and food, and they were always into sharing. While Graham and I abstained, various members of both bands were knocking back whisky shots while the opening band downstairs struck their first few chords. That was when the explosion just outside our dressing room door shook the building.

Wednesday, March 22
Peabody's Down Under
Cleveland, Ohio

It was back to the Cleveland Flats tonight, a disgusting and designated party strip along the river. As we put all of our suits and boots in the upstairs dressing room, we noticed an intense heat right outside the backstage door. We assumed someone was cranking the temperature to warm the place up. The odd thing was the hallway was so hot it felt like a sauna, and the doorknob to the dressing room was too hot to touch! Nonetheless, there were lots of unbothered employees around so none of us made any mention. Just as the Plus Ones were starting, everyone in the club heard a loud BANG. I was down in the club and bore witness to a five-foot-wide waterfall of brown water bursting through the ceiling above the stage, pouring all over the equipment.

Upstairs in the dressing room, an assortment of Donnas and Smugglers were having a booze party. The explosion happened right outside their door. Nick opened it and was immediately sprayed in the face with hot brown liquid (sounds like my last date). The entire hallway was a wall of dirty water, and it was coming down fast. Nick quickly

slammed the door shut. Everyone thought it
was sewage, but Nick could taste the brown
suds and proclaimed that it wasn't shit, so
Dave hastily suggested that "It must be beer!"
Nope, just rusty, gross tap water.

It was rushing under the door and into the
backstage room fast and furious, and also
pouring down onto the stage in a muddy brown
torrent, flowing over the edge down to the
floor. The panicked audience scrambled to get
up on chairs and tables. Water was cascading
down the stairs in such a deluge that no
one from the main floor could get upstairs
to get the band members out. The water level
got higher and higher in the dressing room,
forcing the musicians to climb up on couches,
tables and chairs.

The Cleveland fire department arrived,
sirens blaring. We let them know that people
were trapped upstairs, so three of them
rushed up through the wall of water and burst
into the dressing room to the cheers of the
band members inside. Donna A insisted on
being carried down the stairs by a fireman.
After the water was finally turned off, it
was revealed that the club's water main had
burst due to the extreme heat from upstairs!
Why didn't we say anything? And of course
the pipe cracked right above the stage
and right across from the dressing room
door. What a mess. The equipment is wet but
thankfully okay.

The gig was cancelled, but all three bands still got paid. You would
think it would be a bummer to not get to perform in Cleveland, the

birthplace of "rock 'n' roll," but surprisingly, it came as a relief. It would have been our twenty-fourth show of the tour, and we had had only one night off so far. Suffice to say, there were no complaints about the cancelled show at Peabody's and saying "goodbye Cleveland!"

There was one other weird splash of satisfaction. For over ten years, our onstage footwear had steadfastly remained rubber boots as a shout-out to our wet, West Coast home. For one night only, in a flooded club in Cleveland, no one asked us why we wore "those stupid boots."

The Donnas wouldn't visit the Rock and Roll Hall of Fame in Cleveland with us, but we still had a great time. The Hall of Fame had a grunge exhibit, and we spotted a cub poster among the artifacts! NICK THOMAS PHOTO

forty-two

Kings of the Party

THE DONNAS TOUR came to a close in Salt Lake City after forty shows. We had played every major city in the United States and many smaller ones. We had met movie stars and rock stars and had ridiculous all-night booze parties that devolved into messy orgies, only to wake up to long, hungover, shame-filled drives across a defrosting America. In the afterglow of the last gig (during which a bouncer broke his leg after falling down the stairs while trying to throw out a guy who attacked Jeffy onstage), both bands gathered in the by-then-empty club and popped champagne to celebrate. We didn't know it then, but it was the last major US tour the Smugglers would ever do.

Throughout the tour, the Donnas' formidable bassist Donna F had been trying to live out their new song about getting it on with "Forty Boys in Forty Nights" in real time. While we loaded our vans one final time in the alley behind the club, Donna F announced she was one boy short, then grabbed me by my tie and yanked me towards her. It was a make-out session for the ages, tongues twisting and teeth clacking, until we had to be separated. Then we went at it again. When we finally came up for air, my face was smeared with Donna F's black makeup and her face with my saliva. Later, in the van on our long drive home, Ska-T quietly admitted he had been Boy #38 in Lawrence, Kansas.

WE RESTED UP for a month before embarking on our most ambitious adventure yet, something Lookout dubbed "The Pacific Rim Job Tour 2000": a return trek to Japan and our first tours to Australia and New Zealand, all in one long trip. Nick's travel agent mom booked the entire complicated itinerary. The Smugglers had remained friends with Supersnazz, and bassist Tomoko kindly offered to set up our tour in Japan. It was clear it would be far better organized than our first trip: better venues, more shows on both coasts of the country and great Japanese support bands at every show.

The day we began the Pacific Rim Job Tour was one of the most memorable of my life. We woke up in Vancouver on a Friday, got on a flight bound for Tokyo and landed in Japan on Saturday afternoon in time to play a show that night in downtown Tokyo.

Our pal Maki from the Tokyo band the Lottie Collins met us at Narita Airport. From there, we took a two-hour train ride into Tokyo. After disembarking at a packed rail station, we boarded a subway for another twenty-minute ride, emerging on foot into the hustle bustle of the megacity. After a confusing hike with our guitars and suitcases through the narrow and sweaty streets, we reached the famed Shelter club. We stumbled down the miniature staircase and ended our pan-Pacific marathon journey to reunite with our friends Supersnazz, who greeted us with the news that the show was sold out. We collapsed into their arms, thrilled to be back.

We were weary from our bizarre travel day, but as soon as we counted in the "One, two three …" to our opener "Booze Can," a new song from *Rosie*, the stacked 'n' packed audience detonated, singing along with every word. Crowd enthusiasm can be a remedy for even the most exhausted sacks of shit. Our travel fatigue vanished, and we had one of our most unforgettable shows ever. It was Graham's first time experiencing Japan, and it came on full blast. We got an encore, but when we stumbled back on stage, Nick was nowhere to be found. We played a few songs anyway, assuming he had taken a kamikaze flight to the toilet with an early case of "Bishy-Bishy." (Supersnazz had been forced to teach us this Japanese term for diarrhea, which we used to title a song on *Selling the Sizzle*).

In Nick's absence, we were honoured to have Fink from Teengenerate join us on guitar for a raging version of Chuck Berry's "I'm Talking About

You." We kept on rockin' on our show closer, Brownsville Station's ridiculous "Kings of the Party." We assumed Nick would re-emerge from backstage at some point, but he never did. We later learned that after the final song of our regular set, he had lurched out the back door of the soundproof club, desperate for some fresh air. The door slammed shut behind him. He staggered down a side street, soaking wet in our current look of matching, specially embroidered white tuxedos, and passed out on a woman's doorstep, drained from the epic travel day. The woman arrived home to find a stinking, steaming foreigner in a white tuxedo snoring face down on her doormat.

The rest of the Japanese tour came together like an origami crane, every show a hit, every band we played with excellent, every venue perfect. It was May and the weather was gorgeous. The tour was much more far-reaching geographically than our last trip to Japan had been. We rolled along in a caravan with Supersnazz across the mighty island of Honshu, over the Japanese Alps, through colourful valleys filled with terraced rice fields and farm houses, all the way to the sunny beaches of the west coast. We played in exciting cities and towns like Kanazawa, Niigata, Kyoto and Shizuoka, as well as making return trips to Osaka and Nagoya. On days when the drive was short, Supersnazz took us to all sorts of spectacular Japanese temples and gardens. We stayed everywhere from musicians' tiny bamboo-covered apartments to deluxe hotels with strawberry-scented toilet paper and heated toilet seats.

Our last show in Tokyo was in the heart of Shinjuku, the massive shopping and entertainment district. It was another sold-out success, with a final string of awesome opening bands. It was also Dave's birthday. Supersnazz made him a surprise cake, and by coincidence Dave's dad happened

2000.5.14 (日) タイムテーブル
18:00 OPEN
18:30 START

18:30	**SUPER SNAZZ**
18:50	
18:55	**TREE BERRYS**
19:20	
19:25	**BOOGIE BOY IKUTO**
19:50	
19:55	**THE HAVE NOT'S**
20:25	
20:30	**THE SMUGGLERS**
21:30	

＊ 時間を守ってください。

Out of everyone we performed for all over the world, the Japanese fans were the most rabid.

The lineup at our final show in Tokyo in May 2000. It was Dave's birthday and his dad just happened to be in the city on business. He joined us on stage for the last song, along with a bunch of members of the other bands.

to be in Tokyo on business. He not only came to the show with his business cronies, but also climbed up on stage for some cake and a cheer. By the time we finally got to our closing song, everybody who had helped with the tour was up on stage with us: Supersnazz, the Lottie Collins, the other opening bands, Dave's dad and even Enoki from the astounding Japanese surf band Jackie and the Cedrics, who did us a great honour. Dave threw him his guitar and Enoki cranked out an incredible solo to cap the song, the show and the tour.

We had one last feast in a Shinjuku eatery with all our friends and then collapsed at the first-class hotel digs Supersnazz booked us into for our final night. The next morning we boarded a 747 southbound to Sydney. Could Australia come even close to living up to the rock 'n' roll glory of Japan?

forty-three

Dirty Deeds Done Dirt Cheap

W E HAD OFTEN set final goals for the band over the years, making declarations like "Okay, if we ever make it to Calgary, then we can break up" or "Okay, if we make it to Alabama, then we can break up." For the last few years our dream destination had been Australia. Thanks to the Lookout Records trademark and our close association with the Donnas, an Australian tour came through when a promoter couldn't get the Donnas and took us instead. (That set us up for one of our favourite reoccurring punchlines whenever we were offered a good gig: "Who cancelled?" Unfortunately the promoter usually had an answer.)

We were in a state of disbelief when we stepped out of the Sydney Airport into the blinding sunshine of an early Australian morning. Unlike in Japan, there was no one there to greet us and hustle us through the city to a headlining, sold-out gig. Instead we schlepped our gear onto a bus that wound its way through the sun-baked streets en route to a youth hostel in the back end of town. The culture shock was immediate. What jumped out at us like a great white shark was the city's absolute lack of style. Throughout Japan, we had gawked at the outrageous and completely cool fashion envelopes being pushed, but here in Australia it was as if we had arrived at a seaside resort for the cast of *Little Britain*. Squinting through the dirty windshield of the city bus, we saw mostly lumpy, ruddy white people in bad shorts, loud T-shirts and flip-flops.

Our destination, Billabong Gardens, was a dumpy hostel in Newtown, a bohemian Sydney neighbourhood (Beez later dubbed it "Get-a-Bong Gardens," referring to the other guests' constant reefer madness). We had arrived the day before our first show, but unfortunately Newtown was nowhere near downtown or the beaches Nick and I were hoping to frolic upon. The two of us found the train station and boarded a train bound for downtown Sydney, arriving in the beautiful inner harbour at sunset. We ran gleefully up the famous Opera House steps to take photos and celebrate that we were there. The rest of the band went to see an Australian movie, then afterwards ran into the star of the movie at the corner store across the street from our hostel. No joke! We spent the following day surfing and suntanning at the world-famous Bondi Beach before our first show that night in Sydney.

We had landed the opening slot on a national tour with the Hard-Ons, an Australian punk institution. Forming in 1981, the Hard-Ons were supposedly the most commercially successful Australian indie band of all time, selling over 250,000 albums. They held the record for seventeen consecutive number-one songs on the Australian alternative charts and were renowned in punk circles worldwide. When the Ramones toured Australia, it was the Hard-Ons who opened. They were legends, and thanks to the Donnas being unavailable, the Smugglers were touring with them.

While we were happy to be on the tour, we weren't all that into the Hard-Ons' music, which was a grungy form of punk, an unwelcome throwback to the early 1990s. They also proved to be standoffish; we would rarely see them around the clubs pre- or post shows. Also on the bill was an ex-pat Japanese band called Mach Pelican, three very nice kids who had relocated to Australia to seek their rock 'n' roll fortune. Mach Pelican were obsessed with Lookout Records, which explained why they sounded like a Japanese version of the Queers. All of the gigs were to be bar shows, some in Australia's most renowned punk venues. We would be shocked to see how truly unremarkable those famous venues actually were.

We made it to Australia! To prove it, one of our first stops was the famous stairs leading up to the Sydney Opera House in Sydney Harbour. NICK THOMAS PHOTO

Our Sydney show was at a club called the Excelsior, which more closely resembled the Regal Beagle from *Three's Company* than a punk institution. It was essentially a rundown pub with a very small room for live music in the back. The show was sold out in advance, but our egos were feeling oh so fragile on virgin soil. We had been treated like the Kings of the Party in Japan, but things were going to be different Down Under, since down under was also our place on the bill: we were scheduled to be the first band of the night. We hadn't "opened" a show in years. As Beez put it, "From the Ritz to the shits in forty-eight hours."

To our surprise, the crowd at the front knew our songs. After the show, we found out they were all Canadians travelling and working in Australia. There was a significant audience shift for the Hard-Ons, who attracted an older, mostly male and very punk crowd of shirtless thugs who epitomized an Aussie stereotype we would be forced to deal with for the rest of the tour. Already we were longing for the graciously manic appreciation of the gender-balanced Japanese fans. We would stick pretty close to the Mach Pelican guys for the rest of the trip.

The next morning at the ass crack of dawn, we began a massive, nine-hundred-kilometre trek across the southeast of Australia. We didn't have time to take the coastal route, instead opting for the "short cut," a mind-numbing haul through the Outback. We had ignorantly thought these sorts of epic overland treks between major cities didn't exist much outside of Canada. Wrong. At least Australians liked gigantic roadside attractions, many of which could be seen shimmering in the heat from far off in the distance. On the ride to Melbourne, we visited a four-storey concrete sheep with a sheep museum inside and a thirty-foot plaster statue of 1800s Aussie outlaw Ned Kelly.

Melbourne's sold-out gig, the "anchor date" of the Australian tour, was at a venue called the Tote, described to us as "the CBGB of Oz." We were feeling good and were ready to rock. This time we were also playing right before the Hard-Ons. That did the trick. The Australian crowd fully reacted to us at the Tote, dancing, yelling and trashing stuff off and onstage. Beez was pissed off that none of the lights were shining onto his side of the stage. He literally decided to take matters into his own hands when between songs, he reached up and grabbed an overhead stage lamp, which badly burned both his hands at the touch. The entire club knew about it when he let out a shrill shriek of pain. As our show rolled on and the smell of burnt flesh dissipated, we were taken aback at the Aussie Rules violence that kept erupting on the dance floor. People got into fights, dog-piled on top of each other and smashed glasses and bottles on the stage and each other.

It was more of the same in Adelaide. After a ten-hour drive through more outback scrub (this time we stopped at the Giant Koala, a four-storey, crudely constructed model of a massive, sitting koala made out of chicken wire and plaster, again housing a museum), we played a sold-out club filled with vicious Australian punks who looked like they were straight out of central casting for *Romper Stomper*. During our set, I climbed up onto the PA and thrust my fist in the air, oblivious to the whirling blades of a ceiling fan just inches from my head. Blood from my knuckles sprayed out over the crowd, which seemed to delight them. During the following guitar solo, I wrapped my bloody hand in a towel and kept going, fearful that if we stopped for too long, the heckling would be too intense.

After the show, Beez tried to make his way to our merchandise table

through the Hard-Ons' crowd while carrying a glass of shiraz. A huge Aussie punk spotted him, reached out from the pit, grabbed him by the hair and screamed, "You fookin' Canadian wanka! Get in the pit, mate!" He dragged Beez into the mess of frothing bodies on the dance floor, spilling his wine all over everyone. The wineglass shattered on the dance floor. Beez managed to escape, but the guy caught him and threw him like a rag doll into the mess of shirtless men pounding on each other to the Hard-Ons' relentless beat. Beez made a break for it, only to be caught a third time. He finally worked out a deal with the guy and his buddies by buying them a round of Foster king cans at the bar, which was probably like trying to put out a fire with gasoline. Remembering Denver, Beez managed to befriend the punk. By the end of the night, he was in the bathroom sucking on the guy's massive bong. Yes, the punk had brought his own bong to the gig. Only in Australia.

In Adelaide we stayed at a once-fancy Old West hotel from the late 1800s. It felt like I had just shut my eyes in a state of total exhaustion when I heard Graham's deep voice. "Everything is fuckin' gone, man!" I squinted at his fuzzy, thin frame standing over me. I reached for my glasses. "What's gone? Where?" Graham pointed to the balcony. Dashing outside in my boxer shorts, I glanced around. My heart sank. We had been robbed.

A few hours earlier, we had taken advantage of the sprawling, colonial-style balcony to hang up our soaking wet stage clothes to dry overnight. At some point in the wee hours of the morning, some desperate soul had shimmied up onto our balcony and stolen all five of our embroidered white tuxedos. Gone were our matching jackets, shirts, ties, pants, even our gig gonch. Upon searching the balcony, we realized the thief hadn't quite stolen *everything*; our rubber boots remained lined up in a neat row where we had left them. The guitars and our suitcases were safe; they had been inside the room with us. But we were still shocked at the theft. Under the stage lights, our outfits may have looked pretty good, but those same stage lights had turned our tuxedos into rancid, stinking apparel that was falling apart. Only a truly deprived individual would even touch them, let alone steal them.

We spent a couple of hours searching the back alleys and dumpsters of Adelaide, to no avail, so we switched our search to the Adelaide thrift-store scene. We never saw our five matching white tuxedos again. At the thrift store we pieced together new suits that didn't really match. Dave put together a tweed British gentleman's look, Beez found a waiter's jacket and Graham looked like a guest star from *The Love Boat* in a navy blue, double-breasted, gold-button number. Nick and I both had extra suits in our luggage.

To ease the upset and expense of losing our outfits, our tour manager "Luke the Duke" took us to a wild animal park just outside of Adelaide, where we experienced Australia's weird wildlife up close and personal: wombats, emus, wallabies, Tasmanian devils, dingoes, kangaroos and koalas. I got to hold a koala bear, which didn't go well. In my excitement at cradling the cuddly beast for a photo op, I thought it would be neat to slip my fingers inside its pouch. Instead, I inadvertently poked it somewhere else in its nethers, causing the poor animal to let out a Chewbacca-like squawk. It dug its formidable claws into my leather jacket, which made me squawk and try to shake the animal loose. The Paul Hogan-esque rangers pried the wailing koala from my torso and wasted no time kicking me out of the park. As one of them shoved me through the turnstile, Nick heard me yelling, "I thought it was a marsupial!"

After we had our suits stolen in Adelaide, our tour manager took us to a wildlife park to cheer us up. I got kicked out after trying to stick my finger in this koala bear's pouch. PHOTO COURTESY CLELAND WILDLIFE PARK

forty-four

Supergyration!

F I GET asked the question "What was your most exciting moment as a musician?" my mind races back to an email the Smugglers received while touring the USA with the Donnas. We were in Iowa City, and our tour to Japan and Australia was approaching in the months ahead. The subject line of the email was "NEW ZEALAND?!?" The words jumped out of the screen at me. I nervously opened the message.

The guy on the other end of the email was Jumpin' Johnny Baker, a Kiwi touring impresario who worked with the White Stripes and various other bands. After a few more email exchanges, an extension of our Pacific Rim Job tour was booked to the Land of the Long White Cloud. We were mystified about why we had been invited. Very few Canadian independent bands had ever set foot on a New Zealand stage.

After saying goodbye to our newfound friends Mach Pelican, Luke the Duke and the Spazzys (an Aussie all-female punk band we fell for), we were en route across the Tasman Sea on an Air New Zealand flight bound for the very southern reaches of the Pacific Ocean.

Regardless of our excitement, we couldn't help but second-guess this next leg of the tour. After the grind of Australia, our collective insecurities hinted that we might be on a steady decline, heading into further "markets" with little or no clue about who we were. In one of our darkest Australian hours, lying in a cockroach-infested hostel in Melbourne while an ABBA cover band blared in the packed bar directly beneath our room, we had considered cutting our losses and blowing off New Zealand altogether. We were also nervous, based on the scant touring details Jumpin' Johnny had provided in his emails and on various music scene rumours, that he was a raving lunatic. But we didn't cancel. We woke up the next morning realizing we might never have another chance to visit the place.

When we arrived in Auckland, Beez was randomly chosen for a customs inspection and was held up due to the one remaining piece of our stage wardrobe: rubber boots. They showed up in his suitcase on the X-ray machine and set off a red flag. When asked by the customs agent why he was travelling with rubber boots, Beez panicked. He broke out into a cold sweat, then spat out in a loud shrill voice, "Uh ... the boots? The boots! My boots? Oh! Well ... they ... are ... for ... in ... case ... it ... rains!" The customs agent didn't buy the weather-preparedness story and unzipped Beez's suitcase, removing his rubber boots, which were emblazoned with silver S's on the side.

"What does the 'S' stand for, mate?"

Beez knew he shouldn't say "Smugglers" for several reasons, so he said the first word he could think of: "SHEEP!"

The customs agent never suspected Beez was a musician; he thought Beez was sneaking into New Zealand to work illegally on a sheep farm, and was concerned that his rubber boots might be contaminated. In a country with three million people and sixty million sheep, these sorts of things matter. After swab tests and questions and answers that proved Beez knew absolutely nothing about sheep, he and his rubber boots made it through to the rest of us in the arrivals area.

We found Jumpin' Johnny just outside the airport's main doors. He was snoring in the driver's seat of his van, his head resting on the steering wheel. He had a six-pack of beer sitting on the passenger seat, and was clad in a bright Hawaiian shirt and a black baseball cap that said in red capital letters, "I AM A ROCK 'N' ROLL MACHINE." We were skittish, but when we woke him up he was delighted to see us. We drove into Auckland in Johnny's van with the windows rolled down, soaking in the tropical weather. Craning our necks to take it all in, we entered a beautiful city surrounded by blue waters, squat volcanoes, palm trees and lush vegetation. We were thrilled to be at the end of the earth.

The rumours were completely false about Jumpin' Johnny Baker. As we rolled into Auckland, we started noticing large, full-colour Smugglers posters on every telephone pole. Johnny was a publicity machine, we discovered: he had booked us on several national television and radio shows for interviews and live performances, and he was a top-notch, highly organized promoter who employed a crew of helpers that made the tours run like clockwork. His team even included a travelling DJ, to make sure that great rock 'n' roll records were played before, between sets, and after the show.

Our fears further abated at our first show in Hamilton. We were back in the headlining position, and we took the stage in front of what looked like a friendly crowd. It worked in Japan, so we burst as hard as we could into "Booze Can." The Hamilton kids erupted like Mount Ruapehu. From the first note of the set to the last, they were freaking out, crowd-surfing, charging the stage and, for the last song, grabbing me, hoisting me above their heads like a flying nun and pinning me to the relatively low ceiling, repeatedly mushing my face against it. It was great. Unlike in Australia, where it had felt like us versus the audience every night, this gig felt like a joyous celebration.

We had phased out the kissing contest in Australia for reasons of hygiene and personal safety, but Jumpin' Johnny had read all about it in our tour diaries and had seemingly told everybody in New Zealand, so Kiss the Kiwis we did. The tour took us up and down New Zealand, where media, fans and bands at every stop embraced us like rock stars. We played alongside excellent groups like the Datsuns (who would go on to be swept up in the worldwide garage rock explosion), Shaft, the D4, the

Get Fucked-Ups and Babinski. Following every show there was an after-party at someone's house, often featuring Johnny's DJ, Skinny, blasting out tunes into the wee hours. He started every one of his sets with AC/DC's bagpipe-blaring "It's a Long Way to the Top (If You Wanna Rock 'n' Roll)." We were at the bottom of the earth, but felt like we had finally made it to the top. Conga lines formed; people danced on the tables, on the couches and in the bathroom, and we were shimmying right in step. Within days, it felt like we were a part of the NZ music community.

The drives between towns were short, which left us plenty of time during the day to explore places like Rotorua, famous for the geothermal wonders of boiling volcanic mud, hot springs, geysers, volcanoes and ancient Māori villages, all surrounded by thick, seemingly prehistoric rainforest. Steam constantly rose from the pits, and the grey mud farted and burped before our eyes. The ground was so hot that the pond water

The geothermal mud pools of Rotorua, New Zealand. We had an incredible time in the Land of the Long White Cloud. It was like we had finally found our touring nirvana at the opposite end of the earth. GRAHAM WATSON PHOTO

ASK GRANT

Q: Do you ever regret being in a band?

A: No! It's the greatest thing I've ever done. I'm with my friends in a van seeing the world. And they all love me.

Q: What are your vices?

A: Hooch, street gambling, procrastination, bossing everyone around.

Q: What's the name of your favourite book, film, and TV show?

A: *The Adventures of Tintin*, *Gunga Din*, *Little House on the Prairie*.

Q: How would you like the Smugglers to be remembered in twenty years' time?

A: The Canadian Ambassadors of Rock 'n' Roll.

Q: Who do you most admire?

A: My dad.

Q: Do you have any recurring nightmares?

A: Being unprepared for a gig, like not having set lists written, or doing songs I don't know the lyrics to, or being really late for a show without venue directions. So basically all our actual gigs.

Q: What song do you most enjoy singing live?

A: "Supercar" by the Leather Uppers.

Q: What was the last album you bought?

A: The New Bomb Turks "Information Highway Revisited."

The Smugglers Questionnaire –
Butterfly Juice Zine Issue #14

Happiness found! Graham and Beez rocking out with our New Zealand promoter, Jumpin' Johnny Baker, at one of the many all-night after-parties that followed the gigs.
NICK THOMAS PHOTO

was at a steady boil and the whole place gave off the pungent smell of farts. On other days we'd hike into deep jungle ravines to discover waterfalls cascading down mountainsides. We took ferries across the harbour and rode a gondola to the top of a volcano, racing back down in ridiculously fast and dangerous luge go-carts. We explored Auckland and its awesome record shops and suntanned in parks ringed with palm trees.

In the early evenings before the shows, Johnny had lined up constant mainstream media. One show interviewed us down at the beach, where a pair of rollerblading young women in bikinis recognized us as the camera rolled. We thought for sure Johnny had staged it. He swore he hadn't. Another spot was for a popular national variety TV show called *Space*, where the chirpy, tanned hosts interviewed Beez and me on their couch on their brightly lit, glittering pastel set. After the media blitzes, Johnny would rush us to our gigs, where we'd squeeze ourselves into packed venues brimming with great vibes.

We were having the time of our touring lives. It felt like we had finally found our dream tour, our lost horizon, the rock 'n' roll nirvana we had been searching for since our beat-up VW van pulled out of my parents' driveway bound for Regina a dozen years earlier. The sweet tropical breezes kept us relaxed and happy. We soaked it all in, knowing it couldn't last.

forty-five

Hate to Say
I Told You So

I T WAS THE same effect as staring into a mirror. We were backstage in a massive, freezing arts centre in Switzerland, on the final leg of our *Rosie* world tour, and none of us could really figure out what we were looking at. Graham had entered the dressing room, stopped cold and let out a low "What ... the ... fuck ... Is this a joke or what?" Beez was next. "They loaded in our outfits already? Awesome! Love the Swiss!"

"Those aren't our outfits," Nick answered, perplexed as the rest of us. After the theft of our white tuxedos in Australia, we had decided to streamline our matching stage dress into sharp black outfits with white accents: black pants and black, full-sleeve button-down shirts, white ties embroidered with the Smugglers' "S" and white belts (big at the moment in the "electroclash" musical blip). I had even spray-painted my rubber boots white for full effect. Now, backstage in Switzerland, we were staring at a set of five outfits hung in a row that looked exactly the same. The only way we realized these weren't our clothes was that:

A) they weren't back-of-the-van rumpled, but were instead perfectly ironed and pressed
B) the white ties weren't embroidered with our signature "S"
C) they didn't reek like urine

Whose clothes were they? What band was touring Europe dressed exactly like us?

It took forty years, but following the alt-rock and punk bursts into the mainstream in the 1990s, three-chord, howling garage rock finally broke in the early 2000s. In the USA, the movement was led by the White Stripes, the Strokes and the Yeah Yeah Yeahs. From Australia came the Vines and Jet, and from New Zealand, the Datsuns, the band the Smugglers had just rocked out with. Franz Ferdinand shot forth from Scotland. There was also a considerable Swedish musical invasion, with bands like the Soundtrack of Our Lives, the Caesars, Sahara Hotnights and the (International) Noise Conspiracy pouring onto the charts like spilled vodka and packing venues, first in England, then around the world. Internationally, the Big Three leading this garage rock revival were the White Stripes, the Strokes and a young band from Fagersta, Sweden, called the Hives.

The Hives had formed in 1993 when they were teenagers, with the clear mission to be a band that was "a velvet glove with brass knuckles, both brutal and sophisticated at the same time." Within a few releases, the band was capturing a raw, exciting garage punk energy, doing to the Sonics what the Beatles had done to Little Richard: paying tribute to the original sound but warping it into something their own.

Our friend Mike LaVella from Gearhead Records and Magazine in San Francisco was an original Hives supporter. He released all of their early records, including the Hives' debut album, *Veni Vidi Vicious*, which he licensed from their Swedish label. But it wasn't until British music magnate Alan McGee (the man responsible for discovering Oasis, among many other successful Britpop bands) saw a Hives video on German TV that the band really took off, signing to McGee's newly created Poptones Records in 2001. That record, *Your New Favourite Band*, proved to be the Hives' well-timed breakthrough. Riding on the strength of the Blur-like single "Hate to Say I Told You So," the record reached number seven on the UK charts and went platinum in the UK. "Hate to Say I Told You So" would eventually stomp all over radio and sales charts the world over.

IN THAT BACKSTAGE room in Switzerland in February 2001, it was the Hives' outfits we were staring at. Poptones had yet to release *Your New Favourite Band* in the UK, but "Hate to Say I Told You So" was already a hit in Sweden, and it was catching fire across Europe when our tour schedule collided with theirs in the Alps. The Hives were just as shocked as we were when their members strolled in and saw our outfits hanging on the wall opposite theirs. We didn't know how they would react to the coincidence, but they saw the humour in it, and we hit it off.

The likeness between the two bands didn't stop at the outfits. The Hives' stage show was similar to ours, in that they too were configured in the classic Rolling Stones blueprint of drummer, bassist, two guitars and lead singer. Their lead singer was Howlin' Pelle Almqvist, a dashing motormouth who, like me, thrived on owning and strutting the stage, exhibiting as much false bravado as possible. Unlike me, he possessed pipes that were somewhere in the truly howling range of Gerry Roslie and Bon Scott.

When we first met the Hives backstage at a show we shared in Solothurn, Switzerland, neither band had any idea we dressed EXACTLY the same. It was a bizarre moment, but luckily they were cool about it and we became friends. SCOTT STEWART PHOTO

Our bands also had matching instruments. The Smugglers' guitars and bass were identical rosewood Gibson SGs; the Hives' guitars and bass were white Fenders. Both bands had choreographed moments in their show. The Smugglers had synchronized dance moves throughout our set, whereas the Hives had moments like their "freeze frame" (a pause in a song during which every member remained perfectly still in a rock pose until the drummer came back in). Our guitarist, Nick, had developed a stage-wide flying somersault while soloing on his guitar during our closing song "Kings of the Party." Their guitarist, Nick, had a move in which he would seamlessly spin his Fender Telecaster around his torso by its strap, catch it and keep playing.

Despite our eerie similarities, despite our playing together at a packed arts centre on a cold night in Switzerland, there was one huge difference between the Hives and the Smugglers: they had a hit, and we didn't. The Hives had achieved on their first album what we never did in over a dozen years of trying: they took a five-piece band with a Sonics-meets-Buzzcocks garage rock sound and created a worldwide smash. Having at least one hit is what rock bands need to survive in the long term. The Smugglers never had a breakthrough song or album that a mass of humanity associated with a particular time and place and had a nostalgic desire to hear again and again, year after year, on the radio, on their stereo or live in concert.

Our friendship with the Hives stretched beyond our Swiss one-night stand. We played with them in Vancouver later that year on their first US tour. They kindly invited us to play more shows with them the bigger they got. *Veni Vidi Vicious* was snatched away from Gearhead and re-released in the USA with major distribution, and "Hate to Say I Told You So" cracked the Billboard Hot 100. Still the Hives didn't forget us, inviting us to open for them on their first major headlining tour of the USA, a sold-out, coast-to-coast affair in one-thousand-person-capacity venues. We fatefully turned down the offer.

The big Hives tour coincided directly with the due date of Nick Thomas's second child, and we didn't want to play without Nick. The creeping domesticity in our lives was unavoidable. Everyone was married but me. Nick, Graham and Beez all had kids. Despite the lifelines the Hives threw us, their trajectory left us imagining what might have been as we bounced new babies on our knees. The Hives went on to years of touring the globe, playing to thousands at mega-festivals, on the strength of their

impeccable live show, their perfect branding and even more hit songs and albums.

We wouldn't have traded our DIY club touring experiences around the world for anything, but it was bittersweet to be watching from the sidelines as younger bands reaped the rewards of rock 'n' roll finally bursting from the garage. The Smugglers had surfed the waves of grunge, indie-rock and pop-punk, but when our true genre finally went big, we couldn't keep up. Lookout Records was a shambles, unable to figure out a way to survive in the afterburn of the 1990s pop-punk gold rush. But Mint Records experienced unprecedented success thanks to the New Pornographers, an indie-rock supergroup from Vancouver that Dave had recorded and co-produced. The band featured his old girlfriend, Neko Case, whose solo career was also taking off, and his best friend and one-time Smuggler, John Collins.

The Smugglers still had some good-time gas left in our nearly empty tank, so we gamely put together a new album, *Mutiny in Stereo*, which came out in 2004 on Mint Records in Canada, Screaming Apple in Germany and Lookout in the USA. That would seem to have set us up nicely for another round of international touring, but it never happened.

Mutiny in Stereo landed us the best reviews we had ever received:

> "This might be the strongest record of the Smugglers' career, with no weak moments and a bucketload of great songs. Lawrence's vocals are strong and nuanced, the guitars loud and tough, the arrangements interesting. *Mutiny in Stereo* shows a degree of skill and craft that is lacking in much of today's pop-punk."
> —ALLMUSIC.COM

The Lookout Records 15th anniversary bash in San Francisco. There wouldn't be a twentieth. In early 2012, burdened by heavy debt and owed royalties, Lookout Records closed its doors for good. PHOTO COURTESY NICK THOMAS

Still, if we had learned anything in over sixteen years, it was that an indie rock 'n' roll record will sell only if it's heavily toured. We attempted that in pieces, avoiding the vans and discomfort for jet airliners, becoming weekend warriors in places like Texas, the Maritimes, Las Vegas, Ontario and California. As always, we held a record release party in Vancouver, joined by our old pals Supersnazz, who were touring North America at the time. It was our first hometown show in over a decade that wasn't sold out. I remembered telling myself years earlier to be wary if our draw at home ever started to wane.

THE SECOND NIGHT that changed my life was a warm Sunday evening in May. The Smugglers were playing an ill-fated, poorly promoted all-ages show in San Diego with our friends the Groovie Ghoulies, the last gig of an otherwise successful 2004 tour of California. Since we were in the Golden State, we made it our "beach ball" tour. I had come up with the misguided idea that I would throw twenty or thirty beach balls of all sizes from the stage into the crowd so that the balls could, in theory, be joyously tossed about. It turned out to be ridiculously labour-intensive, and we quickly came to loathe the party ploy for other reasons.

At our first show in Anaheim, we realized the hard way that the balls could not only be thrown back on stage but spiked violently at us. We had beach balls smacking us in the face or in the side of the head or hitting the microphone while we were trying to sing, all of which delighted the devilish offenders in the audience. Graham became something of a beach-ball magnet, with balls bouncing onto his lap and feet or getting caught between his cymbals and the drums, much to his rage. And since there was no room in the van for thirty inflated beach balls, we'd have to deflate the balls each night to pack them, then spend the drive the next day painstakingly blowing them all up again.

That Sunday night in San Diego, the promoter arrived at the venue well after we did, sheepishly admitting he had just got back from his own band's tour and hadn't had time to promote our show. Barely anyone showed up. Those who did seemed completely disinterested. When we threw the beach balls out into the crowd, roughly one ball for every person in attendance, the audience members couldn't be bothered to lift their arms to catch them, and simply let the balls fall to the floor. It was a truly pathetic sight, though at least they weren't getting thrown back at us. Nick was particularly exasperated at the flaccidity of the gig: I had convinced him to allow us to extend the tour to San Diego, which meant him missing his daughter's second birthday back in Vancouver. As we left the venue that night, my emotions were a hot mix of frustration, guilt and annoyance, so much so that I shamefully took it out on the promoter. I picked up one of our forlorn beach balls and spiked it off the back of his head.

After that incident, it only felt right to get the hell out of town. Unfortunately we took a wrong turn and had to drive back right past the club and the fuming promoter on the sidewalk. Heading out of town after a show was never a good decision, but we hit the road for two hours back to Los Angeles to sleep at the house of our friend Ronnie Barnett from the Muffs. Dave complained of feeling ill, so I was bleary-eyed at the wheel of the rental van. I spun the radio dial until I stumbled onto *Rodney on the Roq*, a show hosted by Rodney Bingenheimer, the legendary DJ and Sunset Strip scenester who was responsible for breaking artists like David Bowie, the Ramones, the Sex Pistols, the Go Gos and more on American radio. Once prime-time, Rodney's show was now shelved into a two a.m. Monday timeslot. Within ten minutes of us tuning in, Rodney played "Main Offender" by the Hives. After the song, he announced in his gentle voice that the Hives had signed a worldwide deal with Universal for a rumoured *ten million dollars*. Rolling up the I-5 in the dark, I let that sink in. Hours earlier we had performed in front of thirty lacklustre fans in San Diego. We had been paid *fifty dollars*.

A few months later I found myself at my family cabin in a wild place called Desolation Sound, BC, where I was spending more and more time since the band was touring less and less. I was working on some modest fall touring plans for *Mutiny in Stereo* by making routine trips in a little aluminum skiff to the pay phone on the government wharf to check in with the guys and various show promoters. One of those calls was to Dave Carswell. He sounded resigned when he answered the phone. Dave explained he hadn't been able to shake the sickly, exhausted feeling following the San Diego show. After sixteen years, our Clydesdale of a guitarist was finally burnt out. "I think I'm done," he said in a quiet tone. It didn't quite hit me at the time, but with that phone call, which unfortunately happened to fall on my thirty-third birthday, the Smugglers were no more.

I thanked Dave for his ace guitar chops, his friendship and humour, and said goodbye. I rang our agent Margie Alban next, someone we had been working with since signing to Lookout, and had her call off a string of shows. One of those cancellations painfully included a fan's wedding in our Maritimes hotbed of Moncton, but I knew we couldn't perform without Dave. I hung up the phone, cracked a semi-cold can of Black Label beer, and looked around. I squinted out into the inlet and the mountains of Desolation Sound with a mixed sense of sadness and relief. It was time to start a new chapter. Nick and his family were arriving the next day, and I would break the news to him then, once our fishing lines were in the water. I'd call Beez and Graham soon after that.

The Smugglers were never the biggest band or the most popular, but we lived out many of our musical dreams, fuelled by gasoline and the trifecta of *ambition, good times, denial*. We met countless incredible people and made lifelong friends. In a sense, the Smugglers were the Forrest Gump of rock 'n' roll bands. We were involved with some of the greatest bands, record labels, scenes and musical movements of the era, but at the edge of the spotlight, like an extra mugging for attention. We had strummed our chords of glory in three different decades, released eight albums and collected a lifetime of stories. The Smugglers survived the road and each other, and we had the time of our lives doing it.

Epilogue:
Rock 'n' Roll Was
Never This Fun

WHEN THE SMUGGLERS abruptly stopped being an active band, everyone went their separate ways. I was left to pick up the pieces. The band was in debt, both to our record labels (for tour merchandise) and to me personally (for credit I had extended), so it was a bit messy. The labels took what money they could out of our measly royalties. My personal debt was never paid, but I was okay with that: a small price for the glory.

Not being able to look ahead to the next tour, the next record, the next opportunity for the band had me in a state of withdrawal, but it was liberating, too. I hadn't known how to stop saying yes to everything. Had Dave not hung up his boots, I would have just kept on going, like Clark Griswold in *National Lampoon's Vacation*, refusing to admit that the dream was falling apart around me. *Ambition, good times, denial.*

After a half-hearted attempt to start a children's acoustic band called the Otters (leaving Nick on the hook for a prototype head-to-toe otter costume), I retired from live music to concentrate on my job at the CBC. As a "singer" who was more Monty Hall than Mick Jagger, I was also feeling my age: the Smugglers were a high-energy, very physical band. In the later years gravity was slowly taking over and my voice got blown out so quickly that I often avoided talking to anyone the day of the gig, trying to save my pipes for the show. For a Chatty Cathy like me, that proved a real drag. Once after a Smugglers gig, I did a live broadcast for the CBC sounding like Dirty Harry. My bosses, usually forgiving and supportive, were furious.

In the aftermath of the band's breakup, I developed a type of post-traumatic rock 'n' roll stress disorder: I had a hard time being in night-clubs, once my havens, unless I was working them for the CBC. If I smelled a urinal puck or felt the sole of my sneaker stick to a barroom floor, I felt nauseated. Maybe it was bitterness at no longer being the centre of onstage attention or receiving the backstage VIP treatment. Maybe it was overexposure from doing it for too long. But performing live music—my life's mission from 1986 to 2004—was no longer on my priority list. Offers for the Smugglers to play dwindled to one or two a year: a festival in Spain, a tour of Norway, a special event at Amigos and assorted private parties. We turned them all down.

Then, in the summer of 2016, I received an email from Alex Botkin, a nineteen-year-old promoter for the legendary 924 Gilman Street in Berke-ley, California. The venue that had lit the fuse on the pop-punk explosion of the 1990s would be celebrating its thirtieth anniversary in 2017, Alex said. According to our old pal Larry Livermore, that made Gilman the longest-lived all-ages volunteer-run venue in the United States.

Alex politely asked if the Smugglers would consider performing at the event. His approach reminded me of my teenage self, cold-calling favou-rite bands to ask them if they would play a show. The Smugglers played Gilman several times in the 1990s and we all had great memories of it. During the final gig of a very long US tour, we once performed a Full Monty-like striptease there, giving away more and more of our stage apparel with each song. Besides good times for the Smugglers, Gilman had the weight of history, punk notoriety and a reputation for inclusive ethics. Alex's offer was flattering and possibly redemptive: it could be a chance for us to celebrate and have some fun.

I trepidatiously sent an email to the rest of the band members. To my surprise, everyone agreed to perform. Suddenly, after more than twelve years, we were back in action, booking practices, flights, hotels and a rental van. Even though there was an epic time lapse, everything clicked quickly at our practices. Therein lies the magic of rock 'n' roll: There's a special alchemy that occurs when you reassemble the people who wrote and performed songs together. I had forgotten how exciting it could be.

Over the fall, the gig ballooned into a full-on Lookout Records reunion titled "The Lookouting," with the Mr. T Experience, Pansy Division, Squirtgun, Larry Livermore and the Potatomen, Brent's TV (who had become the Ne'er Do Wells, then the Hi-Fives), Kepi from the Groovie Ghoulies and many others converging over the course of four nights. Many of our friends and family decided to make the trip to Berkeley to see the show, including the wives of every member of the Smugglers. Except my wife. Jill Barber and I met in 2007, so she had completely missed the Smugglers chapter of my life. I wasn't quite sure she "got" what the Smugglers were all about, since she had never seen us live. A singer-songwriter herself, she was used to performing in beautiful soft-seat theatres. She would be disgusted by the apocalyptic European squat-like vibe of Gilman, I thought. We also had two young kids. I was disappointed, but we agreed it would be best for her to stay at home.

Gilman hadn't changed much in the twenty years since we last set rubber boots in the place. It was still a cavernous warehouse covered in graffiti with rules spray-painted on the wall: "No alcohol, no drugs, no stagediving, no dogs, no fucked up behavior, no transphobia, no racism." The only seating was a sunken couch, practically level with the concrete floor, at the very back of the six-hundred-capacity room. The washrooms were now gender-neutral, though, and thanks to a new PA donated by Green Day, the place sounded great.

On the rainy night of January 7, 2017, 924 Gilman was packed with fans from around North America and the world. We reunited with friends in the crowd from the Donnas, the Mummies, the Hi-Fives and many other bands, as well as with fans we had befriended over the years. Nick said it was like rediscovering a family you forgot you had. Just before we took the stage, I texted my wife to make sure the kids were asleep back in Vancouver. She assured me they were.

Our guitar amps buzzed to life. The stage lights at Gilman instantly had us dripping with sweat in our suits. Graham gave the snare a few hard raps and adjusted the cymbal stands. I nervously tapped the microphone to make sure it was on. Dave and Nick tuned up. Beez wondered why more stage lights weren't pointed in his direction. People were pressed against the lip of the stage, with friendly faces smiling up at us for as far back as we could see. The soundwoman's voice crackled through the stage monitor: "Okay, Smugglers, ready when you are."

Graham took a deep breath and gave his drumsticks three quick clicks. And just like that, we threw ourselves into "Rosie." It was equal parts terrifying and exhilarating. People danced, people cheered, and our five-way chemical reaction frothed into forty-five minutes of totally exhausting fun. Even dear old Ska-T was back to work the merchandise table. When we bowed to the crowd at the end of our final song, I felt like I had been repeatedly smacked in the chest by a baseball bat. But I was happy. Really happy.

This was my first time back on stage with the Smugglers in over a decade, at 924 Gilman in Berkeley, California. AARON RUBIN PHOTO

The Smugglers take a final bow after a triumphant reunion show in January 2017.
GLEN WINTER PHOTO

I gave Dave a hug and stumbled off stage. I texted Jill: "We did it!" I pushed my way through the side door to get outside. I desperately needed some air, and maybe somewhere to throw up. I had the word "defibrillator" on my mind when Dave's wife, Polly, stuck her head through the doorway. "Grant! There's a Smugglers fan here who really wants to meet you."

When I turned around, I thought I was seeing a mirage induced by dehydration. Walking through the doorway, looking radiant, was my wife, Jill. I was stunned. She grabbed me and kissed me in the pouring rain. Jill had left the kids with my sister, secretly flown down to Berkeley and slipped into the venue without me spotting her. She wasn't disgusted, she said. She loved the show. She danced! Not only had the Smugglers rocked out one more time, but Jill had provided the best surprise encore I could have ever asked for.

THE END

PAUL CLARKE PHOTO

Where Are They Now?

NICK THOMAS (GUITAR, BACKING VOCALS): Nick has continued to perform, tour and record with several Vancouver rock 'n' roll bands, including playing guitar with the Tranzmitors (with Bryce Dunn on drums), the Evaporators (replacing Dave) and the Vicious Cycles. Nick also co-founded the Flying Vees hockey team with me back in 2004 (the same year the Smugglers ceased) and visits my family in Desolation Sound every summer. By day he works in the diamond mining industry and routinely travels to some of Canada's most remote northern communities. Nick and his wife, Soraya, have three kids—Floyd, Alia and Quinn—and two dogs.

DAVID CARSWELL (GUITAR, BACKING VOCALS): Dave's faux Church of Elvis wedding in Portland back in 1992 proved prophetic. Many years later he kindled a real romantic relationship with Polly Argo while on another Smugglers tour stop in Seattle. That led to an actual legal wedding, this time for keeps, in Canada. After Dave excused himself from the Smugglers, he continued performing and recording with the Evaporators for a few more years. He is now a member of the respected high-art Vancouver indie band Destroyer, as well as guitarist and music director for the Rodney Graham Band. He is constantly adding to his worldwide touring resume, having performed with both groups in Mexico, Korea, Scandinavia and well beyond. Dave also co-owns and operates the recording studio JC/DC with his old pal John Collins.

BEEZ (BASS, BACKING VOCALS): After Beez recovered from his midlife crisis and rejoined the Smugglers in the late 1990s, he became one of our most passionate members, never wanting to stop rocking out. Beez insisted that the Smugglers avoid publicly announcing a breakup, so we never did. Beez and his wife, CC, moved to Olympia, Washington, for several years, raising their son, Charlie. When they returned to Vancouver, Beez joined our beer league hockey team for lack of a band. That didn't turn out well: one afternoon Beez had a heart attack in the locker room after the game. Nick and I were so used to seeing Beez slumped in a sweaty heap in the corner after gigs complaining of aches and pains that we didn't recognize the signs. Luckily we had a doctor on our team who did. Beez survived and thrived. Mostly retired from rock 'n' roll, he is a certified public accountant specializing in US taxes and the unofficial King of Kitsilano. He still loves to sing and is a performer at heart, and pushed for years for the Smugglers' reunion.

GRAHAM WATSON (DRUMS): After the Smugglers wound down like an old dog, Graham planted further roots in his hometown of Nanaimo, where he and his wife, Kathy, have three children—Aidan, Anton and Kiera—and own Threadscape Custom Apparel, a clothing design company. Graham has offered up his rock-steady drumming chops to various bands on Vancouver Island over the years, most notably when Bum reformed for a string of shows, including a triumphant return tour to Spain.

BRYCE DUNN (DRUMS): After quitting the Smugglers, Bryce brought his explosive drumming prowess to a few lucky but non-touring Vancouver rock 'n' roll bands before forming the Tranzmitors with former Smugglers Nick Thomas and Jeffy McCloy. The Tranzmitors have released a string of singles and an LP (a "best of" for the legendary UK punk label Stiff Records), and toured pockets of England, Canada and California. Bryce impressively does most of the legwork for the Tranzmitors, including booking tours and driving the tour van. He is a library technician and lives in Vancouver with his wife, Mary, and their daughter, Ruby.

ADAM WOODALL (HARMONICA, GUITAR, BACKING VOCALS): Adam is the only full-time professional musician to emerge from the Smugglers ranks. His Adam Woodall Band and solo performances in pubs, halls and festivals are beloved fixtures around the North Shore of Vancouver, Bowen Island and the Sunshine Coast. Adam still has an incredible talent for the harmonica, but he sticks mostly to vocals and guitar in his long-running band. He lives in North Vancouver with his wife, Nicole, and two daughters, Emmerson and Elliot.

SEAN POWERS (GUITARIST, ONE-EYED JACKS): The savant-like metal guitar wizard who shredded our USA debut with his "Eruption" solo continued his total obsession with the mastery of the guitar, practising so intensely ("all day, every day," according to his best friend, Jason Carthy), that his wrists eventually gave in to tendinitis. He received cortisone shots in order to keep playing, but his doctor told Sean the only way to end his considerable pain was to stop playing guitar completely. It was a massive blow. He soon began to substitute drugs for his guitar-soloing highs. Sean Harper Powers died of a heroin overdose on November 7, 1993, in a house just three blocks from my parents' home.

SCOTT "SKA-T" STEWART (ROADIE): Ska-T was the Smugglers' official roadie throughout multiple tours of North America and Europe. When we started opting for airplanes over long-haul van travel, we often couldn't afford the sixth seat. Ska-T was regrettably left at home, despite being one of the most fun, positive and hard-working people any of us had the pleasure to know. Ska-T went on to become a site coordinator at Insite, North America's first supervised and clean injection site for intravenous drug users. He now works for the acute care unit in Vancouver's Downtown Eastside. In his free time, he still promotes every ska band that comes to town.

NARDWUAR THE HUMAN SERVIETTE (MENTOR): Nardwuar's band, the Evaporators, celebrated thirty years in 2016, and Nardwuar has hosted his UBC CiTR Radio show weekly for three decades as well, as of 2017. During that time he has become a peerless and unique celebrity interviewer. After a decade on MuchMusic television, Nardwuar has since become a genuine YouTube star. His interviews with musicians and politicians regularly rack up views in the hundreds of thousands, many into the millions. Healthwise, Nardwuar has suffered both a brain aneurysm (1999) and a stroke (2015), but has thankfully recovered from both. Nardwuar released the Evaporators' sixth album, *Ogopogo Punk*, in 2017.

PAUL PREMINGER (DRUMS): After leaving the Smugglers, Paul fulfilled his dream of becoming a chef. He flipped like a flapjack from restaurant to restaurant, often getting scorched in the high-stress world of fine-dining kitchens (he got fired from one of West Vancouver's fanciest restaurants after he lit up a joint while standing under the establishment's patio—directly beneath a chair occupied by former Prime Minister Joe Clark). When Paul's mother passed away he received a large inheritance, which his mom had intended for Paul to use as a down payment on a house. That never happened. Over the course of a year, Paul and his girlfriend spent it all while slipping into a cycle of drug and alcohol addiction. Together they wound up in the single room occupancy hotels of Vancouver's Downtown Eastside. Whenever the Smugglers checked in with him, he kept his behaviour and living conditions a secret. Friends in the know eventually rescued Paul from that scene, and he tried to rebuild his life, becoming a chef again on Gabriola Island. There he had a violent run-in with a biker over a girl. The biker threatened to gut Paul with a butcher knife if he stuck around. Paul hightailed it with some friends and cleaned himself up while living on a water-access-only oyster farm near Desolation Sound, within a ten-minute boat ride of my family cabin. He never let me know he was in the area while he was working in the kitchens of the nearby Lund Hotel and the Laughing Oyster Restaurant.

Paul moved down the road to Powell River a few years later, becoming a chef at a local restaurant, and started playing drums again in a surf band. He had mostly shaken his drug habit, but he couldn't twist from the grip of alcohol. In one of our last correspondences, Paul confessed he hadn't told us of his situation or whereabouts due to embarrassment, and mentioned he had to "quit drinking whisky by the tanker-load."

Paul kindly invited my wife and me to dine at the restaurant he was cooking at in Powell River. He made us a delicious meal, but he refused to meet with us face to face, slipping out the back door shortly after we were served, later citing shame over his physical appearance. Just two months later in October 2009, after relocating to Vancouver to live with his father, Paul Preminger died in his sleep of a heart attack brought on by congestive heart failure. Before he retired to his bedroom that night, his last words had been, "Good night, Dad, I love you."

Acknowledgements

T HANK YOU
To our fan(s), and the person(s) who bought our record(s).
Also to Jill Barber and Joshua and Grace Lawrence; Garth, Jean and
Heather Lawrence; Nick Thomas, David Carswell, Beez, Graham Watson, Bryce Dunn, Adam Woodall, John Collins, Danny Fazio, Jeff McCloy, Ska-T and Nardwuar the Human Serviette; Soraya Thomas, Polly Argo, CC Hammond, Kathy Watson and Mary Hosick; Barbara Pulling, Naomi MacDougall, Silas White, Nicola Goshulak, Anna Comfort O'Keeffe and Zoe Grams; Samantha Haywood, Barbara Miller and everyone at the Transatlantic Agency; Bill Baker, Randy Iwata and Ryan Dyck at Mint Records; Ken Beattie and Killbeat Music; Leeroy Stagger; Paul Clarke; Chris Murphy, Tyler Bancroft, Allison Robertson, Ira Robbins, Lisa Marr and Will Ferguson; Larry Livermore; the CBC Radio 3 community, CBC Music, Sheryl MacKay and *North by Northwest*; *On the Coast, Radio West, All Points West*; Jason Carthy; Whitney Preminger; Paul Preminger Senior; Lookout Records; Denise Donlon; CIMA; Jim Clarke, Brant Palko and everyone at Amigos; The Flame; Screaming Apple Records; 1+2 Records; Jimmy Garcia; Pep Lough; Al and Amy Sharp; Joel Reader; the Vancouver Flying Vees Hockey Club; everyone at Douglas & McIntyre; book clubs everywhere;

Margie Alban; Frank Leone; Heather Peavey; Jeff Cohen, Craig Laskey and everyone at the Horseshoe Tavern; Beng Favreau and Literacy Haida Gwaii; David Wisdom and *Night Lines*; Yvette Ray; Chris Appelgren; Chris Imlay; Molly Neuman; Francisco "Franny" Santelices; Jane Davidson and the Sunshine Coast Festival of the Written Arts; Cathy Bauer; Tristin Laughter; Lee and Peggy Hower; Joe Queer; Dr. Frank and MTX; the Gruesomes; Ronnie Barnett and the Muffs; Clay Reed and the Subsonics; Glen Winter; Paul Thomas; "Smart" Grant Galbraith; Imposible Records; Pat Thomas; "What Wave" Dave O'Halloran; "Timebomb" Tom Smith; Kurt Bloch; Hans Von Seydlitz; Mass Giorgini; Bryan Ward; Pat "the Shanker" Shanks; Brent Hodge; Long Gone John; Mike LaVella; Charlie Demers; Jack Ross; Megan Barnes; Hastings Community Centre; Chris Kelly and Lauren Bercovitch; Joe Kirk; Alex Botkin; Deb and Drew McVittie; Stacy DC; Evelyn Pollen; Bob Kronbauer and VancouerIsAwesome.com; Billy Bones; John and Judy Denery; Brian and Joyce Barber; Sacramento Sandra; What's Up? Hot Dog!, Kessel & March and the Laughing Bean; Pansy Division; Val Mason; Napili Shores; Words on the Water; Alianait Arts Festival; B-Face; Trent Ruane; Gilles Bonnel; Philip "PSTNYC" Turner; Kip Shepard; Mike Sansone; Blair Buscareno; Tunisha Scott; Tomoko and Supersnazz; The Bluesman; Andrea and Sandro Carraro; 924 Gilman Street; Stella Harvey and the Whistlers Writers Festival; Aleck Duncan; Laughing Oyster Books; KJ Jansen and Chixdiggit; Elephant Mountain Literary Festival; Said the Whale; Christy Nyiri, David Look; Joy Kogawa House; Rob Mangelsdorf, Kelsey Klassen and everyone at the *Westender*; Jon Von; Neko Case; Waterkeeper; Allan McMordie and A Whisky Library; 32Books; Ken Kelley; Armchair Books; Baron Cameron; Kate Carswell; Rob Zifarelli; Terry David Mulligan; Elizabeth "Betti-Cola" Colatrella; Galiano Island Literary Festival; Collin Knight; Howard Glassman; Kootenay Library Federation; Word on the Lake; Jon Murphy; Todd Abramson; Scott McCaughey and the Young Fresh Fellows; Joey Kline; Word Vancouver; Calvin Johnson; Candice Pedersen; Sue Miller; KP Sampsell; West Vancouver Memorial Library; Anne DeGrace; North Central Library Federation; Vancouver Folk Music Festival; Antonia Allan; "Jeopardy" Julie Backer and everyone at the North Shore Writers Festival; Squamish Public Library; Talewind Books; Alex Vyskocil, Aaron Chapman and everyone at the Commodore Ballroom; and the Smugglers Not-Forgotten Few: Dave Dykhuizen, Anthony Creery, Dave Wallen and Ross McKenzie. And to Doctor Kevin "Rosie" Rowan, who read it all first, and saved Beez's life.

The Smugglers
Discography

1990
"Up and Down" 7″
(NARDWUAR RECORDS,
CANADA)

1991
At Marineland 10″ LP
(NARDWUAR, CANADA)

1992
*Atlanta Whiskey
Flats* LP
(POPLLAMA, USA)

1992
"At Germany" 7″
(SCREAMING APPLE,
GERMANY)

1993
*In The Hall Of
Fame—All Time
Great Golds* CD
(POPLLAMA, USA)

1994
"Tattoo Dave" 7″
(TOP DRAWER, USA;
SMUGGLERS/
BUM SPLIT)

1994
"The Smugglers/
The Hoods" split 7″
(FOR MONSTERS, ITALY)

1994
Wet Pants Club
LP/CD
(RADIATION, SPAIN)

1994
*Party… Party…
Party… Pooper!*
7″ EP
(MINT, CANADA)

1995
"Talkin' 'Bout You" 7″
(PIN-UP, GERMANY)

1995

Señor Pantsdown
7″ EP

(ROCK & ROLL INC.,
SPAIN)

1995

"Whiplash!" 7″

(1+2, JAPAN)

1996

Summer Games 7″

(MINT/LOOKOUT,
CANADA/USA;
SMUGGLERS/HI-FIVES
SPLIT)

1996

Selling The Sizzle
LP/CD

(MINT/LOOKOUT/
KONKURRENT, CANADA/
USA/NETHERLANDS)

1997

*Buddy Holly
Convention* EP/CD

(MINT/LOOKOUT,
CANADA/USA)

1998

*Growing Up Smuggler:
Ten Year Anniversary
Live Album*

(MINT/LOOKOUT/
IMPOSIBLE/1+2, CANADA/
USA/SPAIN/JAPAN)

2000

Rosie LP/CD

(MINT/LOOKOUT,
CANADA/USA)

2000

*"Smugglers/Mach
Pelican"* split 7″

(CORDUROY, AUSTRALIA)

2002

"Useless Rocker"
7″ picture-disc

(SUPERSONIC
REFRIDGERECORDS,
ITALY)

2004

Mutiny in Stereo
LP/CD

(MINT/LOOKOUT/
SCREAMING APPLE,
CANADA/USA/GERMANY)

2017

*Dirty Windshields—
The Soundtrack:
The Best of the
Smugglers* digital LP

(MINT, CANADA)

*The Smugglers LPs are available
through Mint Records and
worldwide on Spotify and iTunes.*

Recommended
Listening

MANY OF THE titles used in this book are salutes to some of my favourite musicians, bands, singers, songs and albums, and as always I want to give credit where credit is due. It starts with the title of this book. "Dirty Windshields" is a beautiful outlaw country song by Leeroy Stagger from Lethbridge, Alberta. Thank you to Leeroy for his permission to use his title. The song "Dirty Windshields," and many of the other songs, albums and artists mentioned in chapter titles can be found on these records:

Leeroy Stagger, *Radiant Land* (Gold Lake Records, 2012)

The Sonics, *Here Are The Sonics!!!* (Etiquette, 1965)

The Gruesomes, *Gruesomania* (OG, 1987)

Various Artists, *Clam Chowder and Ice vs. Big Macs and Bombers* (Nardwuar, 1991)

Bum, *Wanna Smash Sensation!* (PopLlama, 1993)

Chixdiggit!, *Chixdiggit!* (Sub Pop, 1996)

Stompin' Tom Connors, *My Stompin' Grounds* (Boot Records, 1971)

Library Voices, *Summer of Lust* (Dine Alone, 2011)

Jill Barber, *Chances* (Outside, 2008)

Sarcastic Mannequins, *Little Brother* (Eyecon Industries, 1991)

The Mr. T Experience, *Love Is Dead* (Lookout, 1996)

Mudhoney, "Touch Me I'm Sick" / "Sweet Young Thing Ain't Sweet No More" 7″ (Sub Pop, 1988)

Young Fresh Fellows, *This One's for the Ladies* (Frontier, 1989)

The Blasters, *The Blasters* (Slash, 1981)

Thee Headcoats, *The Kids Are All Square—This Is Hip!* (Hangman, 1990)

Sloan, *Navy Blues* (Murderecords, 1998)

Beat Happening, *Dreamy* (Sub Pop, 1991)

Various Artists, *Joe King Presents More Bounce to the Ounce* (Lookout, 1997)

Shadowy Men on a Shadowy Planet, *Savvy Show Stoppers* (Cargo, 1988)

Rancid, "Roots Radicals" (Epitaph, 1994)

The Hi-Fives, *Welcome to My Mind* (Lookout, 1995)

The Stand GT, "The Cracklefan" 7″ (Mint, 1995)

Magnolias, *Off the Hook* (Alias, 1992)

The Queers, *Don't Back Down* (Lookout, 1996)

Cub, *Come Out, Come Out* (Mint, 1995)

The Muffs, *The Muffs* (Warner, 1993)

Subsonics, *s/t* (Worrybird, 1992)

Pansy Division, *Deflowered* (Lookout, 1994)

Groovie Ghoulies, *Travels With My Amp* (Lookout, 2000)

Supersnazz, *Diode City* (Sympathy for the Record Industry, 1998)

Brownsville Station, *School Punks* (Big Tree, 1974)

The Datsuns, "Super Gyration!" 7″ (Hellsquad, 2000)

The Donnas, *Get Skintight* (Lookout, 1999)

The Tranzmitors, *Tranzmitors* (Stiff, 2007)

The Evaporators, *Ripple Rock* (Alternative Tentacles, 2004)

The Smugglers, *Dirty Windshields—The Soundtrack: The Best of the Smugglers* (Mint, 2017)

Recommended
Reading

Fresh at Twenty: the Oral History of Mint Records, 1991–2011
by Kaitlin Fontana (ECW Press, 2011)

How To Ru(i)n A Record Label: the Story of Lookout Records
by Larry Livermore (Don Giovanni, 2015)

Have Not Been The Same: The CanRock Renaissance, 1985–1995
by Michael Barclay, Ian A.D. Jack and Jason Schneider (ECW Press, 2001)

On A Cold Road: Tales of Adventure in Canadian Rock by Dave Bidini
(McClelland & Stewart, 1998)

Stompin' Tom: Before the Fame by Stompin' Tom Connors
(Viking Press, 1995)

Stompin' Tom and The Connors Tone by Stompin' Tom Connors
(Viking Press, 2000)

Girls to the Front: The True Story of the Riot Grrrl Revolution
by Sara Marcus (Harper Perennial, 2010)

Our Band Could Be Your Life: Scenes from the American Indie Underground,
1981–1991 by Michael Azerrad (Back Bay, 2002)

Deflowered: My Life in Pansy Division by Jon Ginoli (Cleis Press, 2009)

You Can't Always Get What You Want: My Life with the Rolling Stones,
the Grateful Dead and Other Wonderful Reprobates by Sam Cutler
(William Heinemann, 2008)

Girl in a Band: A Memoir by Kim Gordon (Dey Street Books, 2015)

Guilty of Everything by John Armstrong (New Star, 2001)

King Dork by Frank Portman (Delacorte Press, 2006)

Heroes and Villains: The True Story of the Beach Boys
by Steven Gaines (Da Capo Press, 1986)

SHOUT! *The Beatles in Their Generation* by Philip Norman
(Simon and Schuster, 1981)

Unknown Pleasures: Inside Joy Division by Peter "Hooky" Hook
(It Books, 2012)

Live at the Commodore: The Story of Vancouver's Historic Commodore Ballroom
by Aaron Chapman (Arsenal Pulp Press, 2014)

NOFX: *the Hepatitis Bathtub and Other Stories*
by NOFX and Jeff Alulis (Da Capo Press, 2016)

*Nowhere with You: The East Coast Anthems of Joel Plaskett, The Emergency
and Thrush Hermit* by Josh O'Kane (ECW Press, 2016)

Punk USA: *The Rise and Fall of Lookout Records* by Kevin Prested
(Microcosm, 2014)

I, Shithead: A Life in Punk by Joey Keithley (Arsenal Pulp Press, 2003)

The Deadly Snakes: Real Rock and Roll Tonight by J.B. Staniforth
(Invisible, 2012)

Mötley Crüe: The Dirt—Confessions of the World's Most Notorious Rock Band
by Tommy Lee, Vince Neil, Mick Mars, Nikki Sixx and Neil Strauss
(HarperCollins, 2001)

Up and Down with the Rolling Stones: My Rollercoaster Ride with Keith Richards
by "Spanish" Tony Sánchez (William Morrow, 1979)